NORTH SCOTLAND

Scale, 1:2,000,000

Miles

0   10   20   30   40

Highland Line ——

Cape Wrath

Butt of Lewis

MORRISON

MACLEOD OF LEWIS

MACAULAY

MACKENZIE

MACIVER

The Minch

MACLEOD

MACNICOL

MACLEOD OF HARRIS

MACDONELL OF GLENGARRY

L. Maree

N. Uist

MACDONALD

MACQUEEN

MACLEOD OF LEWIS

MACDONALD

MACDONALD OF CLANRANALD

MACLEOD OF LEWIS

MACKENZIE

MACDONELL OF GLENGARRY

MATHESON

CHISHOLM

S. Uist

MACDONALD OF CLANRANALD

MACNICOL

Isle of Skye

MACLEOD OF HARRIS

MACKINNON

MACLENNAN

MACRAE

GRA

Canna

MACDONALD

MACLEOD OF HARRIS

Barra

MACNEILL

MACDONALD OF CLANRANALD

Rum

Eigg

L. Morar

MACDONELL OF GLENGARRY

ATLANTIC

Muck

MACDONALD OF CLANRANALD

L. Shiel

MACDONALD

CAMERO

Fort William

Coll

MACLEAN

MACKINNON

MACGILLIVRAY

MACMASTER MACLEAN

MACINNES

STEWART

HEND

LIVINGSTONE

Tiree

CAMPBELL

MACQUARRIE

Mull

MACLEAN

Oban

MACDOUGALL MACINTYRE

OCEAN

MACALPINE

Iona

CAMPBELL

MAC

MACNAUGHT

MACLEAN

MACALLUM

MAC ARTHU

Colonsay

MACFIE

Jura

MACLEAN

MALCOLM

MACCOLL

MAC LACHLAN

MAC MILLAN

Oronsay

MACEWEN

LAMONT

Pentland Firth

Thurso

SINCLAIR

CKAY

KEITH

GUNN

MURRAY

SUTHERLAND

L. Shin

ROSS

Dornoch Firth

NORTH

SEA

★ *This map gives approximate location of the Clans and Families of North Scotland. Territories located outside the Highland Line (that invisible boundary forming the division between the Highlands and the rest of Scotland) have been determined by reference to reliable records and manuscripts. On a small scale map it is possible to detail only the most prominent names. Absence of any family does not mean that they were landless.*

Moray Firth

MUNRO

URQUHART

BRODIE

INNES

KEITH

Beauly

ROSE

HAY

RASER

Inverness

MACBEAN

GRANT

HAY

L. Ness

MACINTOSH

LESLIE

MACGILLIVRAY

DAVIDSON

Don

RASER

COMYN

SHAW

GORDON

FORBES

SKENE

Aberdeen

MACPHERSON

Balmoral

Aboyne

Dee

CUMMINGS

FARQUHARSON

St. onehaven

NNELL

PPOCH

MURRAY

LINDSAY

BARCLAY

MENZIES

ROBERTSON

GOW

OGILVIE

Esk

Montrose

STEWART

L. Rannoch

CAMPBELL

DUNCAN

L. Tay

MENZIES

FLETCHER

Tay

Dundee

ACGREGOR

OLIPHANT

Firth of Tay

MACNAB

MURRAY

HAY

St. Andrews

MACLAREN

Perth

Earn

DRUMMOND

LINDSAY

STEWART

MACDUFF

BUCHANAN

GRAHAM

ERSKINE

L. Leven

OU

NAPIER

Stirling

BRUCE

Firth of Forth

UN

LIVINGSTONE

Forth

AULAY

L. Lomond

Falkirk

EDINBURGH

THE CLANS AND TARTANS OF SCOTLAND

GENTLEMEN – THE TARTAN!

Here's to it!
The fighting sheen of it,
The yellow, the green of it,
The white, the blue of it,
The swing, the hue of it,
The dark, the red of it,
Every thread of it!

The fair have sighed for it,
The brave have died for it,
Foemen sought for it,
Heroes fought for it.
Honour the name of it,
Drink to the fame of it –

The TARTAN!

Murdoch Maclean.

THE CLANS AND TARTANS OF SCOTLAND

ROBERT BAIN

Enlarged and re-edited by
MARGARET O. MACDOUGALL
F.S.A. SCOT.

Heraldic Adviser
P. E. STEWART-BLACKER
HERALDIC WOODCARVER TO THE
STANDING COUNCIL OF SCOTTISH CHIEFS

With a foreword by The Rt. Hon.
THE COUNTESS OF ERROLL
HEREDITARY LORD HIGH CONSTABLE OF SCOTLAND

FONTANA/COLLINS
GLASGOW AND LONDON

First published, 1938
Second edition, 1946
Third edition, 1953
Fourth edition, 1959
Fifth edition, 1976
Fifth reprint, 1981
First issued in Fontana, 1981
Second impression, 1982
Third impression, 1984
Fourth impression, 1987
Fifth impression, 1988
Sixth impression March 1989

© 1968
Illustrations © 1976
William Collins Sons & Co. Ltd.
Printed in Great Britain
ISBN 0 00 411117 6 (hardback)
ISBN 0 00 636416 0 (Fontana)

CONTENTS

The Countess of Erroll, who has written a Foreword for this book, is chief of the Hays and Lord High Constable of Scotland, an office which was made hereditary for the Hay chiefs by King Robert Bruce in 1314 as a reward after Bannockburn. The Lord High Constable is the senior Great Officer of the Royal Household in Scotland, and as such has " precedence before every other hereditary honour in Scotland after the Blood Royal."

The Lord High Constable is the ritual head of Scottish Chivalry, but the military functions of the office now apply only to purely Scottish bodies such as the Royal Archers and the Atholl Highlanders. On State occasions the Countess of Erroll wears a very curious gold-banded, white-furred red velvet robe of office and carries a gold-tipped silver baton of command. She has her own officer of arms, called Slains Pursuivant, who wears her coat of arms on his tabard.

The Court of the Verge, or Constabulary Court, is presided over by the Lord High Constable, and her jurisdiction is supreme in all matters of assault and riot within four miles of the Queen's person in Scotland. The Lord High Constable's Doorward Guard of Partizans, the oldest of Scottish corps, is maintained now only as a single token doorward, mounted at the foot of the great stairway at the Palace of Holyroodhouse, but when Royal Courts are held at Holyroodhouse Lady Erroll attends on the Queen in person, as senior officer of Scotland's own Royal Household.

FOREWORD

by

THE RIGHT HONOURABLE THE COUNTESS OF ERROLL

27th HEREDITARY LORD HIGH CONSTABLE

This readable and handy book on the Clans and Tartans of Scotland, giving a short account of many widespread families both highland and lowland provides a compact guide for those who wish to learn quickly something of the history and origins of their clan or Name. I mention lowland since it is not always realised that the great lowland Names defended the rights of their members, until after the Union of the Crowns, in much the same way as did the highland Clans until the '45. To-day, this feeling of brotherhood is maintained and kept alive through the Standing Council of Scottish Chiefs and the various Clan Societies.

In too many countries the great historic families are separated from the mass of the people, but in Scotland we have been fortunate in that pride of Name has never depended on wealth and rank, and in that the clan tradition has always prevented class barriers from arising to divide our proud nation. The fact that the Grahams have a ritual head in the Duke of Montrose and that Lords Huntly and Aberdeen are Gordons in no way makes a Graham or a Gordon superior in class to their fellow Scots. In the same way, all the bearers of great Scottish Names share alike in their ancient traditions. It is this brotherhood within clan or Name which links all Scots together and is so marked a feature of our countrymen wherever they may be. We are all one family of Scots, the branches of that family being the clans and Names, and the Chief of Chiefs our Queen.

One great love which all Scots share is their love for the tartan, and in these pages is given the particular tartan which may be worn by each clan or Name and by the other names allied to them. It must be remembered that in many cases there is a choice of different shades and weights, both

7

serviceable and gay. I am happy to see a note on the correct way in which tartan should be worn; there is nothing worse than seeing a girl dressed as an imitation Highlandman in kilt and sporran. Anyone who appreciates the tartan well enough to wear it should wear it correctly.

In particular I understand that much care has been taken to ensure that the illustrations of the heraldic badges, which clansmen are entitled to wear, are authentic representations. In each case they have been checked against the official record in Lyon Register of the chief's personal crest from which they are derived. This in itself makes this book a useful addition to the literature on Scottish clan history. It would of course require many large volumes to give a detailed history of all the clans, but this small book will, I am certain, encourage every Scot to delve deeper into the colourful history and proud traditions of his clan or Name.

Erroll.

HC.

PUBLISHER'S PREFACE

Throughout nearly 40 years and numerous printings since its first publication for the Empire Exhibition in 1938, the publishers have endeavoured to improve the usefulness of this book and extend its scope. The late Robert Bain, responsible for both the first and second editions, created a valuable work, and made sound foundations.

In 1935, a third edition in the present format was prepared by Margaret O. MacDougall with further improvements including coats of arms and clan badges. The publishers are most grateful for her advice and assistance in preparing that edition and a further one in 1959, shortly before her death.

For the fourth edition the introductory matter and appendices were revised, as were many of the clan histories. All the crested clan badges were carefully checked and most of them redrawn. Such a large-scale revision would have been impossible without full co-operation from leading authorities on Scottish history and heraldry. The publishers are especially grateful to Sir Thomas Innes of Learney, Lord Lyon King of Arms, who authoritatively aided B. E. Stewart Blacker in the preparation of the crested clan badges; to Sir Iain Moncrieffe, Albany Herald, who helped in verifying some of the clan histories, and to the Countess of Erroll for her Foreword.

For this fifth edition where all the tartans have been re-reproduced the material was supplied by Messrs Peter MacArthur and Co Ltd of Hamilton, to whom the publishers are indebted for their assistance and advice. The publishers also wish to thank the Scottish National Portrait Gallery for permission to reproduce the portrait by Michael Wright on page 33 and Mr John Prentice of Hugh Macpherson (Scotland) Ltd, Highland Outfitters, Edinburgh, for the photograph of himself wearing a kilt of the Bicentennial tartan on page 35.

EXPLANATORY NOTES

NAME : The form of spelling of Names in this book does not indicate that other forms of spelling are wrong. Many Scottish Names may be spelt in two or more ways, and the editors have simply chosen the one which is most popular, e.g. Macphie, Macfee and Macphee are variations of Macfie, but the last spelling is chosen because it is most commonly used.

CRESTED CLAN BADGES : a clan name followed by " House of——" indicates that the crested clan badge is taken from the arms of a cadet of the clan and not from those of the chief, because the chiefship is vacant. A saltire, which is not a crested clan badge, indicates that no crested clan badge exists.

THE SCOTTISH CLANS

Early History

IT is generally accepted that in pre-Roman times Scotland was inhabited by a people who were mainly Celtic and that they reached this country in three principal waves of immigration. Some came to the East coast by way of the North Sea, others by way of Gaul to the South of England ; the third from the Continent by way of Ireland.

After the departure of the Romans, there were five races settled in Scotland: the Picts, whose origin has been the subject of bitter discussion, who occupied most of the land North of the Forth and Clyde ; the Scots who arrived on the West coast at the beginning of the sixth century and established the Kingdom of Dalriada in what is now Argyll ; the Britons who had been pressed out of England and were settled in Strathclyde ; the Attacotti who inhabited Galloway; and, lastly, the Saxons who had arrived in the South-East of Scotland. About this time, Christianity was introduced into Scotland by St. Ninian about A.D. 396 and by St. Columba about A.D. 563.

The Dalriadic settlement in Argyll was established by Fergus, son of Erc, accompanied by his brothers Lorn and Angus. The territory was subsequently divided among four tribes of the Scots—the Cinel Gabran and the Cinel Comgall descended from grandsons of Fergus, the Cinel Lorn and the Cinel Angus descended from the brothers of Fergus. This is perhaps the earliest instance of the division of the race into district clans that became general in the Highlands some centuries later. Soon after the advent of the Scots there appeared on the West coast one who was to exercise the greatest influence on the history of Scotland—St. Columba. Christianity was previously introduced into Galloway in the South of Scotland by St. Ninian, the results of whose efforts reached as far as the North of Scotland.

The members of the church founded in Iona by St. Columba immediately set to work to Christianise the inhabitants of the portion of Scotland occupied by the Picts. The Saint and his missionaries spread the Gospel where the Druids exercised almost complete control, and through time they extended their labours to England and to the Continent. The Druids whom they succeeded were of three classes—the Bardi or Poets, the Vates or Priests, and the Deo-Phaisten who acted as the instructors of their religion and of law. It is said that they practised the cultivation of memory and that written records were forbidden. Poetry was used to aid the memory and the wonderful feats of the Highland bards in memorising thousands of lines were a survival of Druidical training. The order was presided over by an Arch Druid who exercised great power over the early inhabitants of the country.

For three centuries there was a struggle for supremacy between the Picts and Scots.

About the year 836 Alpin the last King of the Scots was killed in battle and the accession of his son Kenneth MacAlpin marked a new era in the history of Scotland. There is considerable divergence of opinion on the events of this period. Kenneth's capital was at Dunstaffnage in Argyll, but it was removed to Scone where he was crowned in 843 on the Stone of Destiny which has served as coronation stone ever since.

A new element entered into Scottish history in the coming of the Norsemen. In 793 Lindesfarne and the North-east of England was invaded by the Norsemen and a year later they reached the Western Isles. These Sea Raiders were described by the early writers as of two distinct races, the Fingall or fair-haired foreigners were the Norsemen, and the Duthgall or dark-haired foreigners were the Danes. In 798, 802, 806 and on other occasions Iona was burned, and the monks were massacred by these Vikings, if we may use this generic word to describe both races. In 870 Olaf the White, the Norse King who had previously had his headquarters in Dublin, destroyed Dunbarton Castle after a siege of four months. We are informed by the Icelandic *Landnamabok* that Olaf's son Thorstein the Red conquered Caithness, Sutherland, Ross and more than half of Alba. Before the end of the ninth century the Norsemen were masters of the Orkney, Shetland and the Western Isles. The Norse occupation had several setbacks and for a period after A.D. 900 they were expelled from the North of Scotland although they still held their ascendancy over the Western Isles. In 915 the Danes occupied the North of England, so at one period or another the greater part of Scotland was either surrounded by or in the hands of the Norsemen. With periods of varying success the Norse occupation continued until about 1264 when they were finally expelled except from Orkney and Shetland.

It is unnecessary for my purpose to refer individually to the kings who ascended the throne of Scotland until the succession of Malcolm Ceanmore in 1057, although the list contains names of some notable personages including MacBeth.

Malcolm Ceanmore reigned over Scotland for thirty-five years and from his reign may be dated the rise of the Highland clan system attributed to Malcolm's second wife Margaret, granddaughter of Edmund, King of England, who had to flee from England and seek shelter at the Scottish Court. Malcolm had moved his capital to Dunfermline and amongst other questions that came to be discussed was the law of succession, and between the Celtic system of tanistry and the feudalism of the Saxon, Malcolm favoured the latter and encouraged the immigration of a large number of Saxon and Norman nobles from England, to whom he made feudal grants. Queen Margaret exercised great influence over the King and was successful in persuading him to make many innovations, including the discontinuance of Gaelic as the Court language, and the substitution of Roman Catholic practices in the church where they differed from that of the Celtic church. These and other changes led to the alienation of the affection of his Gaelic subjects, who at his death, in 1093, supported the claims of Donald Ban, his brother, to the throne, instead of Malcolm's son Duncan. Donald Ban further increased his popularity by expelling large numbers of the Saxons and Normans whom Malcolm had favoured.

At this time commenced the long succession of rebellions in many parts of the country, which continued with varying success until the last Jacobite rising in 1745, which resulted in the extinction of the Highland clan system. The Crown at this time was engaged in consolidating the Scottish Kingdom, and extending the boundaries of the Central government. King Malcolm IV, who died in 1165, did much in this direction, by crushing a rebellion in Moray, defeating the army of the Lord of the Isles at Renfrew in 1164, and bringing Galloway under control of the Crown.

The Lord of the Isles, whose forces he defeated at Renfrew, was Somerled, the progenitor of that greatest of clans, the Clan Donald, and also of the Clans MacDougall and Mac-Rury. Somerled, who had warred against the Kings of Scotland, was the principal power in freeing the Western Highlands and Islands from the grip of the Norsemen, and, at the time of his death, was ruler of the West Coast from the Isle of Man to Lewis.

It is appropriate at this point that we should consider a condition of Highland polity which afterwards had an important influence on the development of the clans. The greater part of Scotland was divided into large tribal districts, seven in number, corresponding largely to the territorial divisions of the country in Pictish times. In these districts, according to Skene, " The unit was the Tuath or tribe ; several Tuaths formed a Mortuath or great tribe, two or more Mortuaths a Coicidh or province, and at the head of each was a Ri or King, while each province contributed a portion of its territory at their junction to form a central district, in which the capital of the whole country was placed, and the Ri or King who was elected to be its Ard-Ri or sovereign had his seat of government." The Central district, where the four southern provinces met, was in Perthshire and accounts for the choice of Scone as its capital. In the twelfth century the system was modified and the title Ri was no longer held by the heads of the Tuath and the Mortuath ; at the head of the Tuath was the Toiseach, and of the Mortuath the Mormaer (great steward).

The Pictish divisions were seven in number, *Caith* represented by Caithness and Sutherland, *Fidach* represented by Ross and Moray, *Fodhla* represented by Athol, *Fortrenn* represented by Western Perthshire, *Ce* represented by Mar and Buchan, *Ciric* or *Circinn* represented by the Mearns, and *Fibh* represented by Fife. If we add to these the districts of Dalriada, we have divisions that affected the formation of the Highland Clans.

The Development of the Clans

As already mentioned, the rise of the Clan system may be dated from the coming of Queen Margaret to the court of Malcolm Ceanmore. She persuaded the King to adopt Southern customs, alienated his affections from his Gaelic subjects, and made possible the introduction of feudalism which continued during the succeeding reigns. The possession of the land was the principal difference between the old and the new systems. Under the Celtic Patriarchal system the land belonged to the tribe, but feudalism meant that the land passed into the possession of the king to be parcelled out according to his whim or necessity.

From this time we have two systems existing more or less together although not necessarily in harmony. The relationship between the sovereign and the chiefs was changed, but the internal polity of the tribes or clans remained little changed. Certainly when the larger tribes were broken up clans smaller in size than the tribes emerged, and thenceforward clanship was the principle governing the Highland people. The clans generally were confined to districts, restricted often by the configuration of the country. Inland glens, islands and the land bordering sea lochs were favourable districts. Islands, for instance, were held by a single clan, the MacDonalds in Islay, the MacFies in Colonsay, the MacLeans in Mull, Tiree and Coll, while the MacDonalds, MacLeods and MacKinnons in Skye is an instance of several clans occupying one island. On the mainland the Campbells in Mid-Argyll, the Camerons in Lochaber, the Robertsons in Rannoch, the MacKenzies in Ross and the MacKays in Sutherland are examples of clans resident or associated with a district.

Clans consisted generally of " native men " and " broken men." The " native men " were those related to the Chief and to each other by blood ties. This blood relationship is an important fundamental in the clan system and was a strong element in the patriarchal system of government, all being bound together in a common interest. The clan also contained septs or branches composed of clansmen who had become powerful or prominent in some way, and founded families almost as important as that of the Chief. The " broken men " were individuals or groups from other clans who had sought and obtained the protection of the clan. The clan organisation consisted of the chief, the tanist, the chieftains, the captain, the daoin'-uaisle—the gentlemen, and the general body of the clan. An Act passed in 1587 " for the quieting and keeping in obedience of the disorderit and subjectis inhabitants of the Borders, Highlands and Isles " containing a roll of " the clans that have Captains, Chiefs and Chieftans on whom they depend offtimes against the will of their Landlords as well on the Borders as the Highlands " may be considered proof of the existence of the patriarchal system among the inhabitants of the districts named as against the feudal holdings of the landlords, and also gives us three ranks in the clans.

The Chief, who succeeded according to the system of tanistry, dispensed the law in times of peace and led them in war. He governed the clan territory for the benefit of the clan and divided the land in such a way that each member had a portion sufficient for his needs. He " determined all differences and disputes, he protected his followers and he freed the necessitous from their arrears of rent and maintained such who by accidents were fallen to total decay." " At his induction the Chief took his stand on a stone where he took an oath to preserve inviolate all the ancient customs of the people. He was then presented with a sword and a white wand. A bard recounted the Chief's pedigree, enumerated the exploits of his ancestors and exhorted the Chief to emulate their noble example." " The Tanist was the person next in succession to the Chief according to the laws of tanistry. He was nominated and bore the title of Tanist during the lifetime of the Chief, and his special duty was to hold the clan lands in trust for the clan and their posterity." Ceremonies were observed at his induction similar to those of a chief except that he placed one foot on the stone instead of standing on it. The Chieftains were the heads of the houses into which the clan was divided, and the oldest cadet was next to the Chief, and had the post of honour in time of war. In the absence of the Chief he commanded the whole clan.

The Captain was usually the Chief of the clan, but if the Chief was set aside from any incapacity the Toiseach generally bore the title of the Captain of the clan. The titles of Tanist and Toiseach were often borne by the same individual.

The judicial system of the clan was administered by a Brieve (breitheamh) or judge, and the laws had their foundation in and were a survival of the older Celtic law. The office of Brieve was hereditary and a proportion of the fines imposed for offences were perquisites of the office, together with sufficient land to support the Brieve. The judge had the assistance of a council of twelve or fourteen who assisted in the administration of justice. The meetings were held on eminences or moothills, sometimes in a level circle surrounded by higher ground. Some of those moothills and circles are to be seen to this day.

The clan had a definite formation in war, with officers and ranks much the same as military regiments. Each clan had a recognised meeting-place to which the clan was called by beacons or by the fiery cross or crantaraidh, a cross of half-burned wood sometimes dipped in blood. During the '45 the fiery cross travelled through Breadalbane over thirty-six miles in three hours. The officers of the clan had certain well-defined positions, just as certain clans had positions in the fighting line when fighting a common enemy. This honour was jealously guarded, and we know the result at the disaster of Culloden when the place of the MacDonalds on the right wing was usurped by the Stewarts.

In fighting, the first attack was always the fiercest. After discharging their firearms they charged with their claymores, shouting their war-cries. They depended on their first attack for victory, and one of their proverbs, " Better is a good retreat than a bad stand," describes their outlook when the battle went against them. While the clan was at war a number of male members remained at home to till the ground and carry on the agricultural work of the clan.

The social customs of the clans evolved largely from Celtic sources. The Chief was responsible for the good government of his people who, on their part, gave every assistance to him for the mutual benefit of all members of the clan. The custom of fosterage did much to bind members of the clan together. Fosterage consisted in the mutual exchange of the infant members of families, or of sending a child to be reared in another family, the sons of the Chief being included in this practice. The custom had the advantage of enabling one half of the clan world to know how the other half lived. It exacted respect and devotion among families in different grades of clan society that intensified the bonds of clanship. Gaelic proverbs, " Affectionate to a man is a friend, but a foster-brother is as the life blood of his heart," " Kindred to forty degrees, fosterage to a hundred," show the Highland estimation of the custom.

Handfasting was another custom within the clan, parties contracting to live together for a year and a day and if there was no issue within that period were at liberty to dissolve the contract. The Chief was called upon at times to act as match-maker. The existence of these customs was not general, however, and marriage ceremonies were occasions of joyful celebrations including feasting, drinking, and dancing. Women were held in high esteem, and in early times wives were permitted to assist in councils and in settling disputes. " An unfaithful, unkind, or even careless husband was looked upon as a monster " in the Highlands.

Sometimes a sept, or a branch of another clan, too small to protect itself against surrounding clans, might enter into a treaty with a neighbouring clan for protection. The agree-ment was known as a bond of manrent and the parties gave assurances of mutual assistance. The bond was usually qualified, however, to enable the subscribers to remain loyal to their own friends or to the King. Members of the septs had to pay " Calpich " in the same manner as members of the clan. " Calpich " was a payment to the Chief ; on the death of the head of a family, the children or executors were bound to send to their chief their " best aucht whether it be ane mare, or horse, or cow." Cain was another payment made by clansmen by way of rent and consisting of the first fruits of their portion of land.

The Dress of the Clans

We learn from Roman writers that the early Celtic tribes were noted for the excellent weaving of woollen cloth and for the divers colours used in its manufacture. The inheritance of this ability to manufacture woollen cloth and their love of colour in it must have remained with the Celts for we find the existence of it in Scotland at an early period. The dyes were obtained chiefly from plants and the colours of the older tartans were distinguished by their quiet beauty. They had a taste and dignity that is lacking in many of the examples we now see produced with aniline dyes.

The articles of dress, such as the belted plaids, the philabeg and the trews, are well enough known not to require detailed description. The shoes were of untanned hide and the cuaran was like a boot and reached almost to the knee, made of horse or cow hide shaped to the leg and kept in position with thongs. It was a common practice to go bare-legged and bare-footed. A bonnet of knitted wool was generally worn, and a badge common to the clan, generally a flower or plant, was worn on it. The sporran worn in front of the kilt to serve as a purse was usually made of leather and often highly ornamented.

The women wore a curraichd of linen over their heads, fastened under the chin. The tonnag was a small square of woollen cloth or tartan worn over their shoulders, and the arasaid was a long garment of various colours or of tartan, reaching from the head or neck to the ankles, plaited all round, fastened at the breast with a large brooch and at the waist by a belt.

The arms of the clansmen consisted of bows and arrows, spears, swords, dirks, axes, shields and firearms. The Highlanders were often expert bowmen, but archery died out amongst them about the beginning of the eighteenth century on the introduction of firearms. Swords were of two kinds, the older two-handed sword or claymore and the more modern broadsword. The sword was their chief weapon and at hand-to-hand fighting the Highlander had scarcely an equal. The weapon was of excellent workmanship and the Spanish blades of Andrea Ferrara were much sought after. The dirk was a deadly weapon in the hands of a clansman. Shields or targes were a valuable addition to the accoutrements. The musket and the pistol completed the armoury.

Each clan had a slogan or war-cry, often the name of a physical feature in the clan district such as (Campbells) Cruachan, (Buchanans) Car Innes, (Grants) Crag Elachaidh, (MacKenzies) Tulloch Ard, (MacFarlanes) Loch Sloy, and (Stewarts) Creag an Sgaraibh.

The clans, too, carried standards, the Fairy Flag of the MacLeods and the Bratach Ban of the MacKays being existing examples. The duty of bearing the standard was a hereditary one and the custom is recalled to us in the family name of Bannerman.

The Home Life of the Clans

To turn to the more domestic side of clan life, we learn that, although in the thirteenth century many wooden castles were destroyed, in earlier times the houses were generally built of wattle or wicker work strengthened with earth and clay much on the same principle as we see in modern buildings of reinforced concrete. This method continued into fairly modern times. Ruins of duns, castles and churches all through the Highlands proves that they knew the art of building in stone. In later times when smaller stone houses were built they were roofed with heather, turf, rushes or ferns. They were round or square in shape, the windows small, and the smoke from the fire escaped through a hole in the roof.

The furnishings of the house were simple and were made by the Highlanders themselves. The houses and furnishings of the chiefs and principal men of the clan were more elaborate, although they may have lacked many of the valuables and the plate possessed by the noble families of the south. Some of you may remember John Pettie's painting, " The Chief's candlesticks," illustrating the result of a Highland chief's visit to England. When returning home through England the Chief visited a friend who had been with him at an English University. He was invited to a banquet held in his honour at which his host boasted of a beautiful candelabra on the table and said that the Chief could produce nothing so valuable in his Highland home. A wager resulted and the Chief undertook to produce two more valuable candlesticks when his friend visited the Highlands. When his friend came north and was being entertained to dinner, he reminded the Chief of the wager and asked for the candlesticks. Immediately the Chief called for two of his tallest clansmen who stood on either side of his chair holding lighted torches in their upraised hands. The Chief won the bet.

The clansmen were very hospitable to strangers who were given the best accommodation in the house and the best food obtainable. Even fugitives from justice were safe from capture when visiting other clans.

Food was procured by hunting, fishing or cultivation. Beef, mutton, venison, game and poultry were eaten. Cattle and sheep were raised—or stolen—while deer, goats and game birds could be hunted on the high grounds. Milk, cheese and butter were at hand, oatmeal and barley-meal were prepared in various ways, oatcakes, barley-cakes, bannocks, sowens, lithac, drammack and oatmeal brose.

Honey, too, was in use. Fish was not in such common use in inland districts although we know that salmon was plentiful. The old Celtic worship of water deities is supposed to have survived in the Highlands, and the awe of certain lochs and rivers influenced the natives against the use of fresh water fish. In the islands and districts bordering the sea, however, fishing was extensively engaged in even to the extent of exporting the surplus to the Lowlands and foreign countries. In this connection it is worth mentioning as an example of the influence of the clan system in the Western Isles that fishing lines were required to be of equal length to prevent any one obtaining an unfair advantage. The flesh of seals was used as food ; crabs, lobsters and shell fish formed articles of diet and dulse and other seaweeds were used. Herbs and wild fruits made pleasant variety in the diet of the Highlanders. The beverages included whisky, home-brewed beer, and foreign wines obtained through trading.

Occupations and Recreations

Contrary to popular opinion the clans engaged extensively in agriculture ; even when at war a number of the clan remained at home to carry on the work necessary for successful husbandry. The land belonged to the clan and this may account for the continuance of the custom of common grazings in the Highlands. Stock raising was the principal occupation and the crops raised included oats, barley and wheat. Limestone, seaweed, ashes, etc., were used for manure and in spite of climatic conditions creditable crops were obtained. Their implements included the plough, cas-chrom, spade, hoe and harrow. The cas-chrom or foot plough was a useful implement where the arable ground consisted of patches too small for the horse plough or where ground was too steep. It consisted of a strong piece of wood, the thin trunk of a small tree, six or seven feet long, bent almost to a right angle at the lower end and shod with an iron covering, the shod part being flat and broad and from six to nine inches long. A pin was inserted near the lower end for the foot to drive the plough into the ground. A twist on the shaft acting as a lever enabled the operator to turn up a piece of ground about a foot deep and a foot or more long and throw it to the left side in the same way as a horse plough turns over the ground. An expert worker could turn a considerable area in a day.

Harvesting was performed with the sickle or the scythe, and the flail was used to separate the grain from the straw. Grinding was done by the hand-quern in earlier times and later by water mills.

In the summer time cattle were moved to the higher ground in the hill corries for grazing and the younger people with a few of their elders spent a happy time at these summer shielings.

Many enactments affecting agriculture were passed by the old Scottish parliament regulating such work as heather-burning, the shielings, etc.; and doubtless these were observed by the clans when it was to their advantage.

The clans were not immune to illness and disease, and there was often one of their number skilled in the art of medicine and his cures were mainly concoctions of herbs. Certain families seemed to possess an hereditary skill in this art, the Beatons of Islay, Mull, Skye and Sutherland being an outstanding example, and fifteenth and sixteenth century manuscripts of their knowledge are still in existence in the Edinburgh University Library and the British Museum. The surname MacLay, Mac-an-leigh, is indicative of the profession of physicians.

The clansmen were fond of music and dancing. The harp and the bagpipes were the chief musical instruments. Field sports were engaged in to keep them strong and active in times of peace and archery, fencing, and wrestling were popular.

The literature of the clans was almost wholly oral. It consisted chiefly of poetry as might be expected from a race which still retained some influence of the Druid tradition which prevented written records and encouraged the use of poetry.

On the sea-board and in the islands, export trade was engaged in to some extent with the Lowlands, Ireland, England and the Continent. This trade, chiefly in fish, wool and hides, was conducted largely by barter, and was carried in ships belonging to these countries, but the Highlanders themselves possessed sea vessels. The smallest of these vessels (curachs) were constructed with wicker frames and covered with hides and were suitable only for shorter journeys. Larger vessels constructed of wood, known as biorlins, were used for longer voyages. The biorlin of Clan Ranald contained sixteen rowers. The largest vessels were known as lymphads, or galleys, and appear in the heraldry of several of the Highland families. The Highlanders of the west were keen seamen and when John of Lorn was defeated by Bruce at Ben Cruachan he fled for safety to the English King and by him was created High Admiral of the Western Fleet.

Mention of the galleys suggests consideration of the number of clansmen in the Highlands and Islands. There are few definite records to inform us on this point. Angus, Lord of the Isles, is said to have commanded a force of 10,000 men at Bannockburn, where Stewart states twenty-one clans were represented on the side of Bruce, while on the English side four or five clans assisted. The Act of 1587 gives a roll of 105 Landlords and Baillies and a further list of thirty-four clans that have captains, chiefs and chieftains on whom they depend oft-times against the wills of their landlords ; the Act of 1594 adds seven or eight more. The number of individual clansmen is not given, and not until General Wade's report of 1724 do we get an accurate estimate of the number of clansmen in the Highlands. The General reported that the number of men able to carry arms was 22,000 of which number about 10,000 men were vassals to superiors well affected to H.M. government ; most of the remaining 12,000 had been engaged in Rebellion against H.M. and were ready to create new troubles and rise in favour of the Pretender. Two clans which for the most part went into the Rebellion of 1715 without their superiors were 2000 Athol men and 1000 Breadalbin men. A memorial anent the true state of the Highlands . . . 1745 (attributed to Duncan Forbes of Culloden) gives a list of twenty-nine clans and the number of clansmen as 20,650. In this list the Campbells are given as numbering 3000, the MacKenzies 2000, the Duke of Athol 3000 and the combined families of MacDonalds 2200 ; the remaining twenty-five clans all contained fewer than 1000 men each.

It is not generally realised that the population of the Highlands was small considering the amount of trouble it caused the Scottish crown and parliament throughout the existence of the clan system. If we take General Wade's figures of the number of clansmen able to bear arms (22,000) as representing one-sixth of the total population we get the number 132,000 persons ; even if it represented one-tenth we would get no more than 200,000. It might be that in the eighteenth century the population had dwindled to that number only to increase again in the following century, but the astonishing fact remains that the number never reached a quarter of a million.

The End of the Clan System

The clan system ended on the afternoon of 16th April, 1746, when the attenuated battalions of half-starved clansmen composing the army of Prince Charles Edward sustained their first defeat at the hands of the troops of the Duke of Cumberland on the disastrous field of Culloden.

There can be no doubt that the clan system was admirably suited to the circumstances of the times in which it originated and during the time it existed. It was an ideal system in so far as it recognised that land, the basis of life, was not an individual possession, but belonged to the people in common, and that each clansman was in duty bound to assist other members of the clan in time of necessity of any kind, irrespective of his rank. The system was not free from abuses, however, and there have been instances of chiefs demanding contributions that meant considerable sacrifices on the part of members of the clan. Clanship also encouraged clan feuds, and a very slight offence, or suspected insult, often gave rise to long and bitter quarrels resulting in bloody conflicts and massacres. Such feuds kept territories in a state of ferment and prevented the performance of the ordinary acts or duties of a peaceful community. They prevented, too, that union that makes for strength and retarded the normal development which took place in other parts of the country. The effects of such feuds are still evident through the greater part of the Highlands.

ROBERT BAIN

THE DRESS OF THE HIGHLANDER

Tartan

The antiquity of tartan is amply proved by the many references to it in early Scottish literature and in the written accounts of travellers who visited Scotland several hundreds of years ago.

The ancient method of describing tartan was to refer to it as " mottled," " chequered," " striped," " sundrie coloured," " marled " and so on, but the Gaelic word for tartan is *breacan*, meaning chequered, and is aptly descriptive of the check-like arrangement of tartan patterns. When we refer to the sett of a tartan we mean the pattern, and a length of tartan is made up of one sett repeated over and over again until the desired length is made.

For many centuries tartan formed part of the everyday garb of the Highland people and while it was also worn in other parts of Scotland it was in the Highlands that its use continued and developed until it became recognised as a symbol of Clan kinship.

It is believed that the tartans used several centuries ago were simple checks of two or three colours and that these colours were obtained from the dye-producing plants, roots, berries and trees found in the districts where the cloth was woven. These simple checks were district tartans and were worn by the people of the district where they were made. As the people inhabiting a district were generally members of the same clan their district tartan was, in effect, a Clan tartan. Martin Martin in his *Description of the Western Islands of Scotland*, completed circa 1695 and published in 1703, tells us—" Every Isle differs from each other in their fancy of making Plads, as to the Stripes in Breadth and Colours.This Humour is as different thro the main Land of the Highlands, in-so-far that they who have seen those Places, are able, at the first view of a Man's Plad, to guess the Place of his Residence. . . ."

The same writer also tells us that weavers took great pains to give exact patterns of the tartan by having the number and colour of every thread upon a piece of wood. It is well known that these *Maide dalbh* or pattern sticks served as guides for the weavers in making their tartans, and Martin makes it perfectly clear that not only was care taken to keep an exact record of tartan setts but that also the people of each district could be *identified* by the pattern of their tartan.

When chemical dyes came into use weavers were able to enlarge their range of colours and more elaborate patterns were introduced. It is believed that as time passed branches of the larger clans evolved tartans of their own by adding an overstripe or other variation to the basic pattern of their parent clan.

What may be one of the earliest references to Royal use of tartan is contained in the accounts of the treasurer to King James III in 1471 where mention is made of tartan purchased for the King and Queen. King James V wore tartan when hunting in the Highlands in 1538, and King Charles II wore tartan ribbons on his coat at his marriage in 1662.

In a crown charter of 1587, to Hector MacLean of Duart, the feu duty payable on the lands of Narraboll, Islay, was sixty ells of cloth of white, black and green colours. These colours correspond to the colours in the tartan we now call MacLean hunting, but it is doubtful if their arrangement was exactly the same as that in use at the present time. This may be the first Clan tartan.

The antiquity of tartan has never been doubted, but some critics aver that the wearing of a particular pattern by all the members of a clan as a common *clan* tartan is a modern custom dating no earlier than the late eighteenth century. They also claim that prior to that period there were no definite tartans and that clansmen wore whatever patterns the weavers chose to supply.

From the archives of a Highland burgh we learn that southern merchants came to the Highlands to purchase tartan in the sixteenth and seventeenth centuries and the Baillies of that Burgh, to prevent overcharging, fixed maximum prices for tartan, the prices being determined by the number and shades of colours in the cloth. In the same records we read of a housewife who, in 1572, gave coloured wool to a weaver to make into cloth. In suing him before the magistrates she accused him of making the pattern according to his " awin fasoun " (own fashion) and not according to her instructions. She won her case and the weaver was punished ; by her action she has proved that Highland housewives were not prepared to accept, without question, whatever patterns weavers provided.

In other literary sources we read of clansmen dressed in the livery of their chiefs and it is reasonable to infer that the livery was tartan. One of the best known instances is the accusation of Lady Grange who claimed that her abductors, in 1732, were dressed in Lord Lovat's livery. There is a well-known Highland traditional story that during the Jacobite Rising a cadet of Clan Fraser tried to force the Frasers in Stratherrick to join in the attack on Culloden House under threat of " taking away the plaids of the men."

It is known that the clans were organised on military lines and that there were clan regiments. In 1704 the fencible men of Clan Grant in Strathspey, were ordered to rendezvous and to have " ilk ane of thame Heighland coates, trewes, and shorthose of tartan of red and greine sett broad-springed. . . ."

This company of men were all dressed in the same tartan in 1704 and there is reason to believe that other clan regiments were dressed in the tartan or " livery " of their chief.

After the Battle of Culloden in 1746 the government, in an endeavour to purge the Highlands of all unlawful elements, passed an Act of Parliament whereby the Highlander was disarmed and the wearing of tartan made a penal offence. This Act was rigorously enforced and the anxiety of the government to abolish tartan and the,Highland dress suggests that they held more than sentimental meaning for the Highland people.

By the time the Act was repealed in 1785 Highlanders had become accustomed to wearing the same type of dress as other Scots and they showed no great enthusiasm, even if they could afford to do so, to don tartan clothing. Tartan was almost a thing of the past ; many of the old weavers had died and with their passing details of old patterns were lost ; the wooden pattern sticks had rotted away and such fragments of old tartan cloth as remained were so worn and perished they were of little value in adding to the little knowledge that remained of pre-1745 tartans.

The first great tartan revival took place in 1822. George IV, when visiting Edinburgh in that year, suggested that the people should attend the functions wearing their respective tartans. Unfortunately this resulted in many ' original ' tartans being made, since those who had no tartan could always find a tailor to invent one for them. The publication of a book *Vestiarium Scoticum* by the brothers Sobieski Stuart helped to augment the number of spurious tartans, and indeed many tartans existing today owe their existence to this book, although much doubt has been cast on its authenticity. Other 19th century publications added to the confusion but, unlike the *Vestiarium*, they made no claim to antiquity regarding the tartans they exhibited.

To-day the confusion of past uncertainty is being regulated into some semblance of order and patterns are being standardised into recognised settings. The registration of tartans in the Registers at Lyon Court should do much to avoid confusion in the future.

Tartans are described according to the purpose for which they are named.

CLAN TARTANS are patterns for general use by clanspeople. It is not uncommon to find a Clan tartan of recent origin described as " Ancient Clan tartan." The use of the word " ancient " is most misleading, as it is merely an indication that the tartan has been woven in lighter coloured shades.

DRESS TARTANS were originally worn by the ladies of the Clan who preferred lighter coloured patterns. They had a white background and were variations of the Clan pattern. In recent years there has been a tendency to refer to Clan tartans woven in light-weight material as " Dress " tartan. This causes confusion and should be avoided. Clans who do not possess a dress tartan usually wear the Clan pattern, in light-weight material, for evening wear, but this does not justify the description of a Clan tartan as a " Dress" tartan.

MOURNING TARTANS at one time were worn for the purpose for which they were named. They were generally of black and white.

HUNTING TARTANS are worn for sport and outdoor activities. Brown or some other dark hue is the predominant colour. When a Clan possessed a brightly coloured tartan it was unsuitable for hunting purposes, and hunting setts were devised to make the wearer less conspicuous. The colours were arranged so that, when concealed in the heather, the tartan blended with the surroundings.

CHIEFS' TARTANS are the personal tartans of the Chiefs, and should never be worn except by the Chief and his immediate family.

DISTRICT TARTANS are probably the oldest of our tartans from which Clan tartans may have developed. There are a number of District tartans which are, nowadays, worn by the people residing in, or having their place of origin in, the district, always provided they are not entitled to wear a Clan tartan.

While tartan continues to excite the admiration of peoples everywhere, it is impossible to lay down hard and fast rules regarding choice of tartans. In all probability the would-be wearer of tartan will select the " tartan of his fancy." One caution may be voiced. The Royal tartans are for the use of the Royal family and should not be worn by anyone outside the Royal family. Military tartans are for military use only.

Highland Dress

The older form of the Highland dress was the belted plaid, and consisted of " a piece of tartan two yards in width, and four or six in length. This was carefully plaited in the middle, of a breadth suitable to the size of the wearer and sufficient to extend from one side around his back to the other, leaving as much at each end as would cover the front of the body, overlapping each other. The plaid being thus prepared, was firmly bound round the loins with a leathern belt, in such a manner that the lower side fell down to the middle of the knee joint, and then, while there were the foldings behind, the cloth was double before. The upper part was then fastened to the shoulder with a large brooch, or pin, so as to display to the most advantage the tastefulness of the arrangement, the two ends being sometimes suffered to hang down, but that on the right side, which was of necessity the longest, was more usually tucked under the belt."

It was a convenient article of dress as it could be used as a cloak by day, or as a blanket by night.

The feile-beg, or little kilt, is now universally used as modern Highland garb, and consists of the lower part of the belted plaid, which rarely exceeds thirty inches wide and seven to eight yards long. It is pleated and sewn, sufficient cloth being left plain at both ends, which are crossed in front of the body, and the whole sometimes being fastened by a belt round the waist, although a strap and buckle are most common. A silver pin is fastened to the apron a few inches above the lower edge of the kilt.

For ordinary wear the kilt may be made of tartan or tweed and may be box-pleated or knife-pleated ; for dress wear it should be made of tartan of a finer quality of material and should be of the dress tartan of the Clan, if the Clan possesses one. The kilt should be worn with the lower edges reaching not lower than the centre of the knee-cap.

The ordinary or everyday jacket and vest worn with the kilt should be made of tweed, homespun, or other suitable material, preferably with horn buttons. For dress or evening wear the coat should be made of dress cloth or velvet of green or other colour, or of tartan, and may be cut with short tails, and should be ornamented with silver buttons. The vest for evening wear may be made of tartan, black or scarlet cloth. Within the past few years it has become fashionable to wear tartan jackets and vests, a style common in the early nineteenth century.

The sporran, or purse, may be made of leather, or of the head and skin of the badger, seal or other animal. Leather sporrans are preferable for day wear. For evening wear sporrans made of baby seal or other light-coloured skins are worn.

Hose for outdoor wear should be knitted. For evening wear they may be fine knit, woven or cut from the piece. Garters are usually of wool or worsted, and knotted with a garter knot, the end or flashes hanging below the overturn. At present elastic garters with tartan flashes attached are popular.

Shoes for evening wear should be lightweight with silver or gilt buckles. For outdoor wear black or buckskin brogues are correct.

The " Balmoral " style bonnet is the most popular head-wear and it approximates more closely to the old broad bonnet of the Highlander. It is generally blue in colour, but may have a pom-pom of red or other colour. The bonnet should display the wearer's crest, if he is the registered owner of one ; or his chief's crest within a " strap and buckle " to indicate that he is a follower of the chief whose crest badge he wears. In no circumstances should an ordinary clansman wear his chief's crest except in the form permitted and described on page 32. The evergreen plant badge should be fixed behind the crest badge.

A broadsword is worn with court dress, and the wearing of a dirk may have some justification on dress occasions, but it is not necessary. A sgian-dubh, however, may be carried in the right-hand stocking on all occasions.

The kilt is male attire and should never be worn by ladies. A pleated skirt is the correct female attire and under no circumstances should a sporran be worn. For evening wear a tartan skirt of silk or other fine material, with suitable corsage, may be worn together with a sash of silk tartan. The sash is fixed by a brooch to the left shoulder, one end crossing the back and the other carried across the breast, both ends being knotted on the right side.

Many ladies prefer a plain evening frock with tartan sash fixed as above. To meet changing conditions the ancient dress has been simplified to its present form. The survival of the kilt is due almost entirely to the Highland regiments, who have worn it since their inception as military units. The Black Watch, 42nd Regiment (whose tartan is illustrated on page 101) is the premier Highland regiment. This rather sombre tartan is sometimes claimed to have been a Clan Campbell tartan. It has been used as a military tartan since the eighteenth century and in early references to it is called the " Universal," " Government " or " Military " tartan. Many tartans are based upon this Black Watch pattern, the only difference being the addition of overstripes as in the Forbes, Lamont, Gordon, MacKenzie, MacKinlay, Murray of Atholl, and so on.

Those who wear tartan and the Highland dress are helping to preserve the costume of our Scottish ancestors. They recall the romantic days of Scotland's historic past and those who wear them can feel proud that their dress was, for countless centuries, the garb of the Highland people.

Crest Badges

The wearing of crest badges[1] as a symbol of kinship with some Highland Clan or Scottish family is a survival from an old and interesting custom recognised in heraldic law.

In former times many chiefs gave to their followers a metal plate of their crest to wear as a badge. This crest badge was affixed to the Clansman's clothing or accoutrements by a strap and buckle and when not in use the strap and buckle were coiled round the crest badge. This custom is still observed by some chiefs, and is legally competent.

The modern conventional representation of the old metal plate crest badge takes the form of a metal representation of the chief's crest *encircled by a metal strap and buckle* and having the chief's motto cut or engraved on the strap. This is the only form in which a clansman is permitted to display his chief's crest and its use, in the correct and approved manner, indicates that the wearer is a kinsman or follower of the chief whose crest is thus shown. Only the chief and his heir wear the crest without the strap and buckle.

A coat-of-arms, and the crest which forms part of it, is the personal property of the individual in whose name it has been recorded in the Public Registers of All Arms and Bearings in Scotland. It must not be used, in part or in whole, by any other person, and misuse of another's coat-of-arms is an offence liable to action and penalties in Lyon Court.

The Chief's coat-of-arms and banner derived from it indicate the authority, identity and/or presence of the chief just as Royal Arms do for a sovereign.

As symbols of Clan or family kinship crest badges are an ever-present reminder of an old custom and a means of showing our pride of heritage. If we value these things we must not misuse them, as their use in conformity with the Scots heraldic laws gives unity and efficiency to the clan.

Margaret O. MacDougall

---

[1] *For an explanation of the terms used in the description of the crest badges, see notes on Heraldic Terms. (pp.10 and 317)*

About 1670
Portrait of an unknown Highland Chieftain
by Michael Wright from the Scottish National Portrait Gallery,
showing the belted plaid worn at this period.

1831
Highland chiefs dressed in the Stewart and Gordon tartans
from *The Scottish Gael or Celtic Manners* by James Logan.

Contemporary Highland evening dress
showing the continuing vitality of tartan design in the
American Bicentennial tartan created by James D Scarlett.

ANDERSON *or* MACANDREW

House of Airdbreck

CREST BADGE : *An oak tree proper*

MOTTO : *Stand sure.*

GAELIC NAME : *Mac Ghille Aindrais.*

THIS NAME, now fairly widespread throughout Scotland, means " son of Andrew " and in the Highlands is rendered as MacAndrew. In the Lowlands, however, the form of Anderson is more common.

The MacAndrews are regarded as a sept of Clan Chattan, having been associated with that Confederation of Clans from the beginning of the 15th century. In the Kinrara manuscript it is claimed that the MacAndrews came to Badenoch from Moidart about the year 1400.

One famous member of the clan was John MacAndrew of Dalnahatnich, known in Gaelic as Iain Beg Mac-Aindrea. He was a bowman of note and the terror of all who fought against him. Many tales are told of his exploits and his vengeance upon the cattle lifters who raided Badenoch. In 1670 some Lochaber men raided Badenoch and drove away a large number of cattle. They were pursued by a body of men, including Iain Beg, under the command of William Mackintosh of Kyllachy. The cattle lifters were overtaken and in the fight which followed Iain Beg killed most of the raiders. Only one Lochaber man escaped and he carried with him the full story of his comrades' fate at the hands of Iain Beg MacAindrea. The men of Lochaber swore vengeance against little John and made many attempts on his life. As a consequence he led an unsettled exisence for many years but was always able to defend himself. Traditionally some MacAndrews are associated with the MacDonnels of Glengary and wear their tartan.

The most prominent branches of the Andersons were Dowhill, Wester Ardbreck and Candacraig in Strathdon.

36

ANDERSON

ORIGIN OF NAME: *Son of Andrew.*

ARMSTRONG
House of
Gilnockie Mangerston

CREST BADGE: *An arm embowed, proper.*

MOTTO: *Invictus maneo (I remain unvanquished).*

GAELIC NAME: *Mac Ghillielàidir.*

AN ACT passed by the Scottish Parliament in 1587 " for the quieting and keeping in obedience of the . . . inhabitants of the Borders, Highlands and Isles," containing a roll of " the clans that have Captains, Chiefs and Chieftains . . . as well on the Borders as the Highlands," proves that so long ago as the sixteenth century Border families were described as clans, and one of the most important of these families was the Armstrongs.

There is a traditional story that the progenitor of the clan was Fairbairn, an armour bearer of a king of Scotland who went to the assistance of his master when the king had his horse killed under him in battle. Fairbairn, grasping the king by the thigh, set him on his own horse. For this service the king granted Fairbairn lands on the Borders, and gave to him the name Armstrong. The first family of the name on record in Scotland is found in Liddesdale in 1376.

The Armstrongs, a numerous and warlike clan, held lands all along the Borders, chiefly in Liddesdale, where their power was unquestionable. They are said to have been able to muster 3,000 men, and their lawlessness kept the borders in turmoil.

The Armstrongs of Gilnockie were the principal branch of the clan, and John Armstrong of Gilnockie in the early part of the 16th century was captured, through a stratagem, by King James V, and, with over thirty of his followers, was hanged at Carlingrigg. The event is the subject of one of the best of our Border ballads.

ARMSTRONG

ORIGIN OF NAME: *Strong arm (see text).*

BAIRD
House of Auchmeddan

CREST BADGE : *An eagle's head erased, proper.*

MOTTO : *Dominus fecit* (*The Lord made*).

GAELIC NAME : *Mac a'bhaird.*

FOR SAVING his life from a wild boar, King William the Lion is said to have made extensive grants of land to one of his followers named Baird.

A charter was granted to Richard Baird of Meikle and Little Kyp in Lanarkshire, and King Robert the Bruce granted the Barony of Cambusnethan to a Robert Baird. This family of Cambusnethan spread to Banffshire, and later to Auchmeddan in Aberdeenshire. George Baird of Auchmeddan married the niece of the Earl Marischal and the family increased in importance, and supplied a long line of sheriffs to that county. From the Auchmeddan branch came the Bairds of Newbyth and Saughtonhall; and John, who died in 1698, was created Knight Baronet, and made a Lord of Session with the title Lord Newbyth.

General Sir David Baird, Bart., K.C.B., born in 1757, entered the army in 1772, and in command of the 73rd regiment reached Madras in 1780. When seriously wounded he was captured by Hyder Ali, and remained a prisoner until 1784. He and a sergeant were the only two remaining of the original 73rd regiment. He was at the capture of Pondicherry in 1793, and in 1799 he captured Seringapatam. He campaigned in several countries, captured the Cape of Good Hope from the Dutch in 1807, and in the same year was at the siege of Copenhagen. In 1808 he joined Sir John Moore at Corunna. After Moore's death he assumed the chief command, and had the honour of announcing the victory to the government. He received many honours, and died in 1829.

BAIRD

ORIGIN OF NAME: *Place-name, Lanarkshire.*

BALMORAL

*A castle situated on the upper
valley of the Dee, Aberdeenshire,
9 m. from Ballater. Purchased by
Queen Victoria in 1848, it has
always been a favourite of the
Royal Family.*

THE visit of King George IV to Edinburgh in 1822,
and the large number of persons wearing the Highland
dress on that occasion created a general interest in tartans,
and the love of Her Majesty Queen Victoria for all things
Highland, and particularly tartan, led to an increased use
of tartan on all possible occasions.

The Balmoral tartan was designed by H.R.H. the
Prince Consort and was used by Queen Victoria when
making gifts to her friends. It was in general use in the
royal household when the Queen visited the Highlands,
and is reserved for the sole use of the Royal Family.

BALMORAL

ORIGIN OF NAME: *From Gaelic bail (village) and mòral (majestic).*

BARCLAY

CREST BADGE : *Out of a chapeau azure turned ermine a hand holding a dagger, proper.*

MOTTO : *Aut agere aut mori (Either action or death).*

THE Barclays in Scotland are claimed to have descended from the Berkeleys who came to England with William the Conqueror. In 1165 Walter de Berkeley was Chamberlain of Scotland, and in the 12th and 13th centuries the Berkeleys were numerous in Kincardineshire and the east of Scotland. The Barclays of Mathers traced their descent from Alexander, who obtained these lands in 1351 on his marriage to the sister of the Great Marischal of Scotland. His son was the first of the clan to spell his name Barclay. The lands remained in the possession of the family until David Barclay, born in 1580, was compelled for financial reasons to sell his estates. The chiefship passed to the descendants of James Barclay of Mill of Towie in the 19th century.

The Barclays of Urie are descended from Colonel David Barclay, who had served under Gustavus Adolphus of Sweden, and who purchased the estate of Urie in 1647. Robert, his eldest son, became the celebrated apologist of the Quakers. In 1682 he was appointed Governor of East Jersey, but he did not go out, although his brother John settled there. Robert died in 1690.

Other important branches of the family were the Barclays of Collairnie in Fife, the Barclays of Pierston, and the Barclays of Ardrossan. The Barclays of Tolly, in Aberdeenshire, remained in possession of the lands from the 12th till the 18th century, and from this family was descended the famous Russian General, Field Marshal Prince Barclay de Tolly, who died in 1818.

BLACK WATCH

See pages 100-1

BARCLAY

There is a green hunting sett.

ORIGIN OF NAME: *Place-name from Berkeley, England.*

BRODIE

CREST BADGE : *A dexter hand holding a sheaf of arrows, all proper.*

MOTTO : *Unite.*

GAELIC NAME : *Brothaigh.*

FROM earliest times the Clan Brodie was associated with the province of Moray. In the 12th century King Malcolm IV is said to have confirmed their possession of land there, and Michael, Thane of Brodie, received a charter from Robert the Bruce two or three years before the battle of Bannockburn. During the 13th, 14th and 15th centuries the family name appeared frequently in the charters of the period, and John of Brodie assisted the MacKenzies against the MacDonalds at the famous battle of Blair-na-park in 1466. In 1550 Alexander Brodie and over a hundred others were denounced rebels for attacking Alexander Cumming of Altyre.

The family continued prominent in local and national affairs and Alexander Brodie of Brodie, born in 1617, was a Senator of the College of Justice. He represented the county of Elgin in Parliament from 1643 and in 1649 he went to Holland from Parliament to treat with Charles II and to arrange for the conditions of his return to Scotland. He was cited to London by Cromwell to negotiate a union between the two kingdoms, but he avoided employment under the Lord-Protector. He died in 1679.

Alexander Brodie of Brodie, born in 1697, . was appointed Lord Lyon King at Arms in 1727. He died in 1754. Throughout the long history of the family the Brodies became connected through marriage with many of the greatest families in Scotland. Brodie Castle in Morayshire is the seat of the chief.

BRODIE

There is also a hunting tartan.

ORIGIN OF NAME: *Place-name, Morayshire.*
PLANT BADGE: *Periwinkle.*

BRUCE

CREST BADGE: *A lion statant with tail extended, azure, armed and langued gules.*

MOTTO: *Fuimus* (*We have been*).

GAELIC NAME: *Brus.*

SIR ROBERT DE BRUS, a Norman knight, who accompanied William the Conqueror to England is claimed as the progenitor of this clan. The connection of the Brus family with Scotland originated when Robert de Brus was companion at arms to Prince David, later King David I, during his stay at the court of Henry I of England. Brus received from King David a grant of the Lordship of Annandale. He resigned his lands to his son at the outbreak of war with England, and at the battle of the Standard in 1138, the elder Brus, who fought on the English side, is said to have taken his son prisoner. Robert, 4th Lord of Annandale, married a niece of William the Lion, and on this marriage was based the subsequent claims of the family of Bruce to the throne of Scotland. Robert, 6th Lord of Annandale and 1st Earl of Carrick, maintained his claims, but fought on the English side at the Battle of Dunbar. He died in 1304.

His eldest son Robert, 7th Lord of Annandale and 2nd Earl of Carrick, was born in 1274. He was the famous King Robert the Bruce, the victor at Bannockburn in 1314, who after a fierce struggle gained the independence of Scotland acknowledged by the treaty of Northampton in 1328. He died in 1329 at Cardross and was buried in Dunfermline. His heart which was carried by Sir James Douglas reached Spain on its way to the Holy Land, but owing to the death of Sir James was brought back to Scotland and buried at Melrose.

From the Bruces of Clackmannan are descended the Earls of Elgin.

BRUCE

ORIGIN OF NAME: *from French town of Brix.*
PLANT BADGE: *Rosemary.*

BUCHANAN

CREST BADGE : *A dexter hand couped at the wrist, holding up a chapeau tasseled with a rose gules, all within a laurel wreath, proper.*

MOTTO : *Clarior hinc honos* (*Brighter hence the honour*).

GAELIC NAME : *Canonach.*

BUCHANAN OF AUCHMAR traces the origin of the clan to Anselan o' Kyan, son of a king of Ulster, who landed in Argyll about the year 1016. For his services against the Danes, so it is said, he received from King Malcolm II the lands of Buchanan, lying to the east of Loch Lomond. These lands remained in the possession of the family for almost seven centuries until the death of John, 22nd laird of Buchanan, in 1682.

Cadets of the clan included the Buchanans of Auchmar, Spittal, Arnprior, Drumikill, Carbeth and Leny, and the chiefship passed ultimately to the Leny branch.

The clan bore their full share of the military operations of their country. They supported Bruce in his struggle for Scottish independence and the clan was represented in the 7000 men sent from Scotland to assist the French king after the Battle of Agincourt. It is claimed that Sir Alexander Buchanan killed the Duke of Clarence at the Battle of Baugé in 1421. The chief of the clan and Buchanan of Leny fell at Flodden in 1513. The clan took an active part in the Battles of Pinkie and Langside.

The Buchanan lands were sold in 1682 and the principal line became extinct in 1762 following the death of the 22nd chief. The chiefship then passed to Buchanan of Spittal.

George Buchanan, the famous Latin scholar, was born in 1506. Educated at St. Andrews and Paris, he was imprisoned at the instance of Cardinal Beaton, but escaped to France. He was tutor to Mary Queen of Scots, and was afterwards moderator of the General Assembly, and tutor to James VI. From 1570 till 1578 he was Keeper of the Privy Seal. He died in 1582.

BUCHANAN

A hunting tartan has recently become popular.

ORIGIN OF NAME: *from Both-Charain (Canon's Seat). Original name was MacAuslan (Son of Absalon).*
PLANT BADGE: *Bilberry, Oak.*
WAR CRY: *Clar Innis (an island on Loch Lomond).*

CAMERON

CREST BADGE: *A sheaf of five arrows tied with a band, gules.*

MOTTO: *Aonaibh ri cheile (Unite).*

OLD MOTTO: *Mo righ's mo dhuchaich (For king and country).*

GAELIC NAME: *Camshron.*

THE CLAN CAMERON described as " fiercer than fierceness itself " are reputed to be one of the ancient clans of Scotland, and for centuries associated with Lochaber. It consisted originally of three branches, the MacMartins of Letterfinlay, the MacGillonies of Strone, and the MacSorlies of Glen Nevis. The Camerons of Locheil descended from the Strone branch are said to have obtained their lands and the chiefship of the clan through intermarriage with the Letterfinlay branch. For a time the clan were subject to the Lords of the Isles and John assisted Donald, Lord of the Isles, at the Battle of Harlaw in 1411. Later, however, the Camerons withdrew from their association with their powerful allies and a long period of feuds followed.

A notable chief was Sir Ewen of Locheil, born in 1629, who was received in London by King Charles II in 1660, and was knighted in 1680. He fought at Killiecrankie ten years later. The Camerons were always strong adherents of the Stuarts, and Sir Ewen never submitted to Cromwell. When too old for military service, Sir Ewen, in 1715, sent the clan under his son, to help the Earl of Mar. Sir Ewen's grandson Donald, known as " the Gentle Locheil," joined Prince Charles in 1745, and he will ever be honoured as one of the outstanding personalities of the '45. He escaped to France and died there in 1748. The family estates were forfeited, but on their restoration under the General Act of Amnesty of 1784, the Gentle Locheil's grandson, Donald, 22nd chief, resumed possession. Auchnacarry Castle is the home of the chief.

CAMERON

ORIGIN OF NAME: *Camshron from Gaelic cam (wry) and sron (nose), wry-nose.*
PLANT BADGE: *Oak, Crowberry.*
WAR CRY: *Chlanna nan con thigibh a so's gheibh sibh feoil (Sons of the hounds come here and get flesh).*
PIPE MUSIC: *Piobaireachd Dhonuill Duibh.*

CAMERON OF LOCHIEL

CREST BADGE : *A sheaf of five arrows tied with a band, gules.*

MOTTO : *Aonaibh ri cheile (Unite).*

OLD MOTTO : *Mo righ's mo dhuthaich (For king and country).*

GAELIC NAME : *Camshron.*

THE history of the Camerons of Lochiel is inseparably bound up with the history of the clan, as witness the references in the preceding sketch, but in 1528 the lands of the " Captain of Clan Cameron " were erected into the barony of Lochiel by a charter granted by King James V in which the " Captain " is for the first time described as " of Lochiel."

During the time of Sir Ewen, 17th of Lochiel, the castle of Achnacarry was built, and has remained the home of the Camerons of Lochiel until the present day, although the original house was destroyed in 1746, and the present castle was not finished until about 1837. Sir Ewen, who built the original mansion, was the celebrated chief of the clan who waged war against the troops of Cromwell. In the end the Camerons were allowed to retain their arms on their promise to live peaceably, and " no oath was required of Lochiel but his word of honour."

Donald, 19th of Lochiel, " the Gentle Lochiel " whose bravery and heroism was amply proved during the '45, constantly endeavoured to ameliorate the horrors of war as far as possible. He is said to have saved the city of Glasgow from being pillaged during its occupation by the Jacobite army in 1745.

In 1796 Donald, 22nd chief, was by decree of Lyon Court established as chief of the family of Lochiel and as chief of Clan Cameron.

CAMERON OF LOCHIEL

ORIGIN OF NAME: *Camshron from Gaelic cam (wry) and sron (nose), wry-nose.*
PLANT BADGE: *Oak, Crowberry.*
WAR CRY: *Chlanna nan con thigibh a so's gheibh sibh feoil (Sons of the hounds come here and get flesh).*
PIPE MUSIC: *Piobaireachd Dhonuill Duibh.*

CAMERON OF ERRACHT

REGIMENTAL CAP BADGE : *Within a wreath of thistles, the image of St. Andrew holding before him his cross.*

REGIMENTAL MOTTO : *Cameron.*

GAELIC NAME : *Camshron.*

THE Queen's Own Cameron Highlanders wear this tartan, which, according to regimental tradition was designed by the mother of the founder of the regiment. Although widely worn, it is not a Clan Tartan.

The progenitor of the Camerons of Erracht was Ewen, son of Ewen, Chief of the Clan Cameron, by his second wife Marjory Mackintosh, in the first half of the 16th century. At the Jacobite Rising in 1745 Cameron of Erracht supported Prince Charles and was second in command of the Clan Cameron.

Alan Cameron of Erracht, who was born *c.* 1753, served in America and after his return home he raised the original 79th Regiment, Cameron Highlanders, in 1793. He was appointed Lieut.-Colonel Commandant and commanded the regiment throughout the Flanders Campaign of 1794-1795. In 1797 the regiment was disbanded and many of the men joined The Black Watch. A year later Colonel Cameron raised another regiment in the Highlands, also numbered the 79th. In 1804 a second battalion was formed with which the Colonel served in the Low Countries and in the Peninsular War. Colonel Cameron was made a K.C.B. in 1815 and in 1819 was promoted Lieutenant General. He died in 1828.

Since 1873 the regiment has been designated " The Queen's Own Cameron Highlanders." In April, 1798, the officers of the regiment were made burgesses of Inverness and in August, 1953, the freedom of the town was conferred on the regiment. *See also note on page 289.*

CAMERON OF ERRACHT

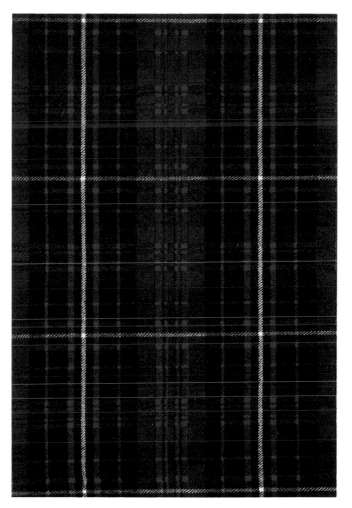

ORIGIN OF NAME: *Camshron from Gaelic cam (wry) and sron (nose), wry-nose.*
REGIMENTAL MARCH PAST: *Pibroch of Donald Dubh.*

CAMPBELL

CREST BADGE : *A boar's head, fesswise, couped, or.*

MOTTO : *Ne obliviscaris (Forget not).*

GAELIC NAME : *Caimbeul.*

KNOWN as the race of Diarmid, the Clan Campbell was for centuries a most powerful influence in Argyll and the West of Scotland. In the 13th century Archibald Campbell obtained the Lordship of Lochow through his marriage with the daughter of the King's Treasurer, and for a long period thereafter the Campbells of Lochow formed one of the chief branches of the clan.

Sir Colin, of Lochow, the progenitor of the Campbells of Argyll, was knighted in 1280, and from him the chiefs of Argyll received the designation, MacCailean Mor, retained by the Dukes of Argyll till the present day. His descendant Sir Duncan was created a peer by King James II in 1445, and Duncan's grandson Colin was created Earl of Argyll in 1457. Archibald, his son, who was Lord High Chancellor, was killed at Flodden in 1513.

Archibald, 5th Earl, although a prominent Reformer, commanded the army of Queen Mary at the Battle of Langside, while his brother Colin supported the young king. Archibald, 7th Earl, commanded the army which was defeated by the Earls of Huntly and Erroll in 1594. His son was the leader of the Covenanters. He was created Marquis in 1641, but in spite of his loyalty was beheaded in 1661. His son Archibald was beheaded in 1685 for his part in the Monmouth rebellion. Archibald, 10th Earl, returned with William of Orange, and by him was elevated to a Dukedom. John, 2nd Duke of Argyll, was created Duke of Greenwich in the peerage of the United Kingdom. John, 9th Duke, married Princess Louise, daughter of Queen Victoria, in 1871.

CAMPBELL

There is also a dress tartan. (The Duke of Argyll wears the 42nd [Black Watch] tartan woven in brighter colours.)

ORIGIN OF NAME: *Caimbeul, from Gaelic cam (wry) and beul (mouth), wry-mouth.*
PLANT BADGE: *Fir club moss, Bog myrtle.*
WAR CRY: *Cruachan.*
PIPE MUSIC: *Baile Ionaraora (The Campbells are coming).*

CAMPBELL OF BREADALBANE

CREST BADGE : *A boar's head, erased, proper.*

MOTTO : *Follow me.*

GAELIC NAME : *Caimbeul.*

THE CAMPBELLS OF BREADALBANE trace their family back to Sir Colin, son of Sir Duncan Campbell of Lochow. From his father he received the lands of Glenorchy, and through his marriage with a daughter of Lord Lorn he received a third part of the lands of Lorn. He built Kilchurn Castle in 1440, and for his valour in Palestine he was made a Knight of Rhodes.

The descendants of Sir Duncan were successful in adding to the possessions of the family, and in course of time these included the lands of Glenlyon, Finlarig, and territory throughout Argyll and Perthshire.

Sir John Campbell, 11th of Glenorchy, was created Earl of Breadalbane in 1681, and was a strong supporter of King Charles II. He was described as cunning as a fox, wise as a serpent, and as slippery as an eel. In 1689 he was employed to bribe the Highland clans to submit to King William III. He died in 1716.

In 1806 John, 14th of Breadalbane, was created a Baron of the United Kingdom, and in 1831 he was raised to a Marquessate. In 1862 by the death of John, 5th Earl, without issue, the United Kingdom titles became extinct, but the Marquessate was restored to Gavin, 7th Earl, in 1885. On the death of the 7th Earl in 1922, without issue, the Marquessate again became extinct, but the Scottish honours devolved upon his nephew, the 8th Earl.

CAMPBELL OF BREADALBANE

ORIGIN OF NAME: *Caimbeul, from Gaelic cam (wry) and beul
(mouth), wry-mouth.*
PLANT BADGE: *Fir club moss, Bog myrtle.*
WAR CRY: *Cruachan.*
PIPE MUSIC: *Bodaich nam Brigisean (The Carles with the breeks).*

CAMPBELL OF CAWDOR (CALDER)

CREST BADGE : *A swan, proper, crowned, or.*
MOTTO : *Be mindful.*
GAELIC NAME : *Caimbeul.*

THE founder of this branch of the Clan Campbell was Sir John Campbell, third son of the 2nd Earl of Argyll, who married Muriel, daughter of Sir John Calder of Calder, in 1510. Sir John died in 1546, but his widow survived him by almost thirty years. On her death the Thanedom of Cawdor passed to her grandson, John, who sold part of his estates in order to purchase Islay, which remained in possession of the Cawdor family till 1726, when it was purchased by Campbell of Shawfield.

Sir John, 8th of Cawdor, who married Mary, daughter of Lewis Pryce, died in 1777, and was succeeded by Pryce Campbell, Member of Parliament for Cromarty and Nairn. John, his son, was born in Scotland but spent most of his life in Wales. He was created Lord Cawdor in 1796. In the following year when 1200 French soldiers landed at Fishguard, the last foreign invasion of Great Britain, Lord Cawdor with a few troops and a large number of peasants, took them prisoners. He died in 1821, and was succeeded by his son, John Frederick Campbell, 2nd Baron Cawdor, who was created Earl of Cawdor in 1827. Cawdor Castle, built about 1454, is one of the finest old castles in Scotland, and is the residence of the chief.

CAMPBELL OF CAWDOR

ORIGIN OF NAME: *Caimbeul, from Gaelic cam (wry) and beul (mouth), wry-mouth.*
PLANT BADGE: *Fir club moss, Bog myrtle.*
WAR CRY: *Cruachan.*
PIPE MUSIC: *Campbell of Cawdor's Salute.*

CHISHOLM

CREST BADGE : *A dexter hand couped at the wrist holding erect a dagger, proper, on which is transfixed a boar's head, couped, proper langued azure.*

MOTTO : *Feros Ferio* (*I am fierce with the fierce*).

GAELIC NAME : *Siosal.*

AN old chief of the clan claimed that only three persons in the world were entitled to use the definite article " The," namely, " The Pope, The King, and The Chisholm." It is claimed by some writers that the Chisholms are of Celtic origin ; others claim that the clan came from the Borders and are of Norman origin. Sir Robert Gordon designates as Chisholm the Thane of Caithness who lived in the latter part of the 12th century. In the Ragman's Roll in 1296 mention is made of Richard de Cheschelme and " John de Cheshome." The homes of the Chisholms were in Roxburgh and Berwick. A descendant, Sir Robert, Lord of Chisholm, succeeded his father-in-law as Constable of Urquhart Castle in 1359. His son, Alexander, married the heiress of Erchless and founded the family of Erchless and Strathglass. This family ceased in the male line, and in 1513 Wiland de Chesholm, of another branch of the family, obtained the lands of Commer and the lands of Erchless and others.

From time to time during the next two centuries there is evidence that the Chisholms were actively engaged in war-like operations. In 1715 the clan served under the Earl of Mar, and in 1745 the Chief with his clan joined Prince Charles, and fought with great valour at the Battle of Culloden. During the Prince's wanderings after the battle, a Chisholm was one of the seven men who sheltered him in Glenmoriston, and afterwards led him across the country to Arisaig. Following The Chisholm's death in 1887 the chiefship passed to the descendants of the heiress of the senior direct line.

CHISHOLM

There is a hunting tartan.

ORIGIN OF NAME: *Place-name, Roxburghshire.*
PLANT BADGE: *Fern.*
PIPE MUSIC: *Chisholm's March.*

CLAN CHATTAN

CREST BADGE: *A cat salient.*

MOTTO: *Touch not the cat but a glove.* (*Touch not the cat without a glove*).

GAELIC NAME: *Clann Gillacatan.*

CLAN CHATTAN, or the " Clan of the Cats," was a very ancient confederation of clans. Originally composed of the Mackintoshes, Davidsons, Macphersons, Mac-Gillivrays and MacBeans, it was later strengthened by the addition of other clans including the Farquharsons.

Gillechattan Mor is claimed to have been the first authentic chief, and from him descended Eva, only child of Dougall Dall, 6th chief. Eva married in 1291, Angus, 6th Laird of Mackintosh, who thus became Captain of Clan Chattan.

The chiefs of Clan Macpherson claimed the chiefship of Clan Chattan on the grounds that they were descended from Muireach, the Parson of Kingussie (1173), who was also Chief of Clan Chattan. Muireach's eldest son was Gillechattan Patrick, grandfather of Eva, and his second son, Ewan Ban, was the progenitor of Clan Macpherson. It is now accepted, however, that the chiefship of Clan Chattan was a heritable honour and that the chiefship was conferred on Eva by her father.

For 200 years the two clans feuded over the chiefship and in 1672 Cluny Macpherson matriculated arms as " the laird of Cluny and the only true representer of the ancient and honourable family of Clan Chattan." The chief of Mackintosh protested and the arms given to Cluny were withdrawn. He was given new arms as a cadet of Clan Chattan.

The 28th chief of Mackintosh who died in 1938 without male issue, had nominated his successor as Chief of Clan Mackintosh but not of Clan Chattan. His death separated the chiefship of both clans and, in 1947, Duncan Alexander Eliott Mackintosh, descendant of the Daviot branch of the Mackintoshes, was granted the arms of Clan Chattan by the Lord Lyon.

CLAN CHATTAN

ORIGIN OF NAME: *Clan of the Cats.*
PLANT BADGE: *Red whortleberry.*
WAR CRY: *Clan Chattan.*

CLERGY

EMBLEM : *The burning bush (see Exodus c. 3 v. 2) has been used as the symbol of the Church of Scotland since the end of the 18th century. To date, the adoption has not been made official.*

MOTTO : *Nec tamen consumebatur (And it was not consumed).*

THAT the clergy in the Highlands in the olden times belonged to the church militant can be proved from many sources. It is recorded of a clergyman in Skye in the 18th century that " he attended church with his two-handed sword, and his servant walked behind him with his bow and case of arrows."

It is recorded of one church, by another author, that when Presbyterianism became the national form of church government in Scotland, " It was not an easy matter even to declare the church vacant and were it not that the Presbytery happened to reckon among its members a certain person of no ordinary trepidity, the ceremony would probably have been indefinitely postponed or omitted altogether." " It is told of Colin Campbell, minister of Ardchattan, the person in question, that, having volunteered to undertake the task, he was met at Kilchoan Church, and angrily denied admittance by MacDonald's friends. But Campbell was dressed in the kilt, and armed with a sword in one hand, and a cocked pistol in the other, set his back against the wall, and resolutely defied the stormy audience in front of him."

Many of the Highland surnames are of ecclesiastical origin, such as Clark, Gilchrist, Gillespie, Gillies, Macclery, Macgilchrist, Macmillan, Macnab, Macniven, Macpherson, Mactaggart, Macvicar.

CLERGY

COLQUHOUN

CREST BADGE : *A hart's head, couped, gules, attired, argent.*

MOTTO : *Si je puis (If I can).*

GAELIC NAME : *Mac a' Chombaich.*

THIS clan takes its name from the lands of Colquhoun in the county of Dunbarton. These lands were granted to Humphrey of Kilpatrick by Malcolm, Earl of Lennox, in the time of Alexander II. Sir Robert Kilpatrick, of Colquhoun, married the daughter of the laird of Luss, and since then the chief has been described as of Colquhoun and Luss.

About 1602 a desperate battle was fought between the Colquhouns and the MacGregors. After a conference between the two clans the Colquhouns hoped to trap the MacGregors in Glenfruin, but their intention was anticipated by Alastair MacGregor of Glenstrae, and after a bloody conflict the Colquhouns were signally defeated and their chief killed. In revenge they made a dramatic representation to the King and the Clan Gregor was proscribed and their name forbidden under pain of death.

Sir John Colquhoun (*c.* 1621–1676), known as the "Black Cock of the West," was a man of ability and learning who took a prominent part in public affairs and was a member of the first parliament after the Restoration.

Sir Humphrey, 18th chief, surrendered his baronetcy for a new grant to himself and his daughter and his son-in-law James Grant, of Pluscarden, with a condition preventing the clan name and estates passing to the Grants of Grant. Owing to this provision two Grants in succession had to resign the estates which then passed to a younger son of James Grant from whom the present Luss family are descended.

COLQUHOUN

ORIGIN OF NAME: *Place-name, Dunbartonshire.*
PLANT BADGE: *Hazel.*
WAR CRY: *Cnoc Ealachain.*
PIPE MUSIC: *The Colquhoun's March.*

CUMMING
CUMIN *or* COMYN

CREST BADGE : *A lion rampant, or, holding in his dexter paw a dagger, proper.*

MOTTO : *Courage.*

GAELIC NAME : *Cuimean.*

THE clan territory of the Cumins was Badenoch, and the chiefs were known as Lords of Badenoch. It is recorded that they came from England following the Norman Conquest, but it is to be remembered that there was a Cumin, Abbot of Iona, in the 7th century.

William de Comyn received a grant of land in Roxburgh, and in 1133 he was appointed Chancellor of Scotland by David I. His nephew Richard had great authority in Scotland, and William, son of Richard, was Justiciary of Scotland, and in 1210 became Earl of Buchan by marriage with Marjory, Countess of Buchan, only child of Fergus, 1st Earl. William's son by a previous marriage became Earl of Menteith and acquired the Lordship of Badenoch by grant from Alexander II. His nephew John, known as the " Red Comyn," was the father of the " Black Comyn " who was one of the six guardians of Scotland during the minority of the Maiden of Norway, and later became a competitor for the Crown of Scotland. The " Black Comyn " married Marjory, sister of John Baliol, and their son John was known, like his grandfather, as the " Red Comyn." Like so many nobles at that time his vacillating policy depended on self-interest. He fought alternately for and against Scotland, until he was stabbed by Bruce, and finally killed by Bruce's followers, Lindsay and Kirkpatrick, at Dumfries in 1306. This was the occasion when Kirkpatrick is alleged to have said " I'll mak siccar." The Comyns were finally defeated at Inverury in 1308, and John, the only son of the " Red Comyn," died in 1325, without issue, thus terminating the direct line of the principal branch of the family.

CUMIN _or_ COMYN

ORIGIN OF NAME: _Place-name, Comines in Flanders._
PLANT BADGE: _Cumin plant._

CUMMING

CREST BADGE: *A lion rampant.
or, holding in his dexter paw a
dagger, proper*

MOTTO: *Courage.*

GAELIC NAME: *Cuimean.*

WHEN ROBERT THE BRUCE secured the throne of
Scotland he generally rewarded his friends at the
expense of his enemies, and the family of Comyn was
among the latter who lost land and titles. However, the
Cummings, to use the modern spelling of the name,
remained numerous in the north-east of Scotland.

The Cummings of Culter traced their descent from
Jardine Comyn, son of the Earl of Buchan, in the 13th
century. The history of the Cummings of Relugas
emerges from the 16th century, but it is the Cummings
of Altyre who have occupied the principal position since
the fall of the Comyns.

The first of the Cummings to be designated as of
Altyre, was Ferquhard, son of Sir Richard Cumming,
in the 14th century, a descendant of the Lords of Badenoch. During the 15th and 16th centuries the Cummings
were actively engaged in public affairs, even to a feud
with the clan Brodie. In 1594 Alexander Cumming of
Altyre commanded a troop of horse in Huntly's army
at the Battle of Glenlivet when the Earl of Argyle was
defeated.

In 1657 Robért Cumming of Altyre married Lucy,
daughter of Sir Ludovick Gordon of Gordonstown, and
when the last Sir William Gordon of Gordonstown died,
more than a century later, Alexander Cumming of Altyre,
being his heir, assumed the name and arms of Gordon of
Gordonstown, and was created a baronet in 1804. He
died in 1806, and his second son Sir William became 2nd
Baronet. Sir Alexander Penrose Gordon-Cumming,
3rd Bart., succeeded his father, and his brother Roualeyn
was the famous traveller and lion hunter in the middle of
last century.

CUMMING

ORIGIN OF NAME: *Place-name, Comines in Flanders.*
PLANT BADGE: *Cumin plant.*

CUNNINGHAM
House of Glencairn

CREST BADGE : *A unicorn's head, argent, crined and armed, or.*

MOTTO : *Over fork over.*

GAELIC NAME : *MacCuinneagain.*

THE family of Cunningham takes its name from the district of Cunningham in Ayrshire. The name occurs as early as the 12th century. About the beginning of the following century the family resigned all their lands in Kilpatrick to the Earl of Lennox. Hervey de Cunningham received from Alexander III the lands of Kilmaurs for his bravery at the Battle of Largs in 1263. The Kilmaurs remained the principal family, and Sir William Cunningham by his marriage to Margaret, daughter of Sir Robert Dennieston of that ilk, added many lands to his family possessions including Glencairn, from which Alexander de Cunningham took his title when created Earl of Glencairn by James III in 1488. He was killed at the Battle of Sauchieburn.

William Cunningham, 8th Earl of Glencairn, born about 1610, was appointed Privy Councillor and Commissioner of the Treasury in 1641, and Lord Justice General in 1646. In 1653 he raised an army in the Highlands in support of Charles II. After the Restoration he was appointed Lord Chancellor of Scotland. He died in 1664. James, 14th Earl of Glencairn, was the friend of our national bard, and when he died in 1791, Burns wrote his well-known " Lament for the Earl of Glencairn." With the death of John, 15th Earl, who died without issue in 1796, the Earldom became dormant.

Many important branches of the family spread all over Scotland. The Cunninghams of Corsehill derive from the second son of the 3rd Earl of Glencairn. The Cunninghams of Caprington trace their ancestry back to the fourteenth century.

CUNNINGHAM

ORIGIN OF NAME: *Place-name, Ayrshire.*

DAVIDSON

CREST BADGE : *A stag's head, erased, proper.*

MOTTO : *Sapienter si sincere (Wisely if sincerely).*

GAELIC NAME : *MacDhaibhidh.*

WHEN the power of the Comyns began to wane in Badenoch, Donald Dubh of Invernahaven, Chief of the Davidsons, having married the daughter of Angus, 6th of Mackintosh, sought the protection of William, 7th of Mackintosh, before 1350, and became associated with the Clan Chattan confederation.

The clan became known as the Clan Dhai from David Dubh of Invernahaven their first chief. Their entry into the Clan Chattan led to a dispute apparently regarding precedence. A portion of Mackintosh's estate lying in Lochaber was let to the Camerons and Mackintosh had difficulty in obtaining rent for it. About 1370 the Camerons decided to attack Mackintosh, who prepared to meet them at the head of several branches of the Clan Chattan. When the forces came in sight of each other, the Macphersons, owing to their dispute with the Davidsons, withdrew from the conflict, and Clan Chattan were defeated. During the night, Mackintosh sent his bard as coming from the Camerons to the camp of the Macphersons and accused them of cowardice. Thus enraged, the Macphersons attacked the Camerons during the night and completely defeated them.

The enmity between the two branches continued, and by some historians the Davidsons are identified with the Clan Dhai, who fought with the Macphersons in the famous Clan Battle on the North Inch of Perth, in 1396, before King Robert I, when only one man of the Clan Dhai and eleven of their opponents remained alive at the termination of the combat.

In the 18th century we find important families like the Davidson's of Cantray and the Davidsons of Tulloch. The latter family came into possession of the lands and castle of Tulloch, near Dingwall.

DAVIDSON

There is also a Davidson of Tulloch tartan.

ORIGIN OF NAME: *Gaelic Daibhidh (David).*
PLANT BADGE: *Red whortleberry.*
PIPE MUSIC: *Tulloch Castle.*

DOUGLAS

CREST BADGE: *On a chapeau a salamander, vert, in fire, proper.*

MOTTO: *Jamais arrière* (*Never behind*).

GAELIC NAME: *Dubhghlas.*

THE origin of this, one of the most powerful families in Scotland, is unknown. Of them it was said, " Men have seen the stream, but what eye ever beheld its source?" In the 12th century they are found in Lanarkshire.

William, of Douglas, who lived in the 12th century, had six sons, five of whom were associated with the Province of Moray. The Douglases were prominent in the struggle for Scotland's independence in the days of Wallace and Bruce, and " the Good Sir James," while carrying Bruce's heart, was killed fighting against the Moors in Spain in 1330. His nephew, William, was created Earl of Douglas in 1357, and became Earl of Mar by his marriage with Margaret, sister of the 13th Earl of Mar. James, 2nd Earl, was killed at Otterburn in 1388, and from him was descended the Queensberry branch. James's half-brother George became Earl of Angus. The Earldom of Douglas was forfeited in 1455 while held by James, 9th Earl.

George Douglas obtained the Earldom of Angus in 1389 when his mother resigned it in his favour. He married Mary, daughter of Robert III. Archibald, 5th Earl, was known as " Bell the Cat " because at a secret meeting of Scottish nobles to discuss means of ridding the Court of the favourites of James III, Lord Gray likened those in conference to mice and asked who had courage to bell the cat. Archibald exclaimed, " I shall bell the cat." Archibald, 6th Earl, was for a long period in rebellion against James V, and kept the young king a prisoner for over three years. William, 11th Earl of Angus, was created Marquis of Douglas in 1633.

Archibald, 3rd Marquis, was created Duke of Douglas in 1703. He died without heir in 1761, and his titles, except the Dukedom, passed to the Duke of Hamilton.

DOUGLAS

ORIGIN OF NAME: *Place-name, Lanark. Meaning "black stream."*
WAR CRY: *A Douglas! A Douglas!*

DOUGLAS

CREST BADGE : *On a chapeau a salamander, vert, in fire, proper.*

MOTTO : *Jamais arrière* (Never behind).

GAELIC NAME : *Dubhghlas.*

THE DOUGLASES OF DRUMLANRIG were descended from Sir William Douglas, who was confirmed in his lands of Drumlanrig by James I in 1412. During the 15th century the Drumlanrig family were actively engaged supporting James I and his successors. In 1628, Douglas of Drumlanrig was created a Viscount, and in 1633 he was raised to the Earldom of Queensberry by Charles I. He administered many important offices in Scotland with great statesmanship, and was created Duke of Queensberry by Charles II in 1684. James, 2nd Duke, was largely responsible for carrying through the Union of 1707. On the death of Charles, 3rd Duke, the title passed to the Earls of March, and later to the Dukes of Buccleuch.

The Earldom of Morton was conferred by James II on James Douglas of Dalkeith, in 1458. He married a daughter of James I, and their son John became 2nd Earl. James, 4th Earl, was the famous Regent Morton. He favoured the Reformation, was concerned in the conspiracy against Rizzio, and was a commander at the Battle of Langside. He was elected Regent in 1572, but his administration was unpopular, and in 1581 his enemies succeeded in bringing him to trial for his part in the murder of Darnley, for which he was executed. Sir William Douglas of Lochleven became 7th Earl of Morton, on the death of the 8th Earl of Angus.

When Archibald, Duke of Douglas, died without issue in 1761, the son of his sister Lady Jane Douglas was served heir to the Duke after protracted lawsuits known as the great " Douglas Cause," but the titles of Marquis of Douglas and Earl of Angus passed to the 7th Duke of Hamilton, who was the heir male.

DOUGLAS, GREY

ORIGIN OF NAME: *Place-name, Lanark. Meaning "black stream."*
WAR CRY: *A Douglas! A Douglas!*

DRUMMOND

CREST BADGE : *Out of crest coronet a goshawk, wings expanded, proper, jessed gules.*
MOTTO : *Gang warily (Go carefully).*
GAELIC NAME : *Drummann.*

THAT GILBERT DE DROMOND, del counte de Dunbrettan, swore fealty to Edward I would point to Drymen being the original territory of the clan.

Sir Malcolm de Drymen supported Bruce at Bannockburn and is said to have been responsible for strewing the ground with the caltrops which had disastrous results for the English cavalry, a circumstance commemorated by the inclusion of caltrops in the armorial bearings of the Drummonds. After Bannockburn he received grants of land in Perthshire with which the Drummonds are associated in more recent times.

Margaret Drummond married King David II in 1369, and Annabella Drummond, who married King Robert III, was the mother of James I.

Sir John Drummond was created Lord Drummond in 1488, and in 1605 King James VI conferred the Earldom of Perth on the 4th Baron Drummond.

The Drummonds were ever loyal to the Stuart kings, and while they received honours from their royal masters such as the Earldom of Melfort conferred on John, second son of the 3rd Earl of Perth, and the title Viscount Strathallan granted to the Hon. William Drummond, they suffered with the Stuarts in their misfortunes. During the Jacobite Risings they continued their support of the Stuarts and the Earl of Perth was created a Duke by James VII after his escape to France. In the '45 the clan followed Prince Charles, and Viscount Strathallan died on the field of Culloden. The Duke of Perth escaped to France and his brother died during the voyage.

The Drummond estates were forfeited, but were restored to the family in 1784 and subsequently passed through the female line to the Earls of Ancaster.

DRUMMOND

ORIGIN OF NAME: *Place-name, Drymen, Stirlingshire.*
PLANT BADGE: *Wild thyme, Holly.*

DUNCAN

House of Camperdown

CREST BADGE : *A ship under sail.*

MOTTO : *Disce pati* (*Learn to suffer*).

GAELIC NAME : *Mac Dhonn-chaidh.*

THE DUNCANS and the Robertsons, or Clan Donna-chaidh, appear to have had the same origin. They were descended from the ancient Earls of Atholl and took their name from the chief Donnachadh Reamhar or " Fat Duncan " who led the clan at the Battle of Bannockburn. The subsequent history of Duncan's descendants is more properly given under the Clan Robertson, but there is here outlined the history of the Duncans of the East of Scotland represented by the family of Duncan of Lundie in Forfarshire.

The Duncans possessed lands in Forfarshire, including the barony of Lundie and the estate of Gourdie. Sir William Duncan was one of the physicians to George III, and in 1764 was created a baronet, but the title became extinct on his death in 1774.

Alexander Duncan of Lundie, provost of Dundee, was a royalist during the Jacobite Rising of 1745. He married Helena, daughter of Haldane of Gleneagles, and their second son, Adam, born in 1731, entered the navy in 1746, and in 1780 he defeated the Spanish at Cape St. Vincent. In 1795 he was appointed commander of the fleet in the North Sea and Admiral of the Blue. He had blockaded the Dutch fleet for two years when the mutiny at the Spithead and Nore spread to all his own ships except the *Venerable*, his flagship, and the *Adamant*. By a stratagem he kept the Dutch in the Texel, and in 1797 he gained at Camperdown one of the most glorious victories in the history of the British Navy. For his services he was created Viscount Duncan of Camperdown by George IV in 1800.

DUNCAN

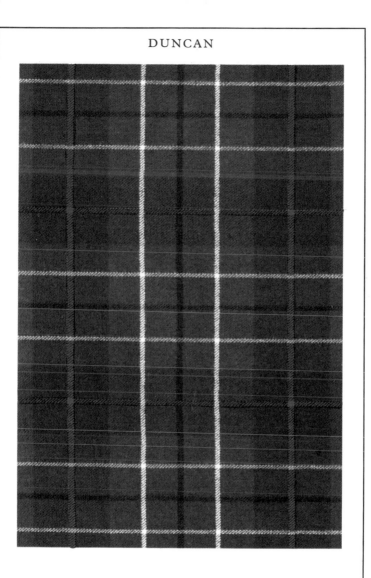

ORIGIN OF NAME: *Donnachadh, from Gaelic donn (brown) and cath (war), brown warrior.*

ELLIOT

CREST BADGE : *A dexter cubit arm in armour, erect, in hand a broadsword, proper.*

MOTTO : *Fortiter et recte* (*With strength and right*).

OLD MOTTO : *Soyez Sage* (*Be wise*).

THE ELLIOTS are a Border clan, although many of the family, it is alleged, took their name from the village Eliot in Forfarshire.

The Elliots of Redheugh were recognised as the principal family. The Elliots of Stobs originated in the 16th century and in 1666 Gilbert Elliot of Stobs was created a baronet of Nova Scotia. George, the youngest son of the 3rd baronet, was born in 1718. He entered the army and served in the War of the Austrian Succession and was wounded at the Battle of Dettingen. He was Governor of Gibraltar when, in 1779, Spain and France laid siege to that important fortress. His defence of the Rock is one of the most glorious achievements in British history. Over 100,000 men, 48 sail of the line, 450 cannon, floating batteries and every conceivable means of warfare were used by the enemy, but the force on the Rock under Elliot remained undefeated. The use of hot shot by the British commenced the complete demoralisation of the enemy. When Lord Howe relieved Gibraltar, the loss of the garrison in nine weeks was 65 dead and 388 wounded. Elliot was created Lord Heathfield, Baron Gibraltar, in 1787. He died in 1790.

Gilbert Elliot, descended from the Stobs branch, was the founder of the Minto family. Born in 1651 he followed the profession of law. His work for religious liberty led to his being condemned for high treason in 1685. He was pardoned, and was constituted a Lord of Session as Lord Minto in 1705. He died in 1718. His great grandson, Gilbert, an eminent statesman, was Governor General of India, 1807–1812. For his services he was created Earl of Minto in 1813. He died in the following year.

ORIGIN OF NAME: *From Old English Elwold.*

ERSKINE

CREST BADGE : *Out of cap of maintenance gules turned ermine, a dexter hand holding a dagger in pale proper.*

MOTTO : *Je Pense Plus* (*I think more*).

GAELIC NAME : *Arascain.*

THIS ancient name is derived from the barony of Erskine in Renfrewshire, which was owned by Henry of Erskine in the 13th century. The family were loyal adherents of Robert the Bruce, to whom they were related by marriage. Sir Robert de Erskine was Great Chamberlain of Scotland. With King David II he exchanged Strathgartney for lands of Alloa. He died in 1385. Sir Robert Erskine assumed the title of Earl of Mar in 1435, but his son, Sir Thomas, was dispossessed of it in 1457, and in 1467 he was created Lord Erskine. John, 4th Lord Erskine, had charge of the infant Mary Queen of Scots in Stirling Castle and Inchmahome, and conveyed her to France. His daughter was mother of the Regent Murray. His son, Alexander, was ancestor of the Earls of Kellie. John, 5th Lord Erskine, was confirmed in the Earldom of Mar. In 1715 the Earldom of Mar was forfeited when John, 11th Earl, formed a party as leader in the Jacobite Rising.

The Erskines of Dun descended from the Erskines of Erskine when Sir Thomas received a charter of the Barony of Dun from King Robert II in 1376. Many of the family of Dun fell at Flodden, and after several generations the estate of Dun passed to the Marquis of Ailsa in 1793. His second son John inherited the property and assumed the name Erskine.

The Erskines of Alva, descended from the House of Mar, are now represented by the Earls of Rosslyn.

James Erskine, son of the 7th Earl of Mar, acquired the Earldom of Buchan by his marriage to the Countess of Buchan.

Thomas, Lord Erskine, third son of the 10th Earl of Buchan, born in 1750, was called to the Bar in 1788. He became Lord Chancellor in 1806.

A green Erksine tartan was invented a few years ago.

ORIGIN OF NAME: *Place-name, Renfrewshire.*

FARQUHARSON

CREST BADGE : *Out of chapeau gules turned ermine a demi-lion rampant, gules, holding in his dexter paw a sword, proper pommelled, or.*

MOTTO : *Fide et fortitudine (By fidelity and fortitude).*

GAELIC NAME : *MacFhearchair*

THIS Aberdeenshire clan was a member of the Clan Chattan Confederation, and took its name from Farquhar, son of Shaw of Rothiemurchus.

A prominent member of the clan was Finlay Mor who carried the royal standard at the Battle of Pinkie where he was killed in 1547. In 1639 the Farquharsons of Monaltrie joined Lord Gordon on the royalist side and six years later they formed part of the army of Montrose. They fought at the Battle of Worcester in 1651, and followed Viscount Dundee. In 1715 they formed part of the Clan Chattan who fought and were defeated at Preston. In 1745 they formed part of the Jacobite army, and distinguished themselves at Falkirk and Culloden. Francis of Monaltrie, known as the Baron Ban, was taken prisoner at Culloden. He was reprieved and was allowed to reside in England. He returned to Scotland in 1766. Farquharson of Balmoral was excepted from the pardon extended to other members of the clan.

The Farquharsons acquired Invercauld by marriage with the MacHardy heiress of Invercauld. In 1595 the Farquharsons acknowledged Mackintosh as their chief in a document signed at Invercauld. The Farquharsons of Invercauld were out in the '15 and in the '45. Anne Farquharson, known as " Colonel Anne," who had married Angus, 22nd chief of the clan Mackintosh, raised the Mackintoshes for Prince Charles, while her husband fought on the side of Hanover.

FARQUHARSON

ORIGIN OF NAME: *Gaelic Fearchar (very dear one).*
PLANT BADGE: *Red whortleberry, Scots fir.*
WAR CRY: *Carn na cuimhne (Cairn of remembrance).*

FERGUS(S)ON

CREST BADGE : *A bee on a thistle all proper.*

MOTTO : *Dulcius ex asperis (Sweeter after difficulties).*

GAELIC NAME : *MacFhearghuis.*

MANY families of the name were established throughout Scotland at an early date. In Perthshire there were the Fergusons of Dunfallandy and Balquhidder, in Aberdeenshire the families of Kinmundy and Pitfour, in Fife the Fergusons of Raith, in Ayrshire the Kilkerran family, and in Dumfries the Fergussons of Craigdarroch. Other families had their homes in Banff, Kincardine and Angus. In Argyll, where the clan is numerous, the Fergusons held lands in Strachur until the beginning of the 19th century, and there appears to be a connection between them and the Fergussons of Kilkerran. The Kilkerran family were active in affairs of state and Sir James, 2nd Baronet, was appointed Lord of Session in 1735, when he took the title of Lord Kilkerran. His son George, Lord of Session in 1799, took the title Lord Hermand. Both were recognised as amongst the ablest lawyers of their time.

The Fergusons of Craigdarroch claim descent from Fergus, Prince of Galloway, in the 12th century, and the family lands have been in their possession since the fifteenth century.

The Fergusons acquired the estate of Raith about a century and a half ago, and one of its members was Gen. Sir Ronald C. Ferguson, colonel of the Cameron Highlanders, who had a distinguished military career and received a special medal at the hands of George III, and the thanks of Parliament, for his services in Portugal.

The Fergussons of Perthshire were recognised as the principal Highland branch of the clan and the chieftainship belonged to the Dunfallandy family, the head of which was designated " MacFhearghuis."

FERGUS(S)ON

There is a district tartan called Ferguson of Balquhidder.

ORIGIN OF NAME: *Gaelic Fearghas (first choice)*.
PLANT BADGE: *Pine, Poplar*.

FLETCHER
House of Dunans

CREST BADGE: *Two naked arms proper shooting an arrow out of a bow sable.*

NO MOTTO.

GAELIC NAME: *Mac an Fhleisteir.*

THE name originated with the making of arrows and is consequently found all over Scotland. The Fletchers followed the clan for whom they made the arrows. In Argyll we find them associated with the Stewarts and the Campbells, and with the MacGregors in Perthshire. In Gaelic the name is found in several forms including Mac-an-Leistear, and Mac-Leister.

For recovering cattle stolen by the MacDonalds in 1497 Stewart of Appin agreed to help the Fletchers when they required assistance. About a century later the Fletchers and the Campbells of Glenorchy entered into a bond. The Fletchers claim to have been the original inhabitants in Glenorchy, and a local saying runs, " It was the clan Fletcher that raised the first smoke to boil water in Orchy." They possessed Achallader for many generations.

The Fletchers of Glenlyon followed the MacGregors for whom they were arrowmakers, and it is on record that a Fletcher saved Rob Roy's life when he was disabled by a dragoon during one of Rob's many conflicts. The Fletchers were out in the '45.

The Fletchers of Dunans were an important family during the 18th and 19th centuries.

The Fletchers of Innerpeffer, in Angus, purchased in 1643 the estate of Saltoun in Haddington. To this family of Saltoun belonged Andrew Fletcher (1653-1716) the celebrated Scottish patriot. He entered the Scots Parliament in 1681, but was later outlawed. At the time of the Revolution he returned to Scotland. He was a powerful advocate of the rights and liberties of the people and several of his limitations of the royal prerogatives were included in the " Act of Security." He was a strenuous opponent of the Union of 1707.

FLETCHER OF DUNANS

ORIGIN OF NAME: *Occupational (arrow maker).*
PLANT BADGE: *Pine tree.*

FORBES

CREST BADGE : *A stag's head, proper.*

MOTTO : *Grace me guide.*

GAELIC NAME : *Foirbeis.*

THIS clan traces its origin to John of Forbes who held the lands of Forbes in Aberdeenshire in the 13th century. In 1303 Alexander of Forbes was killed during the attack on Urquhart Castle by the English, and his son was killed at the Battle of Dupplin in 1332. Alexander Forbes was created a peer by James II in 1442, as Baron Forbes, and he married the granddaughter of King Robert III.

The Forbeses of Culloden were descended from Sir John Forbes of Forbes, through the Forbes of Tolquhoun, and Duncan Forbes, the laird of Culloden who was Lord President of the Court of Session at the time of the '45, exercised his powerful influence to prevent many of the clans from joining the army of Prince Charles. King George II proved an ungrateful sovereign and Forbes received no reward for his loyalty, not even repayment of his own money spent in military service.

The peerage of Pitsligo was conferred on Alexander Forbes in 1633. Alexander, 4th Lord Pitsligo, protested against the Union of 1707 and took part in the Jacobite Risings of 1715 and 1745. His estates were forfeited and on the death of his son the title became dormant. The Forbeses of Craigievar were descended from James, 2nd Lord Forbes. Sir William, 8th of Craigievar, succeeded his cousin as Lord Sempill, Premier Baron of Scotland.

FORBES

ORIGIN OF NAME: *Place-name, Aberdeenshire.*
PLANT BADGE: *Broom.*
WAR CRY: *Lonach.*
PIPE MUSIC: *The Battle of Glen Eurann.*

42ND ROYAL HIGHLAND REGIMENT THE BLACK WATCH

REGIMENTAL CAP BADGE : *Upon the star of the Order of the Thistle and within a wreath of thistles the image of St. Andrew holding before him his cross, all ensigned with an imperial crown, below the Sphinx superinscribed " Egypt."*

MOTTO : *Nemo me impune lacessit (No one attacks me with impunity).*

THIS famous regiment had its origin in the Independent Companies of Highlanders raised in 1729, and commanded by prominent Highlanders loyal to the government. Their duty was to keep peace in the Highlands.

Ten years later the government decided to increase their number and form them into a regiment of 1000 men. The regiment which was numbered the 43rd, but afterwards the 42nd, assembled for the first time on the banks of the Tay, near Aberfeldy, in 1739. They were dressed in the now well-known and popular military tartan, and because of its dark colour and in distinction from the scarlet uniforms of the regular army, the regiment was known as the " Freiceadan Dubh " or " Black Watch."

The regiment has had a long and honourable history, and in 1887 a memorial cairn was erected to the Black Watch on the site of the first muster of the regiment.

ORIGIN OF NAME: *from the Gaelic Freiceadan Dubh (see text).*
REGIMENTAL MARCH PAST: *Heilan' Laddie.*

FRASER OF LOVAT

CREST BADGE : *A buck's head, erased, or tyned argent.*

MOTTO : *Je suis prest (I am ready).*

GAELIC NAME : *Friseal.*

THIS name, said to be of Norman origin, is first found in the south of Scotland in the 12th century. The first recorded Fraser in the Highlands was possibly Sir Andrew who acquired the lands of Lovat through his wife, the daughter of the Earl of Orkney and Caithness, through her descent from Sir David de Graham and from the Bissets.

The Frasers took their share in the feuds of the clans, and in 1544 they espoused the cause of Ranald for the chiefship of Clan Ranald as against the claim of John of Moidart. Ranald had been fostered by Lovat, and a desperate battle was fought on the shores of Loch Lochy between the Frasers and the MacDonalds. This battle is known as Blar-na-Leine—the Battle of the Shirts— because the combatants removed their shirts, and fought with such determination that, when it ended, only five Frasers and eight MacDonalds remained alive. The Frasers opposed Montrose but supported Viscount Dundee. For the part played by the clan in the '45 Lord Lovat, (the Old Fox), was executed, although it was his son who commanded the clan at Culloden. The son was pardoned for his part in the Rising and, in 1757, raised 1800 Frasers for service in America where they fought with distinction.

The title was attainted, and about fifty years later the direct line failed. In 1837 Thomas of Strichen was created Baron Lovat, and from him descended the present Lord Lovat. Lord Saltoun is chief of clan Fraser, but the Frasers of Lovat have for long formed the Highland branch.

FRASER

There is also a hunting tartan.

PLANT BADGE: *Yew*.
WAR CRY: *Caisteal Dhuni*.
PIPE MUSIC: *Lovat's March*.

GORDON

CREST BADGE: *Out of crest coronet a buck's head cabossed, proper, attired or.*

MOTTO: *Bydand (Remaining).*

OLD MOTTO: *Animo non astutia (By courage not craft).*

GAELIC NAME: *Gôrdon.*

THE GORDONS came from the Lowlands to Aberdeenshire in the 14th century when Sir Adam, Lord of Gordon, was granted lands in Strathbogie by King Robert the Bruce. Elizabeth, only child of a later Adam Gordon, married Alexander Seton, who assumed the name of Gordon, and their son was created Earl of Huntly in 1449. A Marquessate was conferred on the 6th Earl in 1599, and a Dukedom on the 4th Marquess by King Charles II in 1684. On the death of the 5th Duke of Gordon the title became extinct, and the Marquessate passed to the Earl of Aboyne, and the estates to the Duke of Richmond, who in 1876 was created Duke of Gordon in the Peerage of the United Kingdom.

The Gordons of Methlic acquired the lands of Haddo in 1533, and in 1642 Sir John was created a Baronet of Nova Scotia. Sir George, who was President of the Court of Session, received the Earldom of Aberdeen in 1682, and John, 7th Earl and 1st Marquess, was Governor-General of Canada and later Lord-Lieutenant of Ireland.

The Gordons of Kirkcudbright were descended from the original stem of Border Gordons and acquired the lands of Lochinvar and Kenmure in the 14th century. In 1633 Sir John Gordon was created Viscount Kenmure and Lord Lochinvar. They were strong adherents of the Stuarts and suffered for their attachment to that unfortunate line.

The regiment, afterwards known as the Gordon Highlanders, was first raised in 1794, with the assistance of Jane, Duchess of Gordon.

GORDON

There is another sett with triple yellow stripes sometimes called Ancient Gordon.

ORIGIN OF NAME: *Place-name, Berwickshire.*
PLANT BADGE: *Ivy.*
WAR CRY: *A Gordon! A Gordon!*
PIPE MUSIC: *The Gordon's March.*

GOW or MACGOWAN

CREST BADGE[1]: *A cat sejant, proper.*

MOTTO: *Touch not the cat bot a glove* (*Touch not the cat without a glove*).

GAELIC NAME: *Mac a'Ghob-hainn.*

THE name Gow is derived from the Gaelic word "Gobha" meaning a blacksmith or armourer, but it may be a shortening of Mac a'Ghobhainn (MacGowan), "son of the smith."

The names Gow and MacGowan are found in connection with several clans—a smith being essential in every clan—but the main Highland branch is believed to be connected with the MacPhersons and the Clan Chattan. This connection is, according to a traditional tale, based on an incident said to have taken place at a Clan conflict on the North Inch of Perth in 1396, when Henry Wynd, known as " an gobh crom " (the crooked Smith)—who was immortalised by Sir Walter Scott as " Hal o' the wynd " in *The Fair Maid of Perth*—took part in the conflict on behalf of one of the clans.

The Gows made their homes chiefly in the shires of Perth and Inverness and amongst the notable bearers of the name were Neil Gow (1727-1807), the Prince of Scottish Fiddlers and composer of many popular reels and strathspeys, and his scarcely less celebrated son, Nathaniel (1766-1831).

The MacGowans appear to be more widely scattered throughout Scotland and in earlier times were found in Stirling, Glasgow, Fife, Dumfries and in the lowlands.

A clan MacGowan is said to have been located in or near Nithsdale in the 12th century.

[1] Gow uses the MacPherson crest badge.

ORIGIN OF NAME: *Occupational; from Gaelic gobha (a smith).*

GRAHAM

CREST BADGE : *A falcon wings displayed, proper, beaked and armed, or, preying on a stork on its back argent, armed gules.*
MOTTO : *Ne oublie (Do not forget).*
GAELIC NAME : *Greumach.*

THERE is a tradition that the Roman Wall across Scotland was breached by a Graham, and from this incident was named " Græme's Dyke." While this story is doubtful the " Gallant Grahams " can at least claim a very ancient origin, stretching back to before the 12th century. The first of the name recorded in Scotland is William de Graham who received the lands of Abercorn and Dalkeith from King David I. Sir John Graham of Dundaff, the " Richt Hand " of Wallace, was killed at the Battle of Falkirk in 1298. The 3rd Lord Graham was created Earl of Montrose by James IV in 1504, and fell at Flodden in 1513. James, 5th Earl, was created Marquis of Montrose in 1644. He was a brilliant soldier and his campaign in Scotland one of the most masterly in military annals. His execution in 1650 is the subject of one of Aytoun's Lays of the Scottish Cavaliers. James, 4th Marquis, was elevated in 1707 to the Dukedom of Montrose. It was to the Marquis of Graham, afterwards 3rd Duke of Montrose, that Highlanders owe the repeal, in 1782, of the Act of 1747 prohibiting the wearing of Highland dress.

Another famous soldier descended from the Montrose family was John Graham of Claverhouse, Viscount Dundee. During his campaign against the Covenanters he gained the name " Bloody Clavers," but to his supporters and to his friends, he was affectionately known as " Bonnie Dundee." He died in his hour of triumph at the Battle of Killiecrankie, in 1689.

Thomas Graham (1750-1843) of Balgowan, in Perthshire, was created Lord Lynedoch for his services in the Peninsular War.

GRAHAM OF MONTROSE

There is a Graham of Menteith tartan.

ORIGIN OF NAME: *Old English graeham (greyhome)*.
PLANT BADGE: *Laurel*.
PIPE MUSIC: *Killiecrankie*.

GRANT

CREST BADGE : *A mountain in-flamed, proper.*

MOTTO : *Stand fast.*

GAELIC NAME : *Grannd.*

THE CLAN GRANT is one of the clans claiming to belong to Siol Alpine and to be descended from Kenneth MacAlpine, King of Scotland in the 9th century.

In the 13th century the Grants appear as Sheriffs of Inverness, and they exerted considerable influence in the north-east of Scotland, and supported Wallace in his struggle. John (Grant), chief of the clan, married the daughter of Gilbert of Glencairnie, and from his elder son sprung the Grants of Freuchie. His younger son was progenitor of the Tullochgorm branch of the clan. From John Grant of Freuchie are descended the Earls of Seafield, the Grants of Corrimony, and the Grants of Glenmoriston.

The Grants were consistently Royalists, and took part in the notable battle on the Haughs of Cromdale which gave its name to the pipe tune made famous by being played by Piper Findlater of the Gordon Highlanders at the Battle of Dargai in 1897.

In the Jacobite Risings the clan supported the Hanoverian side, but the Grants of Glenmoriston supported the Jacobite cause.

Ludovic Grant, of Grant, the then chief, married for his second wife Lady Margaret Ogilvie, daughter of the Earl of Findlater and Seafield, and his grandson succeeded to the Seafield peerage. The 8th Earl died without issue and the titles passed to his uncle, James, 9th Earl of Seafield. The 11th Earl of Seafield was killed in the First World War (1914–18) and the Ogilvie honours passed to his only child, Nina, Countess of Seafield. The chiefship of Clan Grant remained in the Lords Strathspey.

GRANT

The 42nd or Black Watch tartan is worn as a hunting tartan.

ORIGIN OF NAME: *French grand (great).*
PLANT BADGE: *Pine.*
WAR CRY: *Stand fast Craigellachie.*
PIPE MUSIC: *Stand fast Craigellachie.*

GUNN OF KILERNAN

CREST BADGE: *A dexter hand holding a sword in bend all proper.*

MOTTO: *Aut pax aut bellum* (*Either peace or war*)

GAELIC NAME: *Guinne.*

THE territory of the Clan Gunn was in Caithness and Sutherland, and the clan claim to be descended from Olave the Black, Norse King of Man and the Isles, who died in 1237. The clan were noted for their war-like and ferocious character, and continued to extend their possessions until the 15th century, but their continual feuds with other clans led to their settling, at a later date, chiefly in Sutherland. A chief of the clan who flourished in the 15th century was George Gunn, who held the office of crowner, the badge of which was a great brooch. He lived in magnificent style in his castle at Clyth, but was killed by treachery in 1464 when endeavouring to arrange a reconciliation with the Clan Keith, between whom and the Gunns there had been a continued feud. The crowner was one of the greatest men in the country at that time, and his death was avenged about a century loter by his grandson, who killed Keith of Ackergill, his son and twelve followers at Drummoy in Sutherland.

Feuds continued between the Gunns and the Mackays, and the Earls of Caithness and Sutherland, and in 1585 the Earls attacked the Gunns, who, although fewer in number, held the advantage of a position on rising ground. The Gunns killed 140 of their enemies, and only darkness prevented a greater slaughter. The Gunns, however, were later defeated at Lochbroom by the Earl of Sutherland.

GUNN

An alternative pattern has 4 black bars.

ORIGIN OF NAME: *Norse gunn-arr*.
PLANT BADGE: *Juniper*.
PIPE MUSIC: *The Gunn's Salute*.

HAMILTON

CREST BADGE: *On a ducal coronet an oak tree fructed and penetrated transversely ·in the main by a frame saw, proper, the frame or.*

MOTTO: *Through.*

GAELIC NAME: *Hamultun.*

IT is claimed that the first record of the family in Scotland was Walter Fitz-Gilbert from whom is descended the Dukes of Hamilton. Walter witnessed a charter in 1294 conferring on the monastery of Paisley the privilege of a herring fishing in the Clyde.. He was governor of Bothwell Castle for the English during part of the time of the Scottish War of Independence, but later joined Robert the Bruce from whom he received the Barony of Cadzow. The family continued loyal to the Crown, and increased in importance. James, 6th of Cadzow, created Lord Hamilton in 1445, married Princess Mary, eldest daughter of King James II, and widow of the Earl of Arran. From that time on the Hamiltons were frequently heirs presumptive to the throne. James, his son, was created Earl of Arran in 1503, and Duke of Chatelherault in France in 1549. His second son was created Marquis of Hamilton in 1599, and his fourth son was the ancestor of the Earls of Abercorn. James, 3rd Marquis, was created Duke of Hamilton in 1643, and William, 2nd Duke, died from wounds received at the Battle of Worcester in 1651. The latter was succeeded by his niece, Anne, Duchess of Hamilton, who married Lord William Douglas, and through whom the Hamilton titles passed to the Douglas family.

James Hamilton, grandson of the 2nd Earl of Arran, was created Earl of Abercorn in 1603, and in 1790 a Marquessate was conferred on the 9th Earl, whose son the 2nd Marquess was elevated to a Dukedom in 1868.

Other principal families of the name of Hamilton were those of Raploch, of Dalserf, of Preston, East Lothian, of Airdrie, of Silvertonhill, Lanarkshire, and the Earls of Haddington.

HAMILTON

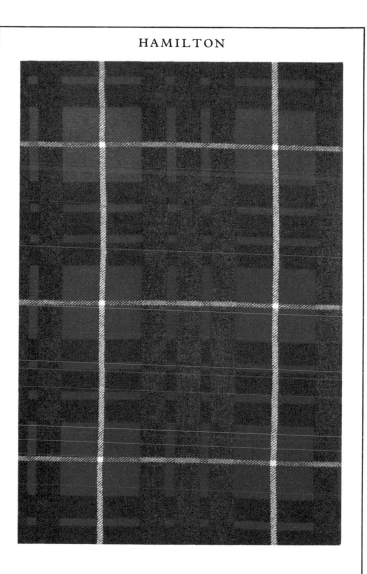

ORIGIN OF NAME: *Place-name in England, Hambledon.*

HAY

CREST BADGE : *Out of a crest coronet a falcon rising, proper, armed and beaked or, jessed, and belled or.*

MOTTO : *Serva jugum (Keep the yoke).*

GAELIC NAME : *Mac Garaidh.*

THE Hays descend from William de la Haye, Butler of Scotland, who was a cadet of the seigneurs de la Haye Hue in Normandy, came to Scotland about 1160, married a Celtic heiress and became Baron of Erroll. The legend that Erroll was acquired by a falcon's flight, in reward for an ancient victory with ox-yokes over Vikings, may be derived from the clan of which she was heiress. Erroll was sold after 1636, when a prophecy attributed to Thomas the Rhymer was apparently fulfilled by the fall of a mistletoe-grown oak associated with strange Hay ritual each All Hallowe'en.

Gilbert, 3rd Baron, was co-Regent of Scotland. Sir Gilbert, 5th Chief, one of the heroes of the Scottish War of Independence, was given Slains Castle in Buchan and made hereditary Constable of Scotland by Bruce himself. Thomas, 7th Chief, married King Robert II's daughter, and William, 9th Chief, was belted Earl of Erroll in 1452. William, 4th Earl, fell at Flodden with 87 Hays. Francis, 9th Earl, in alliance with Huntly defeated Argyll at Glenlivat in 1594, but King James VI personally blew up Slains Castle. Hay of Delgaty was beheaded with Montrose. Charles, 13th Earl, voted against the Union and helped to organise the 1708 Jacobite attempt ; and Mary, 14th Countess (whose heir was son of the beheaded Lord Kilmarnock) raised her men for Prince Charles in 1745. Diana, present Countess of Erroll, Hereditary Lord High Constable, is now 32nd Chief.

Lord Charles Hay, hero of Fontenoy, belonged to the great Border branch that became Lords Hay of Yester in 1488, now represented by the 11th Marquis of Tweeddale, and including Hays of Haystoun, Alderston and Duns. Other branches are Hays of Park and Hayfield.

HAY

There is another tartan known as Hay and Leith.

ORIGIN OF NAME: *French La Haye, place-name in Normandy meaning the stockade.*
PLANT BADGE: *Mistletoe.*

HENDERSON *or* MACKENDRICK

House of Fordell

CREST BADGE : *A dexter hand holding a star argent surmounted by a crescent. or.*
MOTTO : *Sola virtus nobilitat (Virtue alone ennobles).*
GAELIC NAME : *Mac Eanruig.*

THE name Henderson in Gaelic is MacEanruig, sometimes rendered in English MacKendrick, and is found in widely separated districts in Scotland. Those in Caithness and the north claim to be a sept of the Clan Gunn and descended from Henry, son of George Gunn " the Crowner," in the 15th century.

The principal family of Hendersons was the Clan Eanruig of Glencoe for whom it is claimed that they were in that glen of grievous memory centuries before the MacIans (MacDonalds) arrived there. Tradition states that " Iain Fraoch," a brother of John, 1st Lord of the Isles, married a daughter of the chief of the Hendersons of Glencoe and that their son Iain was the founder of the MacIains of Glencoe. He was called " Iain Abrach " from his being born in Lochaber, and the clan came to be known as the Clan Abrach. The Hendersons, who were notable for their strength, always formed the body-guard of the chief, and were the hereditary pipers of the Clan Abrach.

From the Hendersons of Fordell in Angus is descended the famous divine, Alexander Henderson (1583-1646), who filled. a prominent position in the Presbyterian Church of Scotland during the most vital period in her history. With the assistance of Johnston of Wariston he prepared the National Covenant of 1638. He was Moderator of the Glasgow Assembly which outlined Presbyterian organisation in the same year. He drafted the Solemn League and Covenant in 1643, and was a member of the Westminster Assembly which issued the Confession of Faith.

HENDERSON *or* MACKENDRICK

ORIGIN OF NAME: *Henry's son.*
PLANT BADGE: *Cotton grass.*

INNES

CREST BADGE : *A boar's head erased proper.*
MOTTO : *Be traist (Be faithful)*
GAELIC NAME : *Innis.*

THIS clan is of ancient origin and is found in Moray as early as the 12th century, when Berowald, described as Flandrensis, received a charter of the lands of Innes from Malcolm IV in 1160. His grandson assumed the name Innes from his lands and received confirmation of his charter from Alexander II in 1226. By marriage Sir Alexander, 9th of Innes acquired the lands of Aberchirder in the 14th century, and branches of the family established themselves all over the North of Scotland. Alexander, 13th of Innes, had large landed possessions and received many charters between the years 1493 and 1533. Robert, 20th of Innes, was created a baronet in 1625. Sir Harry, 4th Baronet, married a daughter of Duncan Forbes of Culloden. Sir James, 6th Baronet, sold the lands of Innes to the Earl of Fife in 1767, and went to reside in England. On the death of the 4th Duke of Roxburghe, Sir James, as heir-general, claimed the Scottish titles and estates of that family, and the House of Lords decided in his favour. He assumed the name Ker, and succeeded as 5th Duke of Roxburghe. James, 6th Duke, was created Earl Innes in 1836.

Through the Inneses of Innermarkie, the family of Balveny are descended from the Ineses of that ilk. Robert, 5th Baron of Innermarkie, acquired the lands of Balveny in Banffshire. He was created a baronet in 1631. Loyalty to the Stuarts caused the estate to be sold by Sir Robert, 3rd Baronet, and on the death of the 4th Baronet the title passed to James Innes of Orton.

INNES

ORIGIN OF NAME: *Place-name, Morayshire.*
PLANT BADGE: *Great bulrush.*

JOHNSTON
House of Annandale

CREST BADGE : *A winged spur or, leathered gules.*

MOTTO : *Nunquam non paratus (Never unprepared).*

GAELIC NAME : *MacIain.*

THE JOHNSTONS were a powerful clan famous in Border song and story. They derived their name from the barony of Johnston in Annandale, and the name occurs in records of the 13th century. From that time onward they were prominent in Border warfare. The Johnstons supported the crown for generations and in 1633 Sir James Johnston of Johnston was created Lord Johnston of Lochwood by Charles I, and ten years later Earl of Hartfell. The extinct Earldom of Annandale was conferred on the 2nd Earl of Hartfell, who died in 1672. His son was created Marquess of Annandale in 1701. The Marquessate became dormant on the death of George, 3rd Marquess, in 1792.

The Johnstons of Westerhall, in Dumfriesshire, were descended from the same stock, and John, 2nd of Westerhall, was created a Baronet of Nova Scotia in 1700. Sir James, 3rd Baronet, notable for his local improvements, married the eldest daughter of Lord Elibank and had fourteen of a family, several of whom served with distinction in the navy and the army.

The Johnstons of the North claim descent from Stiven de Johnston in the 14th century whose grandson possessed the lands of Ballindalloch. George Johnston of that ilk was created a Baronet of Nova Scotia in 1626. Sir John, 3rd Baronet, was unjustly executed in London in 1690 for being present at the marriage of Captain Campbell of Mamore who was alleged to have abducted Miss Wharton and married her. Campbell escaped to Scotland, but Johnston was betrayed by his landlord for £50. Sir John, 4th Baronet, was out in the '45, and his son was killed at Sheriffmuir.

JOHNSTON

ORIGIN OF NAME: *John's tun (farm)*.
PLANT BADGE: *Red hawthorn*.

KEITH

CREST BADGE: *Out of crest coronet a stag's head erased, proper, attired with tynes or.*

MOTTO: *Veritas vincit* (*Truth conquers*).

GAELIC NAME: *Ceiteach.*

ONE of the most powerful Celtic families, the Keiths held the office of Great Marischal from the 12th century. In the 14th century by a marriage with the heiress of the Cheynes of Ackergill, they took possession of lands in Caithness, and for a long time their settlement there was a source of feuds with the Clan Gunn. An attempt at reconciliation being unsuccessful, a meeting was arranged between twelve horsemen from both sides. The Keiths arrived with two men on each horse, and attacked the Gunns while they were at prayer. In spite of the inequality of numbers both sides fought with desperation until most of the Gunns were killed, including their chief, and the Keiths retired considerably depleted. The surviving Gunns later followed and killed many of the remaining Keiths.

Sir William Keith, Great Marischal in the reign of James II, was created Earl Marischal by the king in 1458, and the family exerted considerable influence in Scotland for centuries afterwards. Marischal College, Aberdeen, was founded in 1593 by the 4th Earl. The soldierly qualities of the Keiths kept them ever in the forefront and one of the outstanding commanders of his time was James, Marshal Keith, younger son of the 9th Earl Marischal, who was out in the Jacobite Rising of 1715. He entered the Russian army in 1728, and was appointed General in 1737. Ten years later he joined the German army and his brilliant leadership won for him a Continental reputation. He was made a Field-Marshal by Frederick the Great, who raised a statue to his memory.

Upon the death of George, last Earl Marischal in 1778, the entailed estates passed to Lord Falconer, and the remainder of his property was divided among his grand-nephews.

KEITH

This tartan is usually called Keith and Austin.

ORIGIN OF NAME: *Place-name, Banffshire.*

KENNEDY

CREST BADGE : *A dolphin naiant, proper.*

MOTTO : *Avise la fin* (*Consider the end*).

GAELIC NAME : *MacUalraig, Ceannaideach.*

THIS ancient clan is found associated with the south-west of Scotland from the 12th century, and the history of the Carrick district of Ayrshire is substantially the early history of the Kennedies. They are claimed to have descended from the 1st Earl of Carrick.

The Kennedies of Dunure acquired Cassillis, and later one of the family married Mary, daughter of King Robert III. Their son was created Lord Kennedy in 1457, and in 1509 the third Lord Kennedy was created Earl of Cassillis. While the family had many illustrious men, Gilbert, 4th Earl, earned an infamous reputation for his dreadful deed of " roasting the Abbot of Crossraguel " in the black vault of Dunure, to obtain possession of the lands of the Abbey. Archibald, 12th Earl of Cassillis, was created Baron Ailsa in 1806, and in 1831 Marquess of Ailsa. Culzean Castle was built between 1775 and 1790 by the 9th and 10th Earls. It was designed by Robert Adam.

Tradition tells that Ulric Kennedy fled from Ayrshire for some lawless deed and settled in Lochaber where his descendants were known as Clan Ulric. The Kennedies of Skye, and other districts of the Highlands, trace their descent from this branch of the family. The Lochaber Kennedies joined forces with the Camerons and are accepted as a sept of that clan.

KENNEDY

ORIGIN OF NAME: *Gaelic ceannaideach (ugly head)*.
PLANT BADGE: *Oak*.

KERR

CREST BADGE: *The sun in his splendour.*

MOTTO: *Sero sed serio (Late but in earnest).*

GAELIC NAME: *Cearr, MacGhillechearr.*

TRADITIONALLY the Kerrs were of Anglo-Norman origin and descended from two brothers who settled in Roxburgh in the 14th century, but it is also claimed that the name is derived from a Celtic word meaning strength. The names, Ker, Kerr and Carr were common on the Borders.

The Kers of Cessford were wardens of the marches and prominent in Border conflicts. They were granted old Roxburgh by James IV, and Sir Walter Cessford fought on the side of James VI at Langside in 1568. Sir Robert, born in 1570, was created Lord Roxburghe in 1600, and in 1616 was elevated to the Earldom of Roxburghe and appointed Lord Privy Seal in 1637. By marriage with the Earl's daughter Jean, Sir William Drummond became 2nd Earl of Roxburghe and assumed the name Ker. John, 5th Earl, supported the Union of 1707, and was created Duke of Roxburghe. John, 3rd Duke, was a noted book-collector, and the sale of his library was a famous event in the literary world. The direct line having failed, Lord Bellenden became 4th Duke, and his death without surviving issue led to a long and confused contest. Sir James Innes succeeded as 5th Duke and assumed the name Ker.

Mark Ker was Abbot of Newbattle in 1547, and his son Mark had the lands of Newbattle erected into a barony in 1587 and in 1606 he was created Earl of Lothian. His son Robert, 2nd Earl, had no male issue, and the title passed through his daughter to her husband William Kerr, son of the 1st Earl of Ancrum, who became 3rd Earl of Lothian in 1631. Robert, 4th Earl, was raised to the Marquessate of Lothian in 1701.

KERR

ORIGIN OF NAME: *British caer*.

LAMONT

CREST BADGE : *A dexter hand, open, pale-ways, couped at the wrist, proper.*

MOTTO : *Ne parcas nec spernas (Neither spare nor dispose).*

GAELIC NAME : *MacLaomainn.*

THE CLAN LAMONT is one of great antiquity and held considerable lands in Argyllshire which were later reduced by the encroachment of the Campbells and other clans. An early name of the clan was Clan 'ic Fhearchair (MacKeracher). The Lamonts' territory latterly was confined chiefly to Cowal.

In the early 13th century Laumun granted to the monks of Paisley certain lands at Kilmun and Kilfinan, and in 1456 John Lamont was Bailie of Cowal. John Lamont of Inveryne was knighted in 1539 and had his lands united into the Barony of Inveryne. At this time his principal seat was Toward Castle, where he entertained Mary Queen of Scots in 1563.

During the disturbed period of the Civil War, several of the Campbell chiefs ravaged the Lamont country with fire and sword, destroying Toward and Ascog Castles, and in 1646 treacherously massacred 200 Lamonts, including thirty-six special gentlemen of the clan, at Dunoon. A memorial commemorating the event was erected on the site by the Clan Lamont in 1906. The massacre formed one of the charges against the Marquess of Argyle for which he was executed in 1661. After the destruction of Toward Castle, Ardlamont became the principal residence of the chief. The family were connected by marriage with many of the titled families of Scotland. John, 19th chief, commanded the Gordon Highlanders at Corunna in 1809.

One of the oldest cadet families, and the only one still possessing the old clan lands, is the Lamonts of Knockdow.

LAMONT

ORIGIN OF NAME: *Norse lawman.*
PLANT BADGE: *Crab apple tree.*

LESLIE

CREST BADGE : *A demi griffin, proper.*

MOTTO : *Grip fast.*

THE family takes its name from the lands of Leslie in Aberdeenshire, and the name became famous not only in Scotland, but in Germany, France, Russia and Poland. In the 12th century Bartholomew, a Flemish noble, obtained the Barony of Lesly, and from him are descended the Earls of Rothes. Sir Andrew de Lesly was one of the signatories to the letter to the Pope in 1320 asserting the independence of Scotland. Walter, his son, married the daughter of the Earl of Ross, and his death without issue led to the famous Battle of Harlaw in 1411.

The title of Earl of Rothes was conferred on George de Lesly of Rothes. His grandson, George, 2nd Earl, was killed at Flodden. The Leslies were concerned in the murder of Cardinal Beaton, and George, 4th Earl, was tried for his part in it, but acquitted. Andrew, 5th Earl, succeeded his father in 1588. He was intimately concerned in the affairs of Mary Queen of Scots. John, 6th Earl, was one of the most powerful leaders of the Covenanters. John, 7th Earl, was created Duke of Rothes in 1680.

General Alexander Leslie, of the Balgonie family, served under Gustavus Adolphus, King of Sweden, with great distinction and rose to be Field-Marshal. Invited back to Scotland to command the Covenanters, he captured Edinburgh Castle with 1000 men. In 1640 he entered England with the Scots army, routed the King's troops at Newburn, and after the Treaty of Ripon, he was created Earl of Leven by Charles I to conciliate the Scots. David, 3rd Earl of Leven, and 2nd of Melville, distinguished himself at the Battle of Killiecrankie.

LESLIE

There is also a red tartan.

ORIGIN OF NAME: *Place-name, Aberdeenshire.*
PLANT BADGE: *Rue.*

LINDSAY

CREST BADGE : *A swan rising from a coronet, proper.*

MOTTO : *Endure fort* (*Endure with strength*).

GAELIC NAME : *MacGhille Fhionntaig.*

LINDSAY, " ane surname of renown," is derived from a place-name, and first appears on the Borders during the 12th century.

William, grandson of the first mentioned Lindsay of Ercildon, acquired the property of Crawford in Lanarkshire, and married the daughter of Henry, Prince of Scotland. Several generations later his descendant Sir David Lindsay of Glenesk was created Earl of Crawford in 1398. He married a daughter of Robert II, and received with her the Barony of Strathnairn, in Invernessshire. He was a brave and chivalrous knight and narrowly escaped death when fighting the forces under the " Wolf of Badenoch." He died in 1407. Bitter feuds existed between the Lindsays and the Ogilvies, and Alexander, 4th Earl, known as Earl Beardie, was severely defeated by the Earl of Huntly in 1452, deprived of all his lands, titles and offices, but after a reconciliation he was pardoned, and died in 1454. His son, David, 5th Earl, was created Duke of Montrose by James III in 1488, the first instance of a Dukedom being conferred on a Scotsman not of the Royal Family. This Dukedom ended with his death in 1495. Later Earls of Crawford were intimately concerned in feuds and rebellions in Scotland, and in military service abroad.

John, 1st Earl of Lindsay, assumed the title of Earl of Crawford in 1644. In 1848 the House of Lords decided that the titles of the Earl of Crawford and the Earl of Lindsay belonged to James, 7th Earl of Balcarres, who thus became 24th Earl of Crawford.

Sir David Lindsay, of the Mount (1490-1567), poet and reformer, and Robert Lindsay of Pitscottie (16th century), author of *The Chronicles of Scotland*, are two of Scotland's celebrated literary men.

LINDSAY

ORIGIN OF NAME: *Place-name, probably Norman.*
PLANT BADGE: *Rue, Lime tree.*

LIVINGSTONE

CREST BADGE : *A demi- savage wreathed about the head and middle with laurel leaves, in dexter a club, in sinister a serpent entwined round the arm, all proper.*

MOTTO : *Si je puis (If I can).*

GAELIC NAME : *Mac an Léigh (Léigh).*

AN ancient name existing before the 12th century, when the name appears in charters as Livingston.

Sir William Livingston, of Gorgyn, near Edinburgh, witnessed a charter of the Earl of Lennox in 1270, and from him descended the Livingstons of Livingston. Sir William received the lands of Callendar from David II in 1347. The lands had been forfeited by Patrick de Callendar and Livingston married his daughter. From the Livingstons of Callendar are descended the Livingstones of Westquarter and Kinnaird, of Bonton and of Dunipace.

Sir James Livingston of Callendar was created Lord Livingston in 1458. Alexander, 5th Lord, had charge of young Queen Mary, but after the Battle of Pinkie she was conveyed to Inchmahome. Alexander, 7th Lord, was raised to the Earldom of Linlithgow in 1600, but the title was attainted in 1716 because James, 5th Earl, engaged in the Rising of 1715. The title of Viscount of Kilsyth conferred on Sir James Livingstone of Barncloich was also attainted for the action of William, 3rd Viscount, in joining the same Rising.

The Livingstones of Argyll claim to be descended from a physician to the Lord of the Isles Mac-an-leigh —son of the physician—being Englished as Livingstone. The Livingstones followed the Stewarts of Appin, and accompanied them at the Battle of Culloden, where Donald Livingstone saved the banner of the Stewarts and conveyed it back to Ballachulish. The family of Livingstones were Barons of the Bachull and received grants of lands in Lismore as keepers of the crozier of the Bishops of Lismore, known in Gaelic as the " Bachull Mor." Dr. David Livingstone, the famous African missionary, was a descendant of the Argyll Livingstones.

LIVINGSTONE

ORIGIN OF NAME: *Place-name, Linlithgow.*

LOGAN

CREST BADGE : *A passion nail piercing a human heart, proper.*

MOTTO : *Hoc majorum virtus (This is the valour of my ancestors).*

GAELIC NAME : *Loganaich or Macgill'innein.*

LIKE the Livingstones, the Logans appear to consist of two distinct families, Lowland and Highland. In the 12th and 13th centuries the name appears frequently, and in 1329 Sir Robert Logan and Sir Walter Logan were killed in Spain when accompanying Sir James Douglas, with the heart of Bruce, on their way to the Holy Land. Lastalrig or Restalrig, near Edinburgh, was the principal possession of the Logans in the south. Sir Robert, of Restalrig, married a daughter of Robert II and in 1400 he was appointed Admiral of Scotland. The last Logan of Restalrig was outlawed and died in his residence Fast Castle in Berwickshire.

Tradition relates that the Logans of the north, "Siol Ghillinnein" (MacLennans), are descended from the Logans of Drumderfit, in Easter Ross. In the 15th century a feud between the Logans and the Frasers ended in a sanguinary battle at North Kessock, in which Gilligorm, the chief of the Logans, was killed, and his widow carried off by the victors. The widow gave birth to a posthumous son of Gilligorm, who from his deformity was known as Crotair MacGilligorm. He was educated by the monks at Beauly and on reaching manhood took Holy Orders at Kilmor in Sleat and in Kilchrinin, Glenelg. Like many others of the Highland clergy at that period he did not remain celibate and his descendants came to be known as Siol Fhinnein or MacLennans. They were numerous in Kintail, and at the Battle of Auldearn in 1645, where they acted as standard bearers to Lord Seaforth, many of them were killed in their gallant defence of the Standard. The name MacLennan is still common in Ross-shire.

LOGAN *and* MACLENNAN

ORIGIN OF NAME: *Logan, a place-name ; MacLennan, Gaelic son of Finnan's servant.*
PLANT BADGE: *Furze.*
WAR CRY: *Druim-nan deur (The ridge of tears).*

MACALISTER

House of Loup

CREST BADGE: *A dexter hand holding a dagger in pale, all proper.*

MOTTO: *Fortiter (Boldly).*

GAELIC NAME: *MacAlasdair.*

THIS branch of the clan Donald traces its history back to the 13th century, and its origin to Alexander, or Alasdair, son of Donald of Isla and great-grandson of the famous Somerled. The clan territory was principally in Kintyre, and in 1481 Charles Macallestar is designated Steward of Kintyre. Later the clan was numerically strong in Bute and Arran.

The principal family was the MacAlisters of Loup whose chieftain in 1493 was Iain Dubh. This family continued to figure prominently in the history of Kintyre, and their name appears in the General Band of King James VI in 1587. Alexander MacAlister of Loup supported James VII and fought under Viscount Dundee at Killiecrankie, and in the following year he was present at the Battle of the Boyne. His son Hector died without issue, and was succeeded by his brother Charles, who married a daughter of Lamont of Lamont. Charles, 12th of Loup, married Janet Somervill, heiress of Kennox, and assumed the name and arms of Somervill in addition to his own.

An important branch of the clan was the MacAlisters of Tarbert, who were Constables of Tarbert Castle, a stronghold on Loch Fyne built by King Robert the Bruce

MACALISTER

ORIGIN OF NAME: *Son of Alexander.*
PLANT BADGE: *Heath.*

MACALPINE

Since MacAlpine is not the name of any single clan, but rather a name covering a number of different clans, there is no crest badge or motto.

GAELIC NAME: *MacAilpein.*

SIOL ALPINE is a name given to a number of clans widely separated and having no apparent connection with each other. It is said to include the MacGregors, Grants, MacKinnons, Macquarries, Macnabs, Macduffies or Macphies, and MacAulays.

The history of the MacAlpines is uncertain and very illusive, and the clan is claimed to be a very ancient one, but its history must be traced through the clans which constituted Siol Alpine the chief of which are described separately.

The traditional home of the MacAlpines was Dunstaffnage, Argyll. The race is claimed to be a Royal one, and descended from King Alpin who was murdered after the defeat of the Scots by the Picts in 834.

The 'clan' is now landless and the family of the chief has not been traced.

MACALPINE

ORIGIN OF NAME: *Son of Alpine.*
PLANT BADGE: *Pine.*
WAR CRY: *Cuimhnich bàs Ailpein* (*Remember the death of Alpine*).

MACARTHUR
House of Hilton and Ascog

CREST BADGE: *Two laurel branches in orle, proper.*

MOTTO: *Fide et opera (By fidelity and work).*

GAELIC NAME: *MacArtuir.*

THE CLAN MACARTHUR is of ancient origin. Highlanders in the west when speaking of olden times used the proverb, " There is nothing older, unless the hills, MacArthur, and the devil." The clan is claimed to be the older branch of the Clan Campbell, and held the chiefship until the 15th century.

The MacArthurs supported King Robert the Bruce in the struggle for the Independence of Scotland, and were rewarded with grants of extensive lands in Argyll, including those of the MacDougalls who opposed the King. The Chief was appointed Captain of the Castle of Dunstaffnage. The clan remained powerful until the year 1427, when John, the chief, was executed by order of King James I and thereafter the power of the clan declined.

The MacArthurs of Strachur remained as the principal family of the clan and it was a member of this family, John MacArthur, born in 1767, who became " the Father of New South Wales." He accompanied the 102nd Regiment (N.S.W. Corps) to Sydney in 1790. He was Commandant at Parramatta from 1793 till 1804. He took an interest in the development of the colony, introduced sheep and improved their breed, and in 1817 planted the first vineyard. Thus he was the founder of the two great Australian industries of wool and wine.

In Skye a family of MacArthurs held land as the hereditary pipers to the MacDonalds of the Isles.

MACARTHUR

ORIGIN OF NAME: *Son of Arthur.*
PLANT BADGE: *Fir club moss, wild myrtle.*
WAR CRY: *Eisd! O'Eisd! (Listen! O Listen!).*

MACAULAY

(Merchant Cadet)

CREST BADGE : *An antique boot, couped at the ankle, proper.*

MOTTO : *Dulce periculum* (*Danger is sweet*).

GAELIC NAME : *MacAmhlaidh.*

Two clans of this name are associated with districts as far apart as Dunbarton and Lewis but they have no family connection with each other.

Aulay, brother of the Earl of Lennox, signed the Ragman's Roll in 1296, but it is as " of Ardincaple " that we consider them first as a clan. They were a branch of the great Clan Alpine, and in 1591 the chief of the MacAulays entered into a bond of manrent with Mac-Gregor of Glenstrae admitting that the former were a cadet of the MacGregors and agreeing to pay the " calp," a tax due to the chief. " Awlay Macawlay of Ardincapill " appears in " The General Band " of 1587 as a vassal of the Duke of Lennox, and again the " McCawlis " appear in the Roll of Broken Clans in 1594. The MacAulays retained the lands of Ardencaple until the 12th chief sold them to the Duke of Argyll in 1767.

The MacAulays of Lewis were followers of " Siol Torquil," or the Macleods of Lewis, and claim to be descended from Aula, or Olave the Black, who was King of Man and the Isles in the 13th century. The Mac-Aulays of Sutherland and Ross, where they were numerous, were probably ·related to the Lewis Mac-Aulays. The Ross-shire MacAulays occupied the district round Ullapool (Olave's home) and enlisted under the banner of the MacKenzies. Thomas Babington, Lord MacAulay (1800-59) the famous essayist and historian, was descended from the Lewis branch of the clan.

MACAULAY

There is also a hunting tartan.

ORIGIN OF NAME: *Son of Olaf*.
PLANT BADGE: *Pine, Cranberry*.

MACBAIN

CREST BADGE : *A grey demi cata-
mountain, salient, on his sinister
foreleg a Highland targe, gules.*
MOTTO : *Touch not the catt bot a
targe.*
GAELIC NAME : *MacBheathain.*

THE Clan MacBean is of ancient origin and is claimed,
by some authorities, to have sprung from the ancient
House of Moray. The name appears in different forms
as MacBean, MacBain, and McVean. An early Scottish
King was known as Donald Ban.

Originally the MacBeans are said to have come from
Lochaber in the suite of the heiress of Clan Chattan and
settled in eastern Inverness-shire. Myles MacBean was a
strong supporter of Mackintosh against the Red Comynn,
and at the Battle of Harlaw in 1411, many of the Mac-
Beans fell fighting for Mackintosh. The principal family
were the MacBeans of Kinchyle, and Kinchyle signs
several important Clan Chattan agreements in 1609, 1664
and 1756. Other families were the MacBeans of
Drummond in the parish of Dores, MacBean of Faillie in
Strathnairn, and MacBean of Tomatin in Strathdearn.

The MacBeans were ever a war-like clan, and at the
Battle of Culloden, Gillies MacBean, filling a breach in a
wall, killed fourteen of the Hanoverian side before he fell.
His feat was almost emulated over a century later by
Major-General William MacBean, who enlisted in the
93rd Regiment as a private, and rose to the command of
the regiment in 1873. He gained the V.C. for attacking
and killing single-handed eleven of the enemy in the
main breach of the Begum Bagh at Lucknow in 1858.
Another member of the clan, Major Forbes MacBean of
the Gordon Highlanders, gained the D.S.O. for his gallant
conduct at the taking of the heights of Dargai in 1897.

MACBEAN or MACBAIN

ORIGIN OF NAME: *Son of Beathan.*
PLANT BADGE: *Red whortleberry, Boxwood.*

MACCALLUM

CREST BADGE : *A castle; argent, masoned sable.*

MOTTO : *In ardua petit (He has attempted difficult things).*

OLD MOTTO : *Deus refugium nostrum (God is our refuge).*

GAELIC NAME : *MacChaluim.*

THE name MacCallum means a follower of Columba, and Argyllshire is the home of the clan.

The history of the clan is so inextricably connected with that of the Malcolms that it is difficult to separate them. In fact, the two names may correctly be considered as applying to the one clan. The Clan Calum is said to have been originally designated as of Ariskeodnish.

Lands in Craignish and on the banks of Loch Avich were granted by Sir Duncan Campbell of Lochow, in 1414, to Reginald MacCallum of Corbarron, with the office of hereditary constable of the castles of Lochaffy and Craignish. Corbarron was bequeathed by the last of the family to Zachary MacCallum of Poltalloch in the 17th century. An earlier Zachary of Poltalloch, a supporter of the Marquess of Argyll, and renowned for his strength, was killed by Sir Alexander MacDonald at Ederline in 1647. He had slain seven of the enemy when he was attacked by Sir Alexander, and was likely to overpower him also, when MacCallum was attacked from behind by a man of the opposing force armed with a scythe. Dugald MacCallum of Poltalloch, who succeeded to the estate in 1779, is said to have been the first to adopt the name Malcolm permanently.

MACCALLUM, ANCIENT

ORIGIN OF NAME: *Son of Callum (bald dove)*.
PLANT BADGE: *Mountain Ash*.

MACCOLL

No arms have been matriculated.

IT is claimed that the MacColls are a branch of the Clan Donald, Coll being a common name in that greatest of all the clans.

Tradition tells that the MacColls were settled round Loch Fyne at an early date and from their proximity to the land of the Campbells they followed that clan. It is related that the MacColls joined with other clans in their feuds with the MacGregors, and from this circumstance found themselves opposed to the Macphersons who were assisting the MacGregors. At Drum Nachder in 1602, the MacColls returning from a raid into Ross were met by the Macphersons when a sanguinary fight took place. The MacColls lost most of their men including their leader. There were MacColls in Appin and during the 1745-46 Jacobite Rising many of them fought in Stewart of Appin's Regiment.

The clan has produced a Gaelic poet of more than ordinary renown. Evan McColl was born at Kenmore on Loch Fyne in 1808. He was the author of *The Mountain Minstrel*, better known under its Gaelic title *Clarsach nam Beann*. He died in 1898 and a monument erected to his memory at Kenmore, Loch Fyne, was unveiled in 1930 by His Grace the Duke of Argyll.

MACCOLL

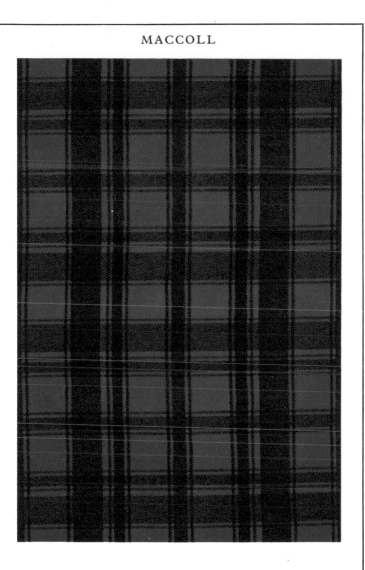

ORIGIN OF NAME: *Son of Coll.*
PLANT BADGE: *Heath.*
PIPE MUSIC: *Ceann na Drochaide Moire (The head of the High Bridge).*

MACDONALD

CREST BADGE : *Out of coronet a hand in armour fessways, holding by its point a cross crosslet fitchy, gules.*

MOTTO : *Per mare per terras (By sea and by land).*

GAELIC NAME : *MacDhòmhnuill.*

THE most powerful of all the Highland clans, the Clan Donald takes its name from Donald, grandson of Somerled, King of the Isles. The clan held extensive territory, and during the struggle of Bruce, Alexander, chief of the clan opposed him. However, Angus Og, his brother, was a strong supporter of King Robert, and with a large number of the clan fought for him at Bannockburn. When Bruce succeeded to the throne, Alexander's possessions were granted to Angus. On the death of Bruce the Clan Donald withdrew their support until they were reconciled to David II. At a later date John, Lord of the Isles, and chief of the clan, divorced his wife Amy, with whom he received the possessions of the Clan MacRury, and married Margaret, daughter of Robert, High Steward of Scotland, afterwards Robert II. The marriage was indirectly the cause of the Battle of Harlaw in 1411. In 1429 Alexander, Lord of the Isles, became Earl of Ross, and in revenge for his previous imprisonment he attacked the Crown lands at Inverness and burned the town. James I imposed a crushing defeat on the Lord of the Isles and Alexander was imprisoned. The Earldom of Ross was annexed to the Crown and the Lordship of the Isles was forfeited in 1493.

Succession passed to the House of Sleat, and subsequently a member of this family was created a Baronet of Nova Scotia. In 1776 Sir Alexander MacDonald was created Lord MacDonald. Lord MacDonald is officially recognised as MacDonald of MacDonald, chief of the name. In 1910 Sir Alexander W. M. Bosville MacDonald proved his right to be 14th Baronet of Sleat, 21st Chief of Sleat.

MACDONALD

ORIGIN OF NAME: *Gaelic Domhnull (world ruler).*
PLANT BADGE: *Heath.*
WAR CRY: *Fraoch Eilean.*
PIPE MUSIC: *March of the MacDonalds.*

MACDONALD OF THE ISLES

CREST BADGE : *Out of coronet a hand in armour fessways, holding by its point a cross crosslet fitchy, gules.*

MOTTO : *Per mare per terras (By sea and by land).*

GAELIC NAME : *MacDhòmhnuill.*

IT is difficult in a short sketch to outline the history of the various branches of the Clan Donald, the families of which are intricately interwoven.

Somerled, Regulus of the Isles, from whom the clan trace their descent, expelled the Norsemen from the Western Isles in the 12th century. He was killed at Renfrew in 1164 when his army did battle with Malcolm IV, and was succeeded by his son Reginald, Lord of the Isles, from whom are descended the clans MacDonald and MacRurie. From Dugall, the brother of Reginald, are descended the Clan MacDugall. Reginald was liberal to the Church and founded the Monastery of Saddell. His son, Donald " de Isla," succeeded him, and under his guidance the clan attained great eminence. He died in 1289 and was succeeded by his son Angus who supported Haco, but did not suffer from the latter's defeat at Largs in 1263. Angus Og supported Bruce and increased the family possessions considerably. His son, John, assumed the title of Lord of the Isles in 1354. His son Donald " of Harlaw " followed as 2nd Lord of the Isles. He married the only daughter of the Countess of Ross, and claimed the Earldom of Ross, but later renounced this claim and became a vassal of the Crown. He died in 1423, and his son Alexander succeeded and became Earl of Ross on the death of his mother. The title was acknowledged by the Crown in 1430. For a period he was Justiciar- of Scotland. He died in 1448 and was succeeded by his son John, 4th and last Lord of the Isles, who rebelled against the Crown and declared his independence. After a long and stormy life, during which the Earldom of Ross was annexed to the Crown, and the Lordship of the Isles forfeited, John died without legitimate issue in 1498.

ORIGIN OF NAME: *Gaelic Domhnull (world ruler).*

MACDONALD OF SLEAT

CREST BADGE : *A hand in armour in fess, proper, holding by the point a cross crosslet fitchy, gules.*

MOTTO : *Per mare per terras* (*By sea and by land*).

GAELIC NAME : *MacDhòmhnuill.*

THE MACDONALDS OF SLEAT are descended from Hugh, son of Alexander, 3rd Lord of the Isles. He died in 1498 and was succeeded by his son John who died in 1502. Donald " Gallach," 3rd of Sleat, was murdered by his half-brother in 1506. During the lifetime of Donald Gruamach, 4th of Sleat, there were many feuds amongst the MacDonalds, and with other clans, and he was one of the nine island chiefs who submitted to the King in 1538. Donald Gorm, 5th of Sleat, claimed the Lordship of the Isles and the Earldom of Ross. He took possession of Trotternish and invaded Kintail, but was killed when attempting to capture Eileandonnan Castle in 1539. Donald Gormeson, 6th of Sleat, died in 1585 and was succeeded by his son Donald Gorm Mor, 7th of Sleat. He raided the Maclean lands in Mull, but after a second defeat Donald was taken prisoner by the Macleans, but was released by order of the Government who were now taking stronger measures to secure peace in the Western Highlands. Donald and other chiefs were imprisoned in Edinburgh, were heavily fined, and then released. In 1610 Donald and five other chiefs attended Edinburgh, agreed to keep the peace, and to submit all disputes to the ordinary courts of law. Donald died without issue in 1616, and was succeeded by his nephew, Sir Donald, 8th of Sleat, and 1st Baronet of Sleat. He was created a Baronet of Nova Scotia in 1625. Sir James, 2nd Baronet, joined Montrose, and in 1651 sent a force to assist Charles II in England. Sir Donald, 4th Baronet, known as " Donald of the Wars," had his estates forfeited for his part in the Rising of 1715. The estate was repurchased for the family during the lifetime of Sir Alexander Mac-Donald, 7th Baronet. Sir Alexander, 9th Baronet of Sleat, was created in 1766 Baron MacDonald of Slate in the peerage of Ireland.

MACDONALD OF SLEAT

ORIGIN OF NAME: *Gaelic Domhnull* (*world ruler*).
PLANT BADGE: *Heath*.

MACDONALD OF THE ISLES,
ANCIENT HUNTING

MACDONALD OF CLANRANALD

CREST BADGE : *On a castle triple towered, an arm in armour, embowed, holding a sword, proper.*

MOTTO : *My hope is constant in thee.*

OLD MOTTO : *Dh'aindeoin co'- theireadh e (Gainsay who dare).*

GAELIC NAME : *MacDhòmhnuill.*

THE MacDonalds of Clanranald take their name from Ranald, younger son of John, 1st Lord of the Isles. In 1373 he received a grant of the North Isles and other lands, and from him are descended the families of Moidart, Morar, Knoidart and Glengarry. During the 15th century there were fierce feuds amongst the branches of the Clan Donald and early in the following century Clanranald received from John, of Sleat, all the latter's estates. On the death of Ranald Bane, 5th chief, the clan, opposing his son Ranald's claim, elected his cousin John of Moidart as chief. Fraser of Lovat supported Ranald, and John of Moidart, with Clanranald, was assisted by the MacDonells of Keppoch and the Clan Cameron in the struggle that followed. The campaign ended in the famous Battle of Blar-na-Leine (Field of the Shirts) in 1544, so called because owing to the heat of the day, the combatants removed their upper garments to enable them to fight more fiercely. The Frasers were defeated and John of Moidart retained the chiefship and possessions of Clan Ranald. The Queen Regent pardoned John and his supporters in 1555. He died in 1584.

The MacDonalds of Clanranald found an outlet for their warlike spirit by serving under the Marquess of Montrose in the 17th century. The clan was represented at Killiecrankie by 500 men under the young chief, a boy of sixteen years of age. At Sheriffmuir the chief of Clanranald was killed, and in the '45 Clanranald was very closely associated with the Rising. It was on Clanranald land that Prince Charles raised his standard, and after Clanranald supporting him throughout all his campaign, it was in Clanranald territory in Benbecula and Uist that the Prince took refuge before embarking for France.

MACDONALD OF CLANRANALD

ORIGIN OF NAME: *Gaelic Domhnull (world ruler).*
PLANT BADGE: *Heath.*
WAR CRY: *Dh'aindeoin co' theireadh e (Gainsay who dare).*
PIPE MUSIC: *Spaidsearachd Mhic Mhic Ailein (Clanranald's March).*

MACDONELL OF GLENGARRY

CREST BADGE: *A raven, proper, perched on a rock, azure.*

MOTTO: *War Cry* (*The raven's rock*).

GAELIC NAME: *MacDhòmhnuill.*

RANALD, younger son of the 1st Lord of the Isles, was the progenitor of Clanranald, and from him are descended the families of Moidart, Morar, Knoidart and Glengarry. From Ranald's son Donald, the MacDonells of Glengarry trace their descent. Donald and his brothers had been dispossessed of their lands by their uncle, Godfrey, and on the execution of Godfrey's son Alexander in 1427, the lands of Glengarry reverted to the Crown, and thereafter the MacDonells became Crown tenants. From Alastair, 4th of Glengarry, the family take their Gaelic patronymic of " Mac 'ic Alasdair." During the late 16th and early 17th centuries there was a bitter feud between Glengarry, who had obtained a portion of the lands of Lochalsh, and the MacKenzies, during which both clans suffered severely. Eneas, 9th of Glengarry, was amongst the first to join Montrose and the Royalist army in 1644, and gave devoted service to Montrose and King Charles II. He was forfeited by Cromwell in 1651, but at the Restoration he was created, in 1660, Lord MacDonell and Aros. The title became extinct on the death of Glengarry in 1680 without male issue. The estates passed to Ranald MacDonell of Scotus. Alexander, 11th of Glengarry, distinguished himself at Killiecrankie in 1689, where he bore the Royal Standard of James VII, and at Sheriffmuir in 1715. In the Rising of 1745, 600 of the Glengarry MacDonells joined Prince Charles under the chief's second son Angus. Glengarry and his son were imprisoned in the Tower of London. With the exception of the ruined castle the estates were sold by the 16th chief whose sons emigrated to New Zealand. On the death of the 18th chief of Glengarry the chiefship passed to the Scotus branch.

MACDONELL OF GLENGARRY

ORIGIN OF NAME: *Gaelic Domhnull (world ruler)*.
PLANT BADGE: *Heath*.
WAR CRY: *Creag an Fhitich (The raven's rock)*.
PIPE MUSIC: *Glengarry's March*.

MACDONELL OF KEPPOCH

CREST BADGE: *A dexter hand holding a cross crosslet, fitche sable.*

MOTTO: *Per mare per terras* (*By sea and land*).

GAELIC NAME: *MacDhòmhnuill.*

KNOWN also as the Clan Ranald of Lochaber, the MacDonells of Keppoch and Garragach are descended from Alastair Carrach, 3rd son of John, Lord of the Isles. Alastair was, in common with the progenitors of Clanranald and Glengarry, a grandson of King Robert II. In 1431 Alastair was forfeited for his part in the insurrection of Donald Balloch, and part of his lands were granted to MacKintosh, chief of Clan Chattan, which caused a long feud between the two clans. John, 4th of Keppoch, was deposed by the clan for delivering a clansmen to the MacKintosh. He was succeeded by his cousin-german Donald Glas, whose son Ranald assisted John of Moidart at Blar-na-Leine in 1544, and for his part in the rebellions was executed in Elgin along with Locheil. Ranald, 9th of Keppoch, an outlaw for most of his life, served in the Swedish army. Donald Glas, 11th Chief, served in the Spanish army. Alexander, 12th of Keppoch, and his brother were murdered in 1663, an event commemorated in Tobair-nan-ceann, the well of the heads, near Invergarry, where the heads of the seven murderers were washed before being placed before Lord McDonell of Invergarry. Coll, 15th of Keppoch, known as " Coll of the Cows " withstood all attempts of the MacKintoshes, assisted by government troops, to capture him, and for forty years he held his lands in Lochaber by right of the sword. He was succeeded by his son Alexander, who with his followers joined Prince Charles Edward in 1745. By intercepting government troops attempting to surprise the gathering at Glenfinnan, they were first to strike a blow in the '45.

Keppoch died fighting single-handed at Culloden. The last chief of Keppoch, in the direct line, died in 1889.

166

MACDONELL OF KEPPOCH

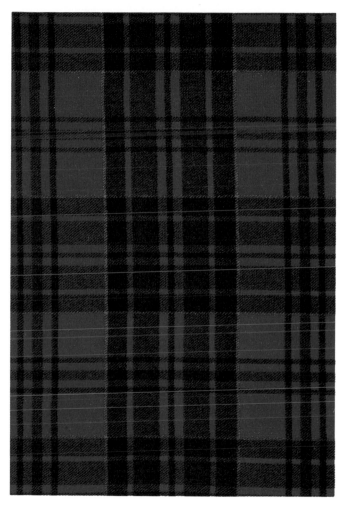

ORIGIN OF NAME: *Gaelic Domhnull (world ruler)*.
PLANT BADGE: *Heath*.
WAR CRY: *Dia's Naomh Aindrea (God and St. Andrew)*.
PIPE MUSIC: *Latha na Maoile Ruadh (The Battle of Mulroy)*.

MACDOUGALL

CREST BADGE : *On a cap of maintenance a dexter arm in armour embowed, fessways, couped, proper, holding a cross crosslet fitchy, gules.*

MOTTO : *Buaidh no bàs* (*To conquer or die*).

GAELIC NAME : *MacDhùghaill.*

THE MACDOUGALLS take their name from Dugall, eldest son of Somerled, from whom they are descended. From Dougall, his son Duncan received the lands of Lorn. Duncan's son, Ewin Lord of Lorn, although he made allegiance to Norway, refused to join King Haco in his ill-fated expedition of 1263. Ewin's son, Alexander, married a daughter of the Red Comyn who was slain at Dumfries, and in consequence the MacDougalls became bitter enemies of Robert the Bruce. In one battle with the MacDougalls Bruce is alleged to have escaped only by discarding his cloak with his brooch, afterwards known as the Brooch of Lorn, and now a treasured possession of the chief of the clan. When Bruce secured his throne he retaliated on the MacDougalls for their opposition, and after their defeat, Alexander submitted to the King, but his son John fled to England, where he was appointed an Admiral in the English fleet. He was later captured in the Western Isles and imprisoned first in Dunbarton and afterwards in Lochleven. On the death of King Robert, John of Lorn was released and his lands restored to him. He married a granddaughter of Robert the Bruce, and his son, John, was the last MacDougall of Lorn. He died without male issue, and the lands passed, through his daughters, to the Stewarts, Lords of Lorn, in 1388.

In 1457, John Stewart, Lord of Lorn, granted to John MacAlan MacDougall the lands of Dunolly. The clan joined in the Rising of 1715, and under their chief, Iain Ciar, were present at Sheriffmuir. On the failure of the Rising the chief's lands were forfeited, but restored when the clan remained loyal to the Crown in 1745.

The eldest daughter of the chief bears the old title " Maid of Lorn."

MACDOUGALL

ORIGIN OF NAME: *Gaelic Dughall (black stranger).*
PLANT BADGE: *Bell heath, Cypress.*
WAR CRY: *Buaidh no bàs (Victory or Death).*
PIPE MUSIC: *Caisteal Dhunolla (Dunolly Castle).*

MACDUFF

CREST BADGE : *A demi-lion rampant, gules, holding in the dexter
paw a dagger, proper, hilted and
pommelled or.*

MOTTO : *Deus juvat (God assists).*

GAELIC NAME : *MacDhuibh.*

TRADITION says that MacDuff was the patronymic of
the Celtic Earls of Fife, and that the first Earl was
MacDuff who opposed MacBeth and assisted Malcolm to
the throne of Scotland. This ancient clan played an
important part in the affairs of Scotland in those days.
The MacDuffs had the privilege of crowning the King,
of leading the Scottish army, and privilege of sanctuary
at the cross of MacDuff in Fifeshire. When Robert the
Bruce was crowned in 1306, Duncan, Earl of Fife, who
had married a niece of Edward I, was opposed to Bruce,
and his sister Isabel, Countess of Buchan, and wife of
Comyn, Bruce's enemy, exercised her family's privilege
and suffered seven years' imprisonment in Berwick for
her courage.

The old Earldom of Fife became extinct in 1353 on
the death of Duncan, 12th Earl, but during the succeeding
centuries traces of prominent families of the names Duff
and MacDuff are found, and William Duff, Lord Braco,
was, in 1759, created Viscount MacDuff and Earl of Fife
in the Peerage of Ireland, and in 1827 James, 4th Earl,
was raised to the peerage of Great Britain as Baron Fife.

Alexander W. G. Duff, Duke of Fife and Earl of
MacDuff, born in 1849, was a successful financier and a
founder of the Chartered Company of South Africa. He
was also a Lord Lieutenant of the County of London,
and married Princess Louise, daughter of King Edward
VII in 1889. He died in 1912 and was succeeded by his
daughter Princess Alexandra Victoria, who married Prince
Arthur of Connaught.

MACDUFF

There are also dress and hunting tartans.

ORIGIN OF NAME: *Gaelic dubh* (*black*).
PLANT BADGE: *Boxwood, Red whortleberry*.

MACEWEN

House of Bardrochat

CREST BADGE : *The trunk of an oak tree from which sprouts forth young branches, proper.*

MOTTO : *Reviresco (I grow green).*

GAELIC NAME : *MacEòghainn.*

ALTHOUGH of ancient origin there are few authentic records of this clan. Skene quoting the MS. of 1450 shows that the Clan Ewen together with the Clan Neil and the Clan Lachlan formed the Siol Gillevray of the Gallgael. The genealogy in the MS. proved the Clan MacEwen existed long before 1450 and that they were known as the MacEwans of Otter. The Rev. Alexander McFarlane, minister of the parish of Kilfinan, writing in 1794, states that : " On a rocky point on the coast of Lochfyne about a mile below the church of Kilfinan is to be seen the vestige of a building called Caisteal mhic Eoghuin or MacEwen's Castle. This MacEwen was the chief of a clan and proprietor of Otter."

Eòghain na h-Oitrich (Ewen of Otter), who gives his name to the clan, lived at the beginning of the 13th century. Gillespie, 5th of Otter, flourished about a century later. Swene MacEwan, 9th and last of Otter, granted lands of Otter to Duncan Campbell in 1432 and resigned the barony of Otter to James I, but it was returned to him with remainder to Celestine, son and heir of Duncan Campbell of Lochow. In 1513 James V confirmed the barony of Otter to Colin, Earl of Argyll, and thereafter Otter remained in the possession of the Campbells.

Without lands the MacEwans became a " broken " clan and found their way to many districts. A large number settled in the Lennox country, others went farther afield to Lochaber, Perth, Skye and the Lowlands, including Galloway.

MACEWEN

ORIGIN OF NAME: *Son of Ewen.*

MACFARLANE

CREST BADGE: *A demi-savage holding in dexter hand a sword and in sinister an imperial crown, all proper.*

MOTTO: *This I'll defend.*

GAELIC NAME: *MacPhàrlain.*

LOCH LOMOND district was the home of several war-like clans, and none more war-like than the MacFarlanes, who claim the moon as their lantern, and who trace their descent from Gilchrist, brother of Maldowen, 3rd of the ancient Earls of Lennox in the 13th century. The great-grandson of Gilchrist was named Bartholomew, and from its Gaelic equivalent Parlan, the clan takes its name.

Duncan, 6th chief of the clan, obtained the lands of Arrochar from the Earl of Lennox, and in 1395 he acquired many of the adjoining lands by marriage. On the death of the last of the old Earls of Lennox without male issue, MacFarlane claimed the title and lands. The conferring of the Earldom on Sir John Stewart of Darnley led to a long enmity between the contesting families that terminated only when a cadet of the Mac-Farlanes married a daughter of the Earl of Lennox in the 15th century. In the following century the clan found an outlet for their war-like spirit in supporting the Earls of Lennox, and Duncan MacFarlane of Tarbet, who was afterwards killed at the Battle of Pinkie, is described as being in command of about 150 men who spoke Irish (Gaelic) and the English-Scottish tongue, well armed in shirts of mail, with bows and two-handed swords. The Mac-Farlanes distinguished themselves at the Battle of Langside fighting against Queen Mary, and claim to have captured three of the queen's standards.

In the 16th and 17th centuries the clan was proscribed and deprived of lands and name. Some members of the clan emigrated to Ireland and the last chief is believed to have emigrated to America in the 18th century.

Walter, 20th chief, who died in 1767, was one of the most famous antiquarians and genealogists of his time.

MACFARLANE

There is a hunting tartan and a black and white sett.

ORIGIN OF NAME: *Son of Parlan (Bartholomew is an Anglicised form of Parlan)*.
PLANT BADGE: *Cranberry, Cloudberry*.
WAR CRY: *Loch Sloy*.

MACFIE

House of Dreghorn

CREST BADGE : *A demi-lion rampant, proper.*

MOTTO : *Pro rege (For the king).*

GAELIC NAME : *MacDubh-shithe.*

COLONSAY is the ancient home of the Macduffies or Macphees, a branch of the great Clan Alpine. The early history of the clan is unknown, but Donald Macduffie witnessed a charter at Dingwall in 1463. The clan was prominent in the history of the Western Highlands, and Macfie of Colonsay was one of the principal chiefs who met Bishop Knox and signed the famous " Statutes of Iona " in 1609. Colonsay passed out of the possession of the clan some years later. In 1615 Malcolm Macfie of Colonsay joined in the rebellion of Sir James MacDonald, and was later delivered to the Earl of Argyll by Coll Kitto MacDonald. In 1623 Coll Kitto was charged with the cruel slaughter of Malcolm and several of his followers. Colonsay passed to the MacDonalds and then to the MacNeils who brought fame to the island.

When the Macfies were dispossessed, some of them followed the MacDonalds and others settled in the Cameron country of Lochaber, and supported that clan at the Battle of Culloden. In Galloway the name took the form of Macguffie and Machaffie.

Ewen Macphee who lived in the middle of the 19th century was famous as the last of the Scottish " outlaws." He enlisted in the army, but deserted as the result of a misunderstanding and settled with his family on an island on Loch Quoich. He recognised no law and no landowner, resided rent free, and defended his home with firearms, his wife being as proficient in their use as her husband. He held it until in his old age he indulged in sheep stealing for which he was ejected.

MACFIE

There is also a black and white sett.

ORIGIN OF NAME: *Gaelic MacDhubhshith (dark of peace)*.
PLANT BADGE: *Pine, Oak*.

MACGILLIVRAY

CREST BADGE: *A stag's head couped proper, tyned or.*

MOTTO: *Dunmaglas.*

GAELIC NAME: *MacGhille-brath.*

THIS clan, one of the oldest branches of the Clan Chattan Confederation, came originally from Morven and Lochaber. They were one of the principal clans in the time of the famous Somerled whose father's name was Gillebride, but they suffered as many others during the conquest of Alexander II. This may have been the reason for the statement of a 16th century historian that about 1268 Gillivray, the progenitor of the Clan vic Gillivray, took protection for himself and posterity of Farquhard Mackintosh, 5th of Mackintosh.

About 1500 the MacGillivrays settled at Dunmaglass in Strathnairn, and in succeeding years added considerably to their possessions and became very influential in that part of the country. The Clan Chattan Bonds of 1609 and 1664 were signed by three members of the clan, being gentlemen and heads of families. The Mac-Gillivrays continued to take a prominent part in public affairs including local clan disputes. (A story is related about Captain William, a son of Farquhar, 6th of Dun-maglass. A local lady disappeared and was reported to have been carried off by the fairies. The captain, learning of wax candles of a particular virtue in possession of a MacQueen, succeeded after many attempts in obtaining the desired charm and restored the lady to her unhappy husband. The candle was preserved in the family for many generations.)

The MacGillivrays took a prominent part in the Jacobite Risings of 1715 and 1745, and at Culloden, Alexander, chief of the clan, led the Clan Chattan regiment which almost wiped out the left wing of the Hanoverian army. The burial place of the MacGillivrays of Dunmaglass is in Dunlichity churchyard.

MACGILLIVRAY

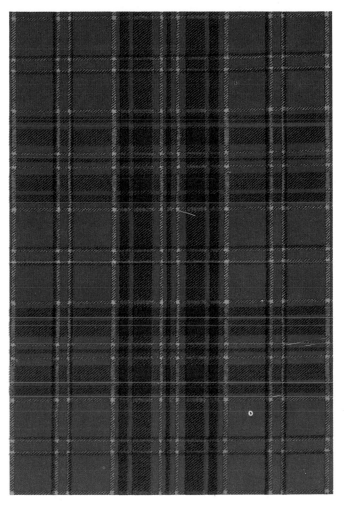

There is also a hunting tartan.

ORIGIN OF NAME: *Gaelic Gillie Bhrath (son of the servant of judgment).*
PLANT BADGE: *Boxwood, Red whortleberry.*
WAR CRY: *Dunmaglas.*

MACGREGOR

CREST BADGE: *A lion's head, erased, crowned with an antique crown, proper.*

MOTTO: *'S rioghal mo dhream (Royal is my race).*

GAELIC NAME: *MacGrioghair.*

" 'S RIOGHAL mo dhream " (Royal is my race) is the claim of this, one of the most famous of Highland clans, and the principal branch of the Clan Alpine. The clan claim descent from Griogar, son of King Alpin, in the 8th century.

The home of the clan was the eastern border of Argyll and the western border of Perthshire, including Glenorchy, Glenstrae, Glenlyon and Glengyle. The earliest possession of the clan, Glenorchy, previously owned by the Campbells, was bestowed on the MacGregors for services rendered to Alexander II in his conquest of Argyll. For a long time the MacGregors maintained possession of their lands by right of the sword, but the enmity of surrounding clans resulted in attempts to displace the clan, and the inevitable retaliation by the MacGregors, who thus earned the reputation of being a turbulent clan. During these conflicts the Campbells were enabled to obtain grants of the MacGregor lands, the name of MacGregor was proscribed, and severe enactments were passed against the clan, whose unfortunate members were prosecuted and persecuted. Charles II, because of their support, repealed the acts against Clan Gregor, but upon the accession of William of Orange the acts of proscription were renewed, and it was not until 1775 that the penal statutes against the MacGregors were finally repealed. After the restoration of their rights a meeting of the clan was held and John Murray of Lanrick, afterwards Sir John MacGregor, Bart., descended from the family of Glenstrae, was recognised as chief.

Rob Roy (1671–1734) the celebrated freebooter and hero of Sir Walter Scott's romance, was a son of Lieut.-Col. Donald MacGregor of Glengyle.

MACGREGOR

This tartan with the red-colour changed to a deep wine is now
popular as a hunting tartan.

ORIGIN OF NAME: *Son of Gregory (flocksman)*.
PLANT BADGE: *Pine*.
WAR CRY: *Ard-choille*.
PIPE MUSIC: *Ruaig Ghlinne Freoine (Chase of Glen Fruin)*.

MACINNES

CREST BADGE : *An arm in band from the shoulder, hand proper, and attired in a highland coatee of the proper tartan of the Clann Aonghais, grasping a bow sable, stringed or.*

MOTTO : *Irìd Ghibht Dhé Agus An Righ* (*Through the Grace of God and the King*).

GAELIC NAME : *MacAonghais.*

THE MACINNESES, or Clan Aonghais, are a Celtic clan of ancient origin. The earliest known territory of the MacInneses was Morven and they are said to have formed part of a branch of the Siol Gillebride, believed to be the original inhabitants of Morven and Ardnamurchan. It is claimed that they were constables of the castle of Kinlochaline.

Hugh MacDonald, the Sleat historian of the 17th century, writing of Morven in the 12th century states that " the principal names in the country were MacInnes and MacGillivray, who are the same as the MacInnes," and then goes on to describe how Somerled coming out of his retirement led these clans and defeated the Norsemen, and expelled them from the district. The MacInneses remained in possession of Morven, and as late as 1645 it appears that a MacInnes was in command of the Castle of Kinlochaline when it was besieged and burnt by Coll Kitto.

When the MacInneses and the MacGillivrays of Morven and Ardgour were broken up, we find, writes Skene, that they acknowledged the Clan Dugall Craignish (Campbell) as their chief.

The hereditary bowmen to the chiefs of MacKinnon were a branch of the MacInneses, and this may be the origin of the MacInneses in Skye in more modern times.

MACINNES

ORIGIN OF NAME: *Gaelic aonghais* (*unique choice*).
PLANT BADGE: *Holly*.

MACINTYRE

House of Camus-na-h-erie

CREST BADGE : *A dexter hand holding a skean 'dhu in pale, on which is affixed a snow ball all proper. Around the wrist a manche of the correct tartan turned or.*

MOTTO : *Per ardua* (*Through difficulties*).

GAELIC NAME : *Mac an t-Saoir.*

THE CLAN MACINTYRE is of ancient origin, with, it is claimed, a close connection with the Clan Donald. The commonly accepted origin of the name is that Mac-an-t-saoir means "the son of the carpenter." A prominent member of the clan gives the derivation as from a MacDonald called Cean-tire from possessing lands in Kintyre. His son John acquired the lands of Degnish in Lorn and was known as John Mac-Cein-teire-Dhegnish. The former derivation may account for the name being found in districts widely separated, as there would be carpenters or wrights in many districts.

The principal family was the Macintyres who possessed the lands of Glenoe on Loch Etive for several centuries until they were forced to part with them in 1806. Members of this family emigrated to America.

A branch of the Macintyres were a sept of the Campbells of Craignish.

The clan was notable for its versatility. The Macintyres of Glenoe were hereditary foresters to the Stewarts, Lords of Lorn. The Macintyres of Badenoch are descended from the bard Macintyre whom William, 13th of MacKintosh, took under his protection in 1496. A family of Macintyres were hereditary pipers to MacDonald of Clanranald, and the Macintyres of Rannoch were hereditary pipers to the chief of Clan Menzies. A branch of the clan resident in Cladich were famous for their weaving of hose and garters.

One of the most famous of Gaelic poets was Duncan Macintyre, Donnacha Ban nan Oran, born in Glenorchy in 1724. He was out in the Rising of 1745, and was later imprisoned for a poem he wrote against the Act proscribing the Highland dress. He died in Edinburgh in 1812.

MACINTYRE, HUNTING

There is another sett called Macintyre of Glenorchy.

ORIGIN OF NAME: *Gaelic Mac-an-t-saoir (son of the carpenter)*.
PLANT BADGE: *Heath*.
WAR CRY: *Cruachan*.
PIPE MUSIC: *Gabhaidh sin an Rathad Mor*.

MACIVER

CREST BADGE : *A boar's head, couped, or.*

MOTTO : *Nunquam obliviscar (I will never forget).*

GAELIC NAME : *Mac Iomhair.*

THE CLAN IVER, known also as Clan Iver Glassary, from Glassary in Argyll, are claimed to have formed part of the army of Alexander II which conquered Argyll in 1221, and received for their services lands in that district. They had come from Glenlyon district, and in Argyll their principal possessions were Lergachonzie and Asknish, and lands in Glassary and Cowal.

The history of the clan after they obtained lands in Argyll is very obscure. It is asserted that in the 13th century branches of the family left Argyll and settled in Lochaber, Glenelg and Ross, and it would appear that the MacIvers were for some time a " broken " clan. In 1564 they appear to have recovered some of their former strength for in that year Archibald, 5th Earl of Argyll, renounced all claims to the calps of any of the Clan Iver, Iver of Lergachonzie agreeing to give the Earl his own calp.

Duncan, who succeeded as chief of the clan about 1572, is described as of Stronshiray and Superior of Lergachonzie. In 1685 Iver of Asknish and Stronshiray forfeited land for aiding Archibald, 9th Earl of Argyll in rebellion. Following the Revolution of 1688, Archibald, 10th Earl, restored the estates of Iver to his son Duncan MacIver on condition that he and his heirs should bear the name and arms of Campbell. Iver was thus the last chief of the MacIvers, and Sir Humphrey Campbell who died in 1818 was the last in the male line of Duncan MacIver of Stronshiray.

Branches of the clan in Argyll all appear to have assumed the name of Campbell. Those in the north and in Lewis retained the name of MacIver.

MACIVER

There is also a black and white sett.

ORIGIN OF NAME: *Gaelic Mac Iomhair (son of Ivar).*
PLANT BADGE: *Bog myrtle, Fir club moss.*

MACKAY

CREST BADGE : *A dexter cubit arm holding erect a dagger in pale, all proper, hilt and pommel or.*

The crest badge shown is that of the Chief and worn by him *alone.* Clansmen wear the crest badge without coronet and feathers.

MOTTO : *Manu forti (With a strong hand).*

GAELIC NAME : *MacAoidh.*

THIS powerful clan was known as the **Clan Morgan** and as the Clan Aoidh. The former name is claimed from Morgan, son of Magnus in the early 14th century, the latter from his grandson Aodh or Hugh. The Mac-Kays are descended from the old Royal House of MacEth.

When Donald, Lord of the Isles, claiming the Earldom of Ross, invaded Sutherland, he was opposed by Angus Dubh and the Clan MacKay, but they were defeated and Angus was imprisoned by the Lord of the Isles. Angus, however, became reconciled and married Elizabeth, daughter of his captor, with whom he received many lands. Angus was killed at the time of the Battle of Drumnacoub in 1429.

In 1626 Sir Donald MacKay of Farr raised an army of 3000 men for service in Bohemia, and afterwards in Denmark. The lands of Strathnaver were sold in 1642 and the remainder of the MacKay country was sold in 1829 to the house of Sutherland. Æneas, grandson of the 1st Lord Reay, was colonel of the MacKay Dutch regiment and settled in Holland, where his family were ennobled with the title of Baron, and when the Scottish succession ceased Baron Eric MacKay van Ophemert, Holland, became 12th Baron Reay.

The MacKays of Argyll, who can be traced back to the 13th century, are said to have no connection with the MacKays of the north.

MACKENDRICK

See pages 118-9

MACKAY

ORIGIN OF NAME: *Gaelic MacAoidh (son of fire).*
PLANT BADGE: *Great bulrush.*
WAR CRY: *Bratach Bhan Chlann Aoidh (The White Banner of MacKay).*
PIPE MUSIC: *MacKay's March.*

MACKENZIE

CREST BADGE : *A mountain in-flamed, proper.* (*Mackenzie more commonly use the badge a stag's head cabossed or, and the motto* ' *Cuidich* '*n righ*'—*Help the King*).

MOTTO : *Luceo non uro* (*I shine, not burn*).

GAELIC NAME : *MacCoinnich.*

IGNORING legendary origins, the MacKenzies claim to be descended from Colin, progenitor of the Earls of Ross. He died in 1278 and was succeeded by his son Kenneth. In 1362 Murdoch, son of Kenneth 3rd Earl, received from David II the lands of Kintail.

In 1491 the MacKenzies defeated the MacDonalds in a fierce battle known as Blair-na-park. The clan supported James IV at Flodden where their chief was captured by the English, and at the Battle of Pinkie the MacKenzies fought for James V. Colin, 11th chief, fought in the army of Queen Mary at Langside. Kenneth, 12th chief, in 1607 received a charter of the lands of Lochalsh and Lochcarron, and it is said that at this time all the lands from Ardnamurchan to Strathnaver were in the possession of the MacKenzies or their vassals. Kenneth was created Lord MacKenzie of Kintail in 1609. Colin, 2nd Lord, was created Earl of Seaforth by James VI in 1623, and was Secretary of State in Scotland to Charles II. Kenneth, 4th Earl, was nominated a Knight of the Thistle by James VII whom he followed to France. William, 5th Earl, joined the Earl of Mar in 1715, was at Sheriffmuir, and later escaped to France. He was attainted and his estates forfeited. In 1726 he was pardoned by George I and died in Lewis in 1740. Kenneth, his grandson, repurchased the forfeited estates and in 1771 was restored to the Earldom of Seaforth. Francis Humbertson MacKenzie, who had succeeded to the estates of Seaforth and Humbertson, was created a British peer in 1797 by the title Lord Seaforth, Baron MacKenzie of Kintail. He died in 1815, his four sons having pre-deceased him, and his eldest daughter married J. A. Stewart of Glasserton who assumed the name Stewart MacKenzie of Seaforth.

MACKENZIE

There is also a dress tartan.

ORIGIN OF NAME: *(Gaelic) MacCoinnich (son of the fair).*
PLANT BADGE: *Holly, Deer-grass.*
WAR CRY: *Tulach Ard.*
PIPE MUSIC: *Caber Féidh.*

MACKINNON

CREST BADGE : *A boar's head erased, argent, in mouth a deer's shankbone, proper.*

MOTTO : *Audentes fortuna juvat (Fortune assists the daring).*

GAELIC NAME : *MacFhionghuin.*

THE MACKINNONS, one of the branches of the Siol Alpine, claim to be descended from Fingon, a great-grandson of Kenneth MacAlpin.

The MacKinnons held lands in Mull and Skye, and from the earliest times appear to have been vassals of the Lords of the Isles. In 1409 Lachlan MacKinnon witnessed a charter of the Lord of the Isles. Until the forfeiture of the Lordship of the Isles, the history of the MacKinnons is bound up with that important family.

The MacKinnons were intimately connected with the ecclesiastical history of Iona, and the last Abbot of that holy island was John MacKinnon, who died in 1550.

Interesting evidence of the connection between the branches of Siol Alpine, who although widely separated, claimed a common ancestry, is to be found in a bond of friendship in 1606 between MacKinnon of Strathardle and Finlay MacNab of Bowaine, and again a bond of manrent between MacKinnon of Strathardle and James MacGregor of MacGregor in 1671.

Ewen, chief of the clan, received from James V a charter of the lands of Mishnish and Strathardle in 1542. The clan was at the Battle of Inverlochy under Montrose. In 1646 Lauchlan, chief, and the clan, supported Charles II at the Battle of Worcester. His second son, Donald, emigrated to Antigua where he died in 1720.

The MacKinnons were out in 1715 and again in 1745 in support of the Stuarts. After Culloden, the chief, although old and infirm, was imprisoned in London but was allowed to return home in 1747. His son Charles had to part with the family estates after they had been in the clan possession for over four centuries. In 1808 the last chief of the main line died, and the chiefship passed to the family of Donald who emigrated to Antigua.

MACKINNON

There is also a hunting tartan.

ORIGIN OF NAME: *Gaelic MacFhionghuin (son of the fair born).*
PLANT BADGE: *Pine.*
WAR CRY: *Cuimhnich Bàs Ailpein (Remember the death of Alpine).*

MACKINTOSH

CREST BADGE : *A cat salient gardant, proper.*
MOTTO : *Touch not the cat bot a glove (Touch not the cat without a glove).*
GAELIC NAME : *Mac an Toisich.*

THE clan name is derived from Mac-an-Toisich and means " son of the chief." The founder of the clan is traditionally said to have been a son of MacDuff, ancestor of the Earls of Fife. The Mackintoshes are one of the clans forming the Clan Chattan Confederation, the chiefship of which devolved on the chiefs of Mackintosh through the marriage in 1291 of Angus, 6th Laird of Mackintosh, to Eva, heiress of Clan Chattan.

The first mention of the Mackintosh as Captain of Clan Chattan is in a charter granted to William Mackintosh by the Lord of the Isles in 1337, and confirmed by King David II in 1359.

The rise of the Mackintoshes led to a period of feuds with the Earls of Moray and Huntly, and the clans Cameron, MacDonells of Keppoch, and Gordon. In 1639 when Huntly supported the King, Mackintosh joined the Covenanters north of the Spey, and he formed part of the army opposing Cromwell, 1650. At the Revolution the Mackintoshes supported the new government and refused to join Viscount Dundee.

They were prominent in the Jacobite Rising of 1715 under Brigadier Mackintosh of Borlum. Angus, chief in 1745, was on service with Loudon's Highlanders when the Rising took place, but Lady Anne his wife, who was a Farquharson of Invercauld, raised the clan for Prince Charles and her strategy was responsible for the Rout of Moy when 1500 of the government troops were put to flight by half a dozen of Lady Mackintosh's retainers. Here the famous piper Donald Ban MacCrimmon, who accompanied the Royalist force, was killed. Following the death in 1938 of the 28th Chief the chiefships of Clan Mackintosh and Clan Chattan were separated.

MACKINTOSH

A hunting tartan was designed about 1929 which received the approval of the Mackintosh, in April, 1951.

ORIGIN OF NAME: *Gaelic Mac-an-toisich* (*son of the thane*).
PLANT BADGE: *Red whortleberry.*
WAR CRY: *Loch Moy.*

MACLACHLAN

CREST BADGE : *Out of crest coronet a castle, triple towered, proper.*

MOTTO : *Fortis et fidus* (*Brave and trusty*).

GAELIC NAME : *Mac Lachlainn.*

THE MACLACHLANS are of ancient origin. As early as 1230 Gilchrist MacLachlan witnessed a charter granted by Lamond, ancestor of the Lamonds. In 1292 Gilleskel MacLachlan received a charter of his lands in Argyll from King John Baliol, and in 1308 Gillespie MacLachlan was a member of the first parliament of Robert the Bruce in St. Andrews. During the 14th and 15th centuries the chiefs of the clan made grants to the Preaching Friars of Glasgow from their lands of Kilbride, near Castlelachlan.

In 1615 the MacLachlans formed part of Argyll's army that opposed the forces of Sir James MacDonald of Isla, and in 1689 they were with Dundee at the Battle of Killiecrankie. During the '45 the clan supported Prince Charles, and the chief who had been appointed A.D.C. to the Prince was killed at the Battle of Culloden. The estates were attainted, but in 1749, Robert, then chief, regained possession of the lands. From him were descended the later chiefs.

There are several branches of the clan in Argyll, Perthshire, Stirlingshire and Lochaber.

MACLACHLAN

There is a yellow dress sett and a sett called
Ancient MacLachlan.

ORIGIN OF NAME: *Gaelic MacLachlainn (son of Lachlan).*
PLANT BADGE: *Mountain ash.*
PIPE MUSIC: *Moladh Mairi (The praise of Mary).*

MACLAINE OF LOCHBUIE

CREST BADGE : *A battleaxe in pale with two branches in saltire dexter a laurel, sinister a cypress, all proper.*

MOTTO : *Vincere vel mori* (*To conquer or die*).

GAELIC NAME : *MacGhille Eoin.*

THE MACLAINES OF LOCHBUIE were descended from Eachan Reaganach, brother of Lachlan the progenitor of the MacLeans of Duart. Eachan, or Hector, received the lands of Lochbuie from John, 1st Lord of the Isles, his brother's father-in-law. Hector's son Charles was the progenitor of the MacLeans of Dochgarroch, a sept of Clan Chattan.

John Og, of Lochbuie, received from James IV charters confirming the lands and baronies held by his progenitors. He was killed with two of his sons in a feud with the MacLeans of Duart, and the surviving son, Murdoch, being an infant, was conveyed to Ireland for safety. Returning when he reached manhood, he captured Lochbuie Castle with the aid of his nurse who recognised him. In Edinburgh, before the king and court, his son John Mor, an expert swordsman, fought and killed a famous Italian fencer who challenged all Scotland.

The MacLaines were strong supporters of the Stuarts, formed part of the army of Montrose, and afterwards fought at Killiecrankie under Viscount Dundee. In later years they found scope for their military activities in the Continental and American wars.

Donald, 20th of Lochbuie, born in 1816, amassed a fortune as an East India merchant, and saved Lochbuie for the family by clearing off all the debt. The estate has now passed out of the family.

MACLAINE OF LOCHBUIE

There is also a hunting tartan.

ORIGIN OF NAME: *Gaelic MacGhille-Eoin (son of the servant of John).*
PLANT BADGE: *Blackberry.*
PIPE MUSIC: *Lament for MacLaine of Lochbuie.*

MACLAREN

CREST BADGE : *A lion's head sabled langued or, crowned with an antique crown or, the four points argent, surrounded by laurel in orle proper.*

MOTTO : *Creag an Tuirc (The Boar's Rock).*

GAELIC NAME : *MacLabhruinn.*

A TRADITIONAL account claims that the MacLarens are descended from Lorn, son of Erc, who landed in Argyll in A.D. 503. The MacLarens are recorded as having been in possession of lands in Balquhidder and Strathearn in the 12th century. In the Ragman Roll in 1296 are three names that have been identified as belonging to the Clan MacLaren—Maurice of Tyrie, Conan of Balquhidder and Laurin of Ardveche in Strathearn, all in Perthshire.

In the 14th century when the Earldom of Strathearn became vested in the crown, the MacLarens were reduced from proprietors of their lands to perpetual tenants. They remained loyal to the crown and fought for James III at Sauchieburn in 1488, for James IV at Flodden in 1513, and for Queen Mary at Pinkie in 1547. They are included in the Rolls of the Clans in 1587 and 1594, appended to an Act of Parliament known as " The General Band." The MacLarens were a war-like clan and had their share of feuds with neighbouring clans. The greater part of the clan followed the Stewarts of Appin, while others followed the Murrays of Atholl. Dugal Stewart, first of Appin, was the natural son of John Stewart, Lord of Lorn, and a daughter of MacLaren of Ardveche.

The clan was out in the '45 and suffered severely at Culloden. MacLaren of Invernenty was taken prisoner and made a remarkable escape near Moffat when being conveyed to Carlisle. The incident is described by Sir Walter Scott in *Redgauntlet*.

John MacLaurin, Lord Dreghorn (1734–1796), proved his claim to the chiefship of the clan before the Lyon Court in 1781 through his descent from a family that had long held the island of Tiree.

MACLAREN

ORIGIN OF NAME: *Gaelic MacLabhruinn (son of Laurence)*.
PLANT BADGE: *Laurel*.
WAR CRY: *Creag an Tuirc (The boar's rock)*.

MACLEAN

CREST BADGE : *A tower embattled, argent.*

MOTTO : *Virtue mine honour.*

GAELIC NAME : *MacGhille Eoin.*

THE CLAN MACLEAN who at one time or another held extensive lands in the Western Isles and mainland are descended from Gilleathain na Tuaidh, Gillian of the Battleaxe, in the 13th century. Two brothers, his descendants, were Lachlan Lubanach, progenitor of the MacLeans of Duart, and Eachan Reaganach, progenitor of the MacLaines of Lochbuie.

The MacLeans were supporters of the MacDougalls of Lorn, but later transferred their allegiance to the MacDonalds, Lords of the Isles, and became one of their most powerful vassals. The MacLeans fought at the Battle of Harlaw, where their chief Red Hector of the Battles was killed. On the forfeiture of the Lordship of the Isles in 1493, the MacLeans, then divided into four separate branches, became independent.

Lachlan MacLean of Duart was killed at Flodden in 1513, and during the 16th and 17th centuries the Mac-Leans were one of the most important clans in the Western Isles. In 1632 Lachlan MacLean of Morven, heir to Hector MacLean of Duart, was created a baronet. MacLeans fought at Inverlochy under Montrose, and at Inverkeithing, and in the latter battle occurred the famous incident of seven brothers in the clan each giving his life to protect his chief, each as he fell shouting " Another for Hector." The sacrifice was unavailing for Sir Hector too was killed. The MacLeans supported Dundee at the Battle of Killiecrankie, and joined the Earl of Mar in 1715. Sir Hector, chief in 1745, was imprisoned in London for two years, but the clan appeared at Culloden under the Duke of Perth.

Sir Fitzroy MacLean, 10th Baronet, repurchased Duart Castle in 1910.

MACLEAN

ORIGIN OF NAME: *Gaelic MacGhille-Eoin (son of the servant of John).*
PLANT BADGE: *Crowberry.*
WAR CRIES: *Bàs no beatha (Death or Life). Fear eile airson Eachainn (Another for Hector).*
PIPE MUSIC: *The MacLean's March.*

MACLEAN
HUNTING TARTAN

CREST BADGE: *A tower embattled, argent.*

MOTTO: *Virtue mine honour.*

GAELIC NAME: *MacGhille Eoin.*

THIS is probably the oldest tartan for which we have documentary evidence. When Hector MacLean, heir of Duart, received a charter of the lands of Nerrabolsadh in Islay in 1587, the feu duty was payable in the form of sixty ells of cloth of white, black and green colours, which describes the hunting tartan of MacLean of Duart.

Thirty years later, when the lands were granted to Rory MacKenzie of Coigeach, the cloth is described as white, black and grey, but when the lands were restored to MacLean of Duart in 1630, the colours of the cloth are described as white, black and grass colour.

The price of the cloth is valued in the charters as equal to eightpence per ell.

MACLEAN, HUNTING

ORIGIN OF NAME: *Gaelic MacGhille-Eoin (son of the servant of John).*
PLANT BADGE: *Crowberry.*
WAR CRIES: *Bàs no beatha (Death or Life). Fear eile airson Eachainn (Another for Hector).*
PIPE MUSIC: *The MacLean's March.*

MACLEOD OF MACLEOD

CREST BADGE : *A bull's head, cabossed sable, horned or, between two flags, gules, staves sable.*
MOTTO : *Hold fast*
GAELIC NAME : *MacLeòid.*

THE CLAN MACLEOD is descended from Leod, son of Olave the Black, who lived in the 13th century. Leod's two sons, Tormod and Torquil, were founders of the two main branches of the clan. From Tormod came the MacLeods of Glenelg, Harris and Dunvegan, and from Torquil the MacLeods of Lewis, Waternish and Assynt.

The Siol Tormod supported Bruce in the War of Independence, and Malcolm, son of Tormod, received a charter from David II about 1343 granting him lands in Glenelg. William, 5th of Glenelg, proved his able leadership by his victories over the Frasers and over the Lord of the Isles. His son John supported the Lord of the Isles at Harlaw in 1411. In 1498 King James IV granted to Alexander 8th the lands of Duirnish and Troternish, and in the charter his father William 7th was described as of Dunvegan.

One of the most distinguished chiefs was Roderick 16th, the famous Rory Mor, who was knighted by King James VI in 1603. He died in 1626. He was held in high esteem by the clan and his death was the occasion of the famous piobaireachd " Rory Mor's Lament," composed by Patrick Mor MacCrimmon. The MacLeods supported Charles I and Charles II, and were present at the Battle of Worcester in 1651 when the clan to the number of 700 were almost wiped out. The memory of this event and the ingratitude of the King may be the reason for the MacLeods refraining from taking part in the later Jacobite Risings. Sir Reginald, 27th chief, who died in 1935, was the last of the male line of the Dunvegan MacLeods. His daughter Dame Flora, Mrs. MacLeod of MacLeod, succeeded him as 28th chief.

MACLEOD OF MACLEOD

ORIGIN OF NAME: *Gaelic MacLeòid (son of Leod, from Norse ljot, ugly).*
PLANT BADGE: *Juniper.*
PIPE MUSIC: *MacLeod's Praise.*

MACLEOD

CREST BADGE : *A bull's head, cabossed sable, horned or, between two flags, gules, staves sable.*

MOTTO : *Hold fast.*

OLD MOTTO : *Murus aheneus esto (Be then a wall of brass).*

GAELIC NAME : *MacLeòid.*

THE SIOL TORQUIL branch of the Clan MacLeod is descended from Torquil, son of Leod.

In the 14th century King David II granted to Torquil MacLeod a charter of the barony of Assynt in Sutherland. Lewis had been held by this branch of the clan as vassals of the MacDonalds, and with the acquisition of other lands in Raasay, Waternish and Gairloch, the Siol Torquil rivalled the Siol Tormod in importance and disputed the chiefship of the clan.

Torquil, who was chief of this branch of the MacLeods, had his estate forfeited in 1506 for assisting Donald Dubh MacDonald in his rebellion to obtain the forfeited Lordship of the Isles. The forfeited estate of Lewis was restored to Malcolm, brother of the attainted Torquil in 1511. In the 16th century the history of the Siol Torquil became a succession of feuds, not only with other clans, but between members of their own clans, and when the main lines became extinct in the early 17th century, the chiefship of this branch later passed to the MacLeods of Raasay, though Raasay was sold by the 11th Laird in 1846.

DRESS MACLEOD

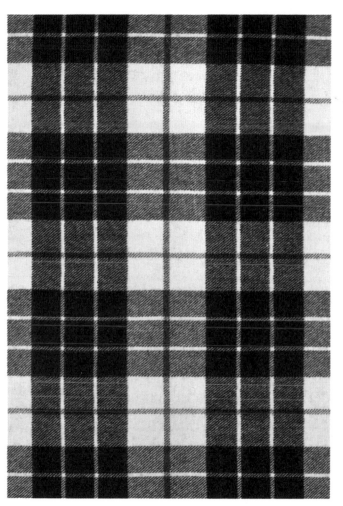

ORIGIN OF NAME: *Gaelic MacLeòid (son of Leod, from Norse ljot, ugly).*
PLANT BADGE: *Red whortleberry.*

MACMILLAN

CREST BADGE : *A dexter and a sinister hand brandishing a two-handed sword, proper.*
MOTTO : *Miseris succurrere disco* (*I learn to succour the distressed*).
GAELIC NAME : *MacGhille-Mhaolain.*

THERE are several origins suggested for the Clan Macmillan, and the fact that they were found in widely separated areas makes the problem more difficult. Skene suggests that they were connected with the Clan Chattan, and Buchanan of Auchmar claims their descent from the Buchanans. The name Macmillan is of ecclesiastical origin and a like origin is claimed for the name Buchanan. The armorial bearings of both clans contain a rampant lion.

The Macmillans were in the Loch Arkaig district in the 12th century when it is alleged they were removed to the crown lands round Loch Tay. About two centuries later they were driven from Lawers, and the greater number settled in Knapdale, while the others travelled farther south and the branch in Galloway is claimed to be of the latter number. Macmillan of Knap was considered to be the chief of the clan, and when the Knapdale Macmillans became extinct, the chiefship passed to the family of Dunmore, an estate lying on the side of Loch Tarbet opposite Knapdale, but that family also is now extinct. The clan is still associated with districts originally in the possession of Macmillans, i.e. Lochaber, Argyllshire and Galloway.

In 1951 the chiefship, by decree of Lyon Court, passed to the representative of the Laggalgarve line.

DRESS MACMILLAN

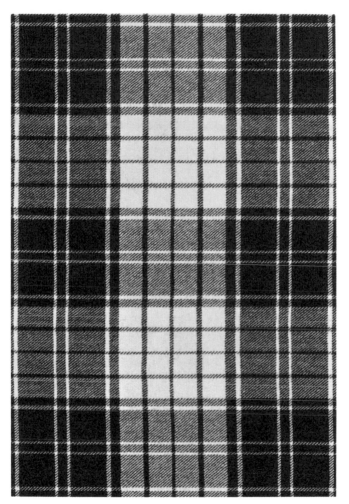

ORIGIN OF NAME: *Gaelic MacMhaolain (son of the bald or tonsured one).*
PLANT BADGE: *Holly.*

MACNAB

CREST BADGE : *A savage's head affronté, proper.*

MOTTO : *Timor omnis abesto* (*Let fear be far from all*).

GAELIC NAME : *Mac an Aba*

THE CLAN MACNAB, a branch of the great Siol Alpine, are of ecclesiastical origin, being termed in Gaelic Clann-an-Aba (children of the Abbot), and claim descent from the abbots of Glendochart, where the clan lands were for several centuries. They were an important clan as early as the 12th century, but they joined the Mac-Dougalls in their fight against Robert the Bruce.

After Bannockburn the Macnabs lost all their possessions except the Barony of Bovain, in Glendochart, which was confirmed to them by a charter from David II to Gilbert Macnab in 1336. Finlay, 4th chief, added considerably to the family estates towards the end of the 15th century. In 1552, Finlay, 6th chief, mortgaged the most of his lands to Campbell of Glenorchy, but the clan refused to acknowledge the superiority of Glenorchy. In 1606, Finlay, 7th chief, entered into the famous bond of friendship with his cousin, Lachlan MacKinnon of Strathardle, which is often quoted as proof of the common descent of the two clans.

The Macnabs under their chief, " Smooth John," supported the Stuarts during the Civil Wars, and served under Montrose, and the chief was later killed at the Battle of Worcester. In the Rising of 1745 the chief sided with the Government, but the clan supported Prince Charles Edward. Francis, 12th and last chief in the direct male line, was a noted character in his time, and the subject of Raeburn's famous portrait. He died in 1860.

Archibald C. MacNab, 22nd Chief, repurchased the MacNab lands in 1949.

MACNAB

There is also a chief's tartan.

ORIGIN OF NAME: *Gaelic Mac-an-Aba (son of the Abbot).*
PLANT BADGE: *Heath, Pine, Crowberry, Bramble.*
PIPE MUSIC: *Macnab's Salute.*

MACNAUGHTON

CREST BADGE : *A castle embattled, gules.*

MOTTO : *I hope in God.*

GAELIC NAME : *MacNeachdainn.*

THE progenitor of this ancient clan is alleged to be Nachtan Mor who lived about the 10th century. The clan is supposed to be one of those transferred from the province of Moray to the crown lands in Strathtay by Malcolm IV. About a century later they possessed lands bordering on Loch Awe and Loch Fyne, and in 1267 Gilchrist MacNaughtan and his heirs were appointed by Alexander III keepers of the Castle of Fraoch Eilean in Loch Awe. The MacNaughtans also held the castles of Dubh-Loch in Glen Shira, and Dunderave on Loch Fyne.

Donald MacNaughtan opposed Bruce and lost most of his possessions, but in the reign of David II the fortunes of the MacNaughtans were somewhat restored by the grant of lands in Lewis. Alexander, chief of the clan, who was knighted by James IV, was killed at the Battle of Flodden in 1513. The MacNaughtans remained loyal to the Stuarts and after the Restoration the chief, Alexander, was knighted by Charles II. His son John fought at Killiecrankie in 1698. The estates passed out of the family about 1691, having been forfeited to the crown.

At a meeting of the clan held in 1878 it was resolved that Sir Francis E. MacNaughten of Dunderawe, Bushmills, Ireland, was the lineal descendant of the family of the chief through Shane Dubh, the grandson of Sir Alexander MacNaughtan who fell at Flodden, and who went to Ireland in 1580.

MACNAUGHTON

ORIGIN OF NAME: *Gaelic MacNeachdainn (son of Nechtan, pure one).*
PLANT BADGE: *Trailing azalea.*
WAR CRY: *Fraoch Eilean (Heathery Island)*

MACNEIL(L) OF BARRA

CREST BADGE: *A rock.*

MOTTO: *Vincere vel mori* (*To conquer or die*).

GAELIC NAME: *MacNèill.*

THERE were two main branches of the Clan MacNeill, the MacNeills of Barra and the MacNeills of Gigha, but the former is now recognised as the chief. Neil Og is recorded to have received lands in Kintyre from Robert the Bruce. The clan were vassals of the Lords of the Isles, and in 1427 Gilleonan received from his overlord a charter of Barra and the lands of Boisdale in South Uist, which charter was confirmed in 1495 by James IV after the forfeiture of the lands of the Lords of the Isles.

The MacNeills of Barra subsequently supported the MacLeans of Duart, while the MacNeills of Gigha followed the MacDonalds of Isla. The Barra MacNeills were prominently concerned in the actions of the Mac-Leans for the next two centuries, and in the feuds of the MacLeans and the MacDonalds the two branches of the MacNeills were found often fighting on opposing sides.

General Roderick MacNeill of Barra, last of the direct line, had to part with the island, which he sold in 1838. He died in England in 1863. Robert L. MacNeill of Barra re-acquired parts of the island in 1938 and has restored Kisimul Castle.

When Neil, the last chief of the MacNeills of Gigha, was killed in 1530, the chiefship passed to the MacNeills of Taynish, and in 1590 Hector of Taynish repurchased Gigha, which had been sold in 1554. In 1780 Gigha was sold to the MacNeills of Colonsay, who had obtained Colonsay from the Duke of Argyll in 1700 in exchange for the lands of Crerar. Colonsay remained with the MacNeill family until the death of Sir James C. MacNeill, V.C., in 1904, when it was sold to Lord Strathcona.

MACNEILL OF BARRA

There is also a MacNeill of Colonsay tartan.

ORIGIN OF NAME: *Gaelic MacNèill (son of Neil, champion).*
PLANT BADGE: *Dryas, Seaware.*
WAR CRY: *Buaidh no bàs (Victory or Death).*
PIPE MUSIC: *MacNeil of Barra's March.*

MACNICOL or NICHOLSON

CREST BADGE : *A hawk's head erased, gules.*

MOTTO : *Sgorra Bhreac*

GAELIC NAME : *MacNeacail.*

IN the old Statistical Account, the Rev. William MacKenzie, in his description of the parish of Assynt, writes : " Tradition and even documents declare that it was a forest of the ancient Thanes of Sutherland. One of these Prince · Thanes gave it in vassalage to one Mackrycul, who in ancient times held the coast of Coygach, that part of it at the place presently called Ullapool." Mackrycul has been identified as the Gregall mentioned in the genealogy of the MacNicols in the MS. of 1450, and on the marriage of Torquil MacLeod to the daughter of the last of the MacNicol chiefs, the lands of Assynt passed to the MacLeods.

When Assynt passed to MacLeod, the Clan MacNicol appear to have emigrated to Skye, where the MacLeods had extensive possessions, and the lands of Scorrybreck near Portree were in possession of MacNicols or Nicolsons for several centuries. The clan played an important part in the history of Skye and from time to time their names appear in local records. The Rev. Donald Nicolson, who was chief of the Scorrybreck family at the end of the 17th century, was minister of Troternish for over thirty years. He was a strong Episcopalian, and resigned his charge in 1696 only because of his opposition to Presbyterianism which had become the established church. Norman, the last chief of Scorrybreck, emigrated to New Zealand.

There was also a strong branch of the MacNicols resident in Argyllshire.

MACNICOL

ORIGIN OF NAME: *Gaelic MacNeacail (son of Nicol, conquering people).*
PLANT BADGE: *Trailing azalea.*

MACPHERSON

CREST BADGE : *A cat sejant, proper.*

MOTTO : *Touch not the cat bot a glove* (*Touch not the cat without a glove*).

GAELIC NAME : *Mac a' Phearsoin, MacMhuirich.*

MACPHERSON is a name of ecclesiastical origin. The clan formed a branch of the Clan Chattan Confederation, and disputed with the Mackintoshes the leadership of that great confederation.

There seems to have been several families of Macphersons, but the family of Cluny emerged as the most important. The Macphersons are mentioned in the roll of broken clans in the Act of Parliament of 1594—they are not in the Act of 1587. Andrew is in Cluny in 1603, and in 1609 he signed the Clan Chattan Bond, taking the burden of the Brin, and other families of the Macphersons. In 1640 Donald Macpherson of Cluny was a faithful Royalist. In 1715 the Macphersons were active under their chief, Duncan, on the Stuart side, and during the Rising of 1745 Ewen Macpherson of Cluny with 600 of the clan joined Prince Charles, and behaved with great gallantry at several engagements, but did not arrive in time to take part in the Battle of Culloden. Cluny, however, actively assisted Prince Charles to escape capture. After that disaster the house of Cluny was burned to the ground and for nine years the chief remained in hiding, chiefly on his own estate. In spite of a reward of £1000 he was never captured, and ultimately escaped to France in 1755. The Cluny estates were forfeited, but in 1784 they were restored to Duncan, son of Ewen of the '45. Cluny Castle was rebuilt but following the death of the 17th Chief the estate was sold. There is a Clan Museum at Newtonmore.

MACPHERSON

ORIGIN OF NAME: *Gaelic Mac-a-Phearsoin (son of the Parson).*
PLANT BADGE: *Boxwood, White heather.*
WAR CRY: *Creag Dhubh Chloinn Chatain (The Black Rock of Clan Chattan).*
PIPE MUSIC: *Macpherson's March.*

MACQUARRIE
OF ULVA

CREST BADGE: *Out of an antique crown a bent arm in armour holding a dagger.*

MOTTO: *An t'Arm breac dearg. (The red tartaned army).*

GAELIC NAME: *MacGuadhre.*

THE clan are one of the branches of the great Clan Alpine.

When Alexander II invaded the Western Highlands in 1249 he was joined by Cormac Mor, chief of the Macquarries, but the king's death in Kerrera brought trouble to the clan. It is not until the death of John Macquarrie of Ulva in 1473 that we find any authentic record of the clan. Twenty years later John's son, Dunslaff, was chief of the clan. The clan lands were the islands of Ulva and part of Mull, and after the forfeiture of the Lords of the Isles, the clan acquired independence. They then followed the MacLeans of Duart, and supported Donald Dubh MacDonald in his effort to restore the Lordship of the Isles. In 1505 the Macquarries, with their powerful leaders, the MacLeans of Duart, submitted to the Government, and in 1517 Dunslaff Macquarrie was included in the petition of Laughlan MacLean of Duart for a free remission for all offences, and this was granted by the Privy Council.

The Macquarries never recovered from the blow suffered in 1651, when the chief, Allan Macquarrie, and most of the clan were killed at the Battle of Inverkeithing, and Lachlan, 16th of Ulva, who had entertained Dr. Johnson and Boswell in 1773, was forced to sell his lands in 1778. He died in 1818, aged 103, and was the last known chief of the Macquarries.

Major-General Lachlan Macquarrie was Governor of New South Wales during the convict period, and under his wise government the colony prospered. He laid out the city of Sydney, and returned home in 1821, to the great regret of the colonists. His name is commemorated in Macquarrie Island and other place-names.

MACQUARRIE

ORIGIN OF NAME: *Gaelic son of Guaire (proud or noble)*.
PLANT BADGE: *Pine*.
WAR CRY: *An t'Arm breac dearg (The red tartaned army)*.
PIPE MUSIC: *The red tartaned army*.

MACQUEEN OF CORYBROUGH

CREST BADGE: *A wolf rampant ermine holding a pheon gules point downward argent.*

MOTTO: *Constant and faithful.*

GAELIC NAME: *MacShuibhne.*

THE CLAN MACQUEEN were of West Highland or Hebridean origin and originally appear to have been associated with Clan Donald. The name is found in many forms, Cuinn, Suibne, Sweyn, MacCunn, MacSween, MacSuain and MacSwan.

In the 13th century there were MacSweens in Argyllshire at Castle Sween, and the name remained in that district in the form of Swene and Macqueen for three or four hundred years thereafter.

Macqueens, MacSwans and MacSweens are numerous in Skye and Lewis, and the Macqueens held the lands of Garafad in Skye for several centuries.

Early in the 15th century when Malcolm, tenth chief of the Mackintoshs, married Mora MacDonald of Moidart, the bride was accompanied by several of her clansmen, including Revan Macqueen, who settled in the Mackintosh country and subsequently formed septs of the Clan Chattan. Revan Macqueen fought under Mackintosh at the Battle of Harlaw in 1411.

The Macqueens settled in Strathdearn, and in the 16th century we find them in possession of the lands of Corrybrough, and figuring prominently in the district. The Clan Chattan Bond of 1609 was signed by Donald Macqueen of Corrybrough, for himself, and taking full burden of John Macqueen in Little Corrybrough and Sween Macqueen in Raigbeg. The lands of Corrybrough passed out of the possession of the Macqueens in the 18th century.

Robert Macqueen, Lord Braxfield, the eminent lawyer, belonged to a Lanarkshire family of Macqueens. His reputation as a judge of political prisoners was not a flattering one.

MACQUEEN

ORIGIN OF NAME: *Gaelic MacShuibhne (son of the good going).*
PLANT BADGE: *Boxwood, Red whortleberry.*

MACRAE

House of Inverinate

CREST BADGE : *A dexter hand grasping a sword, all proper.*
MOTTO : *Fortitudine (With fortitude).*
GAELIC NAME : *MacRath.*

THE name Macrae, in Gaelic MacRath (Son of Grace), is supposed to be of ecclesiastical origin. The clan appears to have inhabited the lands of Clunes in the Beauly district in the 12th and 13th centuries, and removed to Kintail in the 14th century. The founder of the Kintail branch is said to be Fionnla Dubh Mac-Gillechriosd who died in 1416. Duncan, 5th of Kintail, whose arrow caused the death of Donald Gorm of Sleat at Eilean Donan in 1539, was granted the lands of Inverinate about 1557, and these remained in the family for over 200 years. In 1677 Alexander, eldest son of Rev. John Macrae of Dingwall, received a wadset of the lands of Conchra and Ardachy, and became the progenitor of the Macraes of Conchra.

The Macraes were loyal followers of the MacKenzies, Lord of Kintail and Earls of Seaforth, and the Mac-Kenzies owed not a little of their importance to the help of the Macraes. At various dates Macraes were Constables of Eilean Donan Castle, Chamberlains of Kintail, and Vicars of Kintail. Rev. Farquhar Macrae who was born at Eilan Donan in 1580 was a man of considerable influence and importance, and his grandson, Donnachadh nam Pios (Duncan of the silver cups), was the compiler of the famous Fernaig Manuscript, 1688-93. It contains Gaelic poems by himself and other Gaelic poets, and forms an important contribution to Gaelic literature.

The Macraes took a prominent part in the Civil Wars and were conspicuous for their bravery at Sheriffmuir. They were not out as a clan in the '45, but many individuals took part in the Rising.

MACRAE

There is a hunting tartan and a pattern called MacRae of Conchra or Sheriffmuir tartan.

ORIGIN OF NAME: *Gaelic MacRath (son of Grace).*
PLANT BADGE: *Fir club moss.*
WAR CRY: *Sgur Urain (A mountain in Kintail).*
PIPE MUSIC: *The Macrae's March.*

MALCOLM

CREST BADGE : *A tower, argent.*

MOTTO : *In ardua petit (He aims at difficult things).*

OLD MOTTO : *Deus refugium nostrum (God is our refuge).*

GAELIC NAME : *Mac Mhaol Chaluim.*

THE equivalent of the name Malcolm in Gaelic is Calum, consequently we find the names used indiscriminately in older records, and facts relating to the Malcolms and the MacCallums may be considered as referring to the same clan in the Highlands. There is a genealogy of the Clan Malcolm in the Gaelic MS. of 1450.

Sir Duncan Campbell, of Lochow, granted lands in Craignish and on the banks of Loch Avich to Reginald MacCallum of Corbarron in 1414, with the office of hereditary constable of the castles of Lochaffy and Craignish. Corbarron was bequeathed by the last of the family to Zachary MacCallum of Poltalloch. The Mac-Callums were in Poltalloch previous to 1562, and Dugald MacCallum of Poltalloch, who succeeded to the estate in 1779, is said to be the first to adopt the name Malcolm permanently. Dugald Malcolm of Poltalloch was succeeded by his cousin Neil Malcolm in 1778 and died in 1802.

John W. Malcolm, of Poltalloch, was created Lord Malcolm in 1896. He died in 1902.

The name Malcolm is found in Stirlingshire and Dunbartonshire as early as the 14th century.

In 1665 Charles II conferred a baronetcy of Nova Scotia on John Malcolm of Balbeadie and Grange, Fifeshire. This family also acquired the lands of Lochore and, later, lands in Dumfriesshire.

MALCOLM

There is also a dress tartan.

ORIGIN OF NAME: *Gaelic MacColuimb (devotee of St. Columba).*
PLANT BADGE: *Mountain ash.*

MATHESON
House of Lochalsh

CREST BADGE : *Out of an eastern crown, or, a naked arm holding a drawn sword, proper.*

MOTTO : *Fac et spera* (*Do and hope*).

GAELIC NAME : *MacMhathain.*

THE Gaelic MS. of 1450 derives the Clan MacMathan, or Matheson, from the same source as the MacKenzies, and as the chief of the Mathesons is reported in 1427 to have had 2000 men, the Clan Matheson was then as powerful as the more famous MacKenzies.

The clan was divided into two main branches, those of Lochalsh and those of Shiness in Sutherland. Of the former was John Dubh Matheson, who was Constable of Eilean Donan Castle when Donald Gorm of Sleat attacked it in 1539. Donald Gorm was killed by an arrow of the defenders and John Dubh by an arrow of the besiegers. From John Dubh's son, Murchadh Buidhe, of Fernaig and Balmacarra, are descended the families of Bennetsfield, Iomaire and Glas-na-Muclach. The Mathesons of Sutherland were an offshoot from the Lochalsh family and are mentioned in the 15th century. They are represented by the Mathesons of Shiness, Achany and the Lews.

John Matheson of the Lochalsh family purchased Attadale in 1730. John, 4th of Attadale, married Margaret, daughter of Donald Matheson, of Shiness, and their son Alexander, born in 1805, was the first baronet of Lochalsh. Sir Alexander made a large fortune in the East, and on his return he purchased estates in Ross-shire extending to over 220,000 acres at a total cost of £773,020, and spent £300,000 in land improvement and building.

James Sutherland Matheson, of the Shiness family, born in 1796, was one of the founders of the firm of Jardine, Matheson & Co. He purchased the island of Lewis in 1844 and was created a Baronet in 1851 for his munificence to the people of Lewis during the famine of 1845-46.

MATHESON

There is also a green hunting tartan.

ORIGIN OF NAME: *Bear's son.*
PLANT BADGE: *Broom.*
WAR CRY: *Achadh da thearnaidh* (*Field of the Two Declivities*).

MAXWELL
House of Corruchan

CREST BADGE: *A stag lodged in front of a holly bush proper.*

MOTTO: *Reviresco* (*I flourish again*).

SIR JOHN MAXWELL, Chamberlain of Scotland about 1231-1233, died in 1241 and was succeeded by his brother Sir Aymer. This Sir Aymer had two sons, Herbert and John, from whom have descended many prominent Maxwell families.

Herbert Maxwell, descendent of the above Herbert, was created Lord Maxwell about 1445, and was succeeded by his son Sir Robert and, from his son, Sir Edward, descend the Maxwells of Monreith.

John, 3rd Lord Maxwell, was killed at Flodden in 1513. In 1581 John, Lord Maxwell, was created Earl of Morton, but this honour was later taken from him. He was killed in a fray with the Johnstons in 1592 and his son, in 1608, in revenge for his father's death slew Sir James Johnston. He escaped arrest but later returned to Scotland and was executed in 1613. His brother, Sir Robert, who succeeded him was created Earl of Nithsdale *circa* 1620. The 2nd Earl supported Montrose in 1644 and he was succeeded in 1667 by his cousin John, 4th Lord Herries. The 5th Earl joined in the Jacobite Rising of 1715, was captured at Preston and sentenced to death for high treason. Aided by his wife he escaped from the Tower of London and died in Rome in 1744. His daughter married William Haggerston-Constable and their grandson, William Constable-Maxwell, proved his claim to the Lordship of Herries in 1858. His son, who succeeded him, died in 1908 when the Scottish Barony devolved upon his daughter the Duchess of Norfolk. William Maxwell of Carruchan, established, in Lyon Court, his claim as heir male of the Maxwells.

Among the prominent Maxwell families are those of Pollock, Cardoness, Monreith and Farnham.

Caerlaveroch Castle was the seat of the Maxwells.

MAXWELL

ORIGIN OF NAME: *Place-name* (*Maccus's Wiel*).

MENZIES

CREST BADGE : *A savage head affronté, erased, proper.*

MOTTO : *Vill God I Zall* (*Will God I shall*).

GAELIC NAME : *Méinn, Méinnearach.*

THE name is found in various forms, Menzies, Mengues, Mingies, and Meyners. It appears in charters in the 12th and 13th centuries, and in 1249 Robert de Menyers was Lord High Chamberlain. His son, Alexander, possessed the lands of Durisdeer—an indication of Anglo-Norman origin of the family—Weem, Aberfeldy and Glendochart, which passed to his son Robert, while his lands in Fortingall passed to his son Thomas. The last mentioned lands passed to the Stewarts through marriage.

At Bannockburn the Menzies supported Bruce, who granted several charters of lands to members of the clan. David Menzies was appointed Governor of Orkney and Shetland in 1423 under the King of Norway. In 1487 Sir Robert de Mengues received a grant of land erected into the Barony of Menzies. A century later the " Menyessis, in Athoill and Apnadull " appear in the Roll of the Clans, 1587. Sir Alexander Menzies of Castle Menzies was created a Baronet of Nova Scotia in 1665, and the baronetcy continued until the death of Sir Neil, 8th Baronet, in 1910.

A distinguished branch of the clan was the Menzieses of Pitfoddels. At the Battle of Invercarron in 1650 young Menzies of Pitfoddels carried the Royal Standard. This branch is now extinct. The last Chieftan of the Pitfoddels branch founded the Roman Catholic College of Blairs.

Menzies of Culdares is said to have introduced the first larches into Scotland from the Tyrol in 1738. Two of the original trees are still to be seen in the grounds of the Duke of Atholl.

MELVILLE *see* pp. 254-5

MENZIES, HUNTING

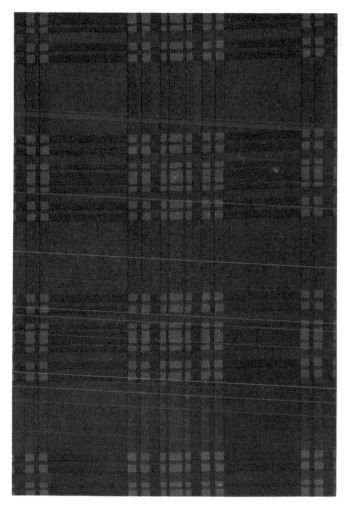

There is also a red and white sett and a black and white sett.

ORIGIN OF NAME: *Norman de Meyners.*
PLANT BADGE: *Menzies heath, Mountain ash.*
WAR CRY: *Geal 'us Dearg a suas (Up the White and Red).*
PIPE MUSIC: *Menzies' March.*

MONTGOMERY

CREST BADGE : *A female figure proper, antiquely attired, argent, holding in dexter an anchor or, in sinister a savage's head held by the hair, couped of the fist.*

MOTTO : *Gardez bien (Look well).*

GAELIC NAME : *MacGumerait.*

THE MONTGOMERYS are a lowland clan of Anglo-Norman origin. Roger de Montgomery, a Regent of Normandy, followed William the Conqueror to England where he was created Earl of Arundel. His grandson, Robert de Montgomery, came to Scotland in the train of Walter, the first high steward of Scotland in the reign of David I. Robert, who received the manor of Eaglesham, for long the principal home of the Montgomerys, witnessed the foundation charter of the monastery of Paisley in 1160.

Sir John Montgomery, 7th of Eaglesham, distinguished himself at the Battle of Otterburn in 1388 by capturing Henry Percy, called Hotspur. With Percy's ransom Montgomery built Polnoon Castle. He married Elizabeth de Eglinton, and obtained the lands of Eglinton and Ardrossan. Sir Alexander Montgomery was Governor of Kintyre and Knapdale in 1430, and some time later was created Lord Montgomery. Hugh, 3rd Lord Montgomery, was created Earl of Eglinton in 1507. Hugh, 2nd Earl, supported Queen Mary and was taken prisoner at the Battle of Langside in 1568. Hugh, 5th Earl, died without issue and the earldom passed to his cousin, Sir Alexander Seton, who took the name and arms of Montgomery.

George Montgomery, second son of Sir Alexander, 1st Lord Montgomery, was progenitor of the Montgomerys of Skelmorlie, and in the " Roll of Landlords in the Highlands and Isles where broken men dwelt, 1587," is mentioned " The Laird of Skelmourlie, for Rauchry." This was Sir Robert Montgomery of Skelmorlie, and Rauchry appears to be the island of Rathlin.

During the Plantation of Ulster at the end of the 16th century, Lady Montgomery of Eglinton set up linen and woollen manufactures in Ireland and encouraged the making of tartan there.

240

MONTGOMERY

There is another sett with green and blue.

ORIGIN OF NAME: *Place-name, Norman.*

MORRISON

CREST BADGE: *Issuant from waves of the sea azure crested argent, a mount vert, thereon an embattled wall azure, masoned argent, and issuing therefrom a cubit arm naked proper, the hand grasping a dagger hilted or.*

MOTTO: *Castle Eistein.*

GAELIC NAME: *MacGhille Mhoire.*

ACCORDING to tradition the Clan Morrison is said to be of Norse origin and descended from a family who were shipwrecked on the shores of the island of Lewis and saved by clinging to driftwood, and for this reason, so it is said, a badge of driftwood was chosen.

The Morrisons were one of the ancient clans of Lewis, and for a long period the Morrisons of Habost held the office of brieve or judge, and were known as Clan-na-breitheamh. Hugh Morrison was brieve during the latter half of the 16th century. He was accused by the Government of harbouring rebels, and his son John incurred the displeasure of the MacLeods for the betrayal of Torquil Dubh MacLeod who was beheaded by the MacKenzies in 1597. The Morrisons in consequence had to take refuge on the mainland, and as many as sixty families are said to have fled to Sutherland. Neill MacLeod of Lewis, who accompanied some of the " Fife Adventurers " to Edinburgh in 1600, carried with him the heads of ten or twelve of the Clan Morrison whom he had killed. Neill was pardoned for his offences.

On the abolition of the brieveship in the 17th century the Morrisons gravitated to the church and many of their number became prominent clergymen.

A branch of the clan in Harris were celebrated smiths and armourers and one of this family was the famous Gaelic poet John Morrison (1790-1852). Another branch was long established in Skye.

There were Morrisons in the counties of Perth, Stirling and Dunbarton, but they had no connection with the Lewis clan.

MORRISON

ORIGIN OF NAME: *Son of Maurice*.
PLANT BADGE: *Driftwood*.
WAR CRY: *Dun Uisdean*.

MUNRO

CREST BADGE: *An eagle displayed wings inverted, proper.*

MOTTO: *Dread God.*

GAELIC NAME: *Mac an Rothaich.*

EASTER ROSS has always been the home of the Munros. It is claimed that the first Munro of Foulis was Hugh who died in 1126. About a century later George Munro of Foulis had a charter from the Earl of Sutherland. Robert, who had a charter from Bruce, led his clan at the Battle of Bannockburn. Robert, 8th of Foulis, married a niece of Euphame, daughter of the Earl of Ross and Queen of Robert II. William, 12th of Foulis, knighted by James IV, died in 1505, and Robert Mor, 15th chief, was a staunch supporter of Mary Queen of Scots. He received many favours from her son James VI.

During the 17th century the Munros engaged actively in the Continental wars, and Robert, 18th chief, joined the army of Gustavus Adolphus. He raised 700 men of his own clan for service in Sweden, and greatly distinguished himself there, where the Scots received the name of " The Invincibles." At that time there were " Three generals, eight colonels, five lieut.-colonels, eleven majors and above thirty captains, all of the name of Monroe, besides a great number of subalterns."

Sir Robert Munro, 6th Bart., commanded the Black Watch at the Battle of Fontenoy in 1745, when, using their own method of fighting—alternately firing and taking cover—for the first time in a Continental battle, they introduced a system of infantry tactics that has not been superseded. On the death of the 11th Baronet his eldest daughter became Heretrix of Clan Munro.

Sir Thomas Munro, born in Glasgow in 1761, had a distinguished career in India, and Mr. Canning speaking in the House of Commons in 1819 said of Munro, " England never produced a more accomplished statesman, nor India, fertile as it is in heroes, a more skilful soldier."

MUNRO

The 42nd (Black Watch) tartan is worn as a hunting sett.

ORIGIN OF NAME: *Gaelic Rothach (man from Ro).*
PLANT BADGE: *Common club moss.*
WAR CRY: *Caisteal Folais'n a Theine (Castle Foulis in flames).*
PIPE MUSIC: *Bealach na Broige.*

MURRAY

CREST BADGE: *A mermaid holding in her dexter hand a mirror, and in the sinister a comb all proper.*

MOTTO: *Tout Prêt (Quite ready).*

GAELIC NAME: *MacMhuirich.*

THIS powerful clan had its origin in one of the ancient tribes of the Province of Moray. The clan name is found in many districts of Scotland, and the principal family is said to be descended from Freskin, who received lands in Moray from David I. His grandson, William, because of extensive possessions in Moray is described as *de Moravia*. He acquired the lands of Bothwell and others in the South of Scotland, and several of his sons founded other houses, including the Murrays of Tullibardine. He died in 1226 and his son, Sir Walter, was the first described as *of Bothwell*. Sir Walter's son, Sir William de Moravia, dominus de Bothwell, died without issue in 1293, and was succeeded by his brother, Sir Andrew, who was the celebrated patriot and staunch supporter of Sir William Wallace. His son, also Sir Andrew, with Wallace, sent the famous letter dated 11th October, 1297, to the Mayors of Lubeck and of Hamburg informing them that the Scottish ports were again open for trade. He was Regent of Scotland after the death of Robert the Bruce, and died in 1338.

Sir William de Moravia acquired the lands of Tullibardine in Perthshire in 1282 through his marriage with a daughter of Malise, seneschal of Strathearn. Sir William Murray of Tullibardine, who succeeded in 1446, had seventeen sons, many of whom founded prominent families of Murray. Sir John, 12th of Tullibardine, was created Lord Murray in 1604, and Earl of Tullibardine in 1606. William, 2nd Earl of Tullibardine, claimed the Earldom of Atholl by right of his wife, but died before the patent was granted. His son, John, however, obtained the title of Earl of Atholl in 1629, and became the first Earl of the Murray branch.

MURRAY OF TULLIBARDINE

ORIGIN OF NAME: *Place-name, Morayshire.*

MURRAY OF ATHOLL

CREST BADGE: *A mermaid holding in her dexter hand a mirror, and in the sinister a comb all proper.*

MOTTO: *Tout Prêt (Quite ready).*

GAELIC NAME: *MacMhuirich.*

JOHN, 1st Earl of Atholl of the Murray branch, obtained the title in 1629, and the Earldom of Tullibardine was conferred on his uncle, Sir Patrick Murray. Atholl was a staunch Royalist, and his son John, 2nd Earl, strongly supported Charles I. He married Lady Amelia Stanley, daughter of the Earl of Derby, through whom he acquired the lordship of the Isle of Man. In 1670 he succeeded to the Earldom of Tullibardine, and in 1676 he was created Marquis of Atholl. Disappointed at his reception by William of Orange, he joined the Jacobites. He died in 1703. John, 2nd Marquis, was created Duke of Atholl in 1703, and was a bitter opponent of the Union of 1707. He died in 1724, and was succeeded by his third son, James. John's first son predeceased him, and his second son, William, with his brothers Charles and George, were engaged in the Jacobite Risings of 1715, 1719, and 1745. Lord George who unfurled Prince Charles's standard at Glenfinnan was the brilliant Lieut.-General of the Prince's army.

James, 2nd Duke of Atholl, claimed the English barony of Strange through the line of the Earl of Derby, and as his son and eldest daughter died young, he was succeeded by his daughter Charlotte, who married her cousin, John Murray, eldest son of Lord George Murray of Jacobite fame. John Murray succeeded his uncle as 3rd Duke of Atholl and holder of many other titles of the Murray family.

Other branches of the clan include the Murrays of Polmaise, of Abercairney, of Auchtertyre, of Elibank, and many others, the Earls of Dunmore, and the Earls of Mansfield.

MURRAY OF ATHOLL

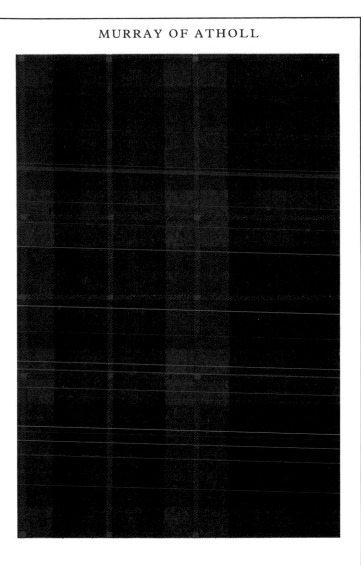

ORIGIN OF NAME: *Place-name, Morayshire.*
PLANT BADGE: *Butcher's broom, Juniper.*
PIPE MUSIC: *Atholl Highlander.*

NAPIER

(Lord Napier and Ettrick)

CREST BADGE : *A cubit arm, the hand grasping a crescent argent.*
MOTTO : *Sans tache (Without stain).*

ACCORDING to tradition the Napiers were descended from the ancient Earls of Lennox, and John de Napier who held lands in the county of Dunbarton is recorded in a charter of the Earl of Lennox in 1280. He is also recorded in the Ragman Roll of 1296, and he assisted in the defence of Stirling Castle in 1303. A descendant of his, William de Napier, was governor of Edinburgh Castle in 1401. William's son, Alexander, who owned the lands of Merchiston, was provost of Edinburgh in 1437, and his son, Sir Alexander Napier of Merchiston, was comptroller to James II in 1440, Provost of Edinburgh in 1455, Vice-Admiral of Scotland and Ambassador to England in 1461, and held several other offices.

Archibald Napier of Merchiston obtained Gartness, Rusky, and other lands in 1509. His son, Alexander, was killed at Flodden in 1513, and the latter's son was killed at Pinkie in 1547. John Napier of Merchiston, born in 1550, was the celebrated inventor of logarithms and considered the greatest mathematician of his age. His son, Sir Archibald, was a Lord of Session and was created Baron Napier of Merchiston in 1627. He was a strong supporter of Charles I. Archibald, 3rd Lord Napier, died a bachelor, and the titles passed through the female line to the Scotts of Thirlestane. Francis, 5th Lord Napier, was the father of the Hon. George Napier, of whom it was said, " A better or braver soldier never served his country," and the grandfather of Admiral Sir Charles Napier, one of the most distinguished of British naval commanders. Francis, 9th Lord Napier, entered the Diplomatic Service, and was British Minister at Washington, and at The Hague. He was the chairman of the Crofters' Commission.

NAPIER

ORIGIN OF NAME: *English. The Napier had charge of the Royal linen.*

OGILVIE

CREST BADGE : *A woman naked from the waist up draped azure pinned or holding a portcullis gules.*

MOTTO : *À fin* (*To the end*).

GAELIC NAME : *Mac Ghille Bhuidhe.*

THE OGILVIES take their name from Gilbert, a descendant of the ancient Earls of Angus, who was granted the barony of Ogilvie by William the Lion about 1163. The family acquired the barony of Cortachy about 1370. In 1392 Sir Walter Ogilvie of Auchterhouse was killed in a battle with the Clan Donnachaidh. His son, the Sheriff of Angus, styled Lord Ogilvie, was killed at the Battle of Harlaw in 1411. Sir Walter, son of the Sheriff, was Lord High Treasurer, and built the tower of Airlie. He acquired by marriage the barony of Lintrathen, and died in 1440. From Sir Walter, his younger son, were descended the Earls of Findlater and Seafield, and the Lords of Banff.

Sir James Ogilvie of Airlie was created Lord Ogilvie of Airlie in 1491. The Ogilvies were Royalists during the Civil Wars, and James, 1st Earl of Airlie, gave gallant service to the cause. James, 2nd Earl, taken prisoner at Philiphaugh, and sentenced to death, escaped from the castle of St. Andrews on the eve of his execution, dressed in his sister's clothes. The Ogilvies engaged actively in the Jacobite Risings of 1715 and 1745. David, 5th Lord Ogilvie, son of John, 4th Earl of Airlie, who joined Prince Charles with the Clan Ogilvie, was attainted and fled to France. Receiving a free pardon, he returned in 1783, and died in 1813. His son, Walter Ogilvie of Airlie, assumed the title of 7th Earl in 1812, but it was not restored until 1826, when his son David was confirmed in it by Act of Parliament. David, 8th Earl of Airlie, was killed at the battle of Diamond Hill, South Africa, in 1900, gallantly leading his regiment in a charge which saved the guns.

OGILVIE OF AIRLIE

There is another sett, also a hunting tartan.

ORIGIN OF NAME: *Place-name, Angus.*
PLANT BADGE: *Evergreen Alkanet, Whitethorn, Hawthorn.*

OLIPHANT and MELVILLE

CREST BADGE: *Unicorn couped argent, crined and armed, or.*

MOTTO: *A tout pourvoir (Provide for all).*

DAVID DE OLIFARD, who accompanied King David I from Winchester in 1141, is said to be the progenitor of the house of Oliphant.

The title of Lord Oliphant was conferred on Sir Lawrence Oliphant, a descendant of the above David de Olifard, in 1458. From Sir Lawrence's second son, William, the Oliphants of Gask were descended, while his third son, George, was styled of Bachilton.

The Oliphants of Gask were ardent Jacobites, and Laurence Oliphant of Gask and his eldest son were attainted for their participation in the Jacobite Rising of 1745. The famous Scottish poetess Lady Nairne (Carolina Oliphant), 1766-1844, was of the Gask family and was named Carolina in honour of Prince Charlie.

The Melvilles are a Lothian family, the first member having settled in Scotland during the reign of King David I. He called his manor " Mala Ville," hence the name Melville. In early days the Melvilles held many important offices under the crown.

Eventually the family died out and the Barony of Melville came into the family of Ross of Halkhead through marriage with the Melville heiress. The title Earl of Melville was conjoined with that of the Earl of Leven.

The tartan here illustrated was for long known under the trade name of " Oliphant and Melville." A different pattern under the name Melville is found in some early collections of tartan.

OLIPHANT (*and* MELVILLE)

ORIGIN OF NAMES: *Oliphant, from elephant, indicating great strength; Melville, see Text.*

RAMSAY

CREST BADGE : *A unicorn's head, couped, argent, armed and crined, or.*

MOTTO : *Ora et labora* (Pray and work).

GAELIC NAME : *Ramsaidh*.

THE RAMSAYS are an ancient family of Anglo-Norman origin. The first of the name recorded in Scotland was Simon de Ramsay, who was granted lands in Lothian by David I. He was the ancestor of the Ramsays of Dalhousie. The names of many of the family appear in charters between that date and 1296 when that of William de Ramsay appears in the Ragman Roll. He later supported Bruce and signed the letter to the Pope asserting the independence of Scotland in 1320.

During the next three centuries the Ramsays were prominently engaged in the Border Wars, with raids into England. In 1618 George Ramsay, of Dalhousie, was created Lord Ramsay of Melrose, a title changed a few months later to Lord Ramsay of Dalhousie. His son, William, was created Earl of Dalhousie by Charles I in 1633. During the War of the Spanish Succession, William, 5th Earl, was colonel of the Scots Guards sent to support Archduke Charles of Austria. He died in Spain in 1710. George, 9th Earl, had a distinguished military career in various parts of the world and in 1815 was created Baron Dalhousie in the peerage of the United Kingdom. His son, James, 10th Earl, was created Marquess of Dalhousie in 1849. He was Governor-General of India from 1847 till 1855. When he died in 1860 the title of Marquess became extinct. The Scottish titles Earl of Dalhousie and Baron Ramsay devolved on his cousin Fox, 2nd Lord Panmure, 11th Earl of Dalhousie.

The Ramsays of Bamff, Perthshire, are descended from Adam de Ramsay of Bamff, a baron in the 13th century. In 1666 a baronetcy of Nova Scotia was conferred on Sir Gilbert Ramsay. Sir George, 6th Bart., was killed in a duel with Capt. James Macrae of Holmains in 1790.

RAMSAY

ORIGIN OF NAME: *Place-name, South Scotland.*

ROB ROY
MacGregor

CREST BADGE : *A lion's head, erased, crowned with an antique crown, proper.*

MOTTO : *'S rioghal mo dhream (Royal is my race).*

GAELIC NAME : *Rob Ruadh.*

THE ROB ROY tartan of red and black checks, perhaps the best known of all the Scottish tartans, was used by Robert MacGregor possibly because of the proscription of the clan name of MacGregor.

Rob Roy was the younger son of Lieut.-Col. Donald MacGregor of Glengyle, and his mother was a Campbell of Glenfalloch, and a granddaughter of Sir Robert Campbell of Glenorchy. He was born about 1660. In early life he was a gentleman cattle drover, and became involved in financial difficulties with the Duke of Montrose. The Duke obtained possession of Rob Roy's lands of Craig Royston, and Rob declared that in future the Duke would provide him with cattle and that the Duke would regret the quarrel. For thirty years Rob carried out this threat and continued to take all the cattle, goods and money he required.

Rob Roy was a brilliant swordsman and led a very adventurous life as an outlaw. The government erected a fort at Inversnaid and garrisoned it with an English regiment to keep the MacGregors in order, but Rob Roy captured the fort, disarmed and dispersed the garrison, and set fire to the fort. Rob, escaping all attempts to capture him, died at home in Balquhidder in 1734, and was buried in the churchyard there, where his grave and that of his wife Helen are still visited by many admirers of his romantic life.

ROB ROY

ORIGIN OF NAME: *from Gaelic Rob Ruadh (red Rob).*
PLANT BADGE: *Pine.*

ROBERTSON

CREST BADGE : *A dexter hand holding an imperial crown, all proper.*

MOTTO : *Virtutis gloria merces* (*Glory is the reward of valour*).

GAELIC NAME : *Mac Raibeirt* (*MacDhonnachaidh*).

THE ROBERTSONS, known as Clan Donnachaidh, are claimed to be descended from the Celtic Earls of Atholl. The clan takes its Gaelic name from Donnachadh Reamhar (Stout Duncan) the staunch friend of Bruce, who led the clan at Bannockburn. It was from Robert Riach (Grizzled Robert) that the clan took the name of Robertson. This Robert was the chief who captured the murderers of James I and delivered them to the Government, and for this action he received, in 1451, a crown charter erecting his lands into the barony of Struan. About a century later the Earl of Atholl seized about half of the Struan lands under a wadset and the Robertsons never recovered them.

The Robertsons were loyal adherents of the Stuarts and accompanied Montrose in all his campaign, and after the Restoration Charles II settled a pension on Robertson of Struan. Alexander, the celebrated poet, chief of Struan, born about 1670, was studying for the church when he succeeded to the chiefship, but he left the cloisters and joined Dundee in 1688. He was attainted, but received a remission in 1703. He was out again in 1715, and was captured at Sheriffmuir, but escaped to France. He was pardoned in 1731, but joined Prince Charles in 1745 with the clan ; he was then too old to fight and returned home in Sir John Cope's carriage. He died in 1749.

The Robertsons of Lude are the oldest cadet family. Other families are the Robertsons of Inches, of Kindeace, of Auchleeks, of Kinlochmoidart, etc. The Chief of the clan is styled Struan-Robertson.

ROBERTSON

Also a hunting tartan and an "Ancient Robertson" pattern.

ORIGIN OF NAME: *Son of Robert.*
PLANT BADGE: *Fine-leaved heath, Bracken.*
WAR CRY: *Garg'n uair dhuis gear (Fierce when raised).*
PIPE MUSIC: *Teachd Chlann Donnachaidh (The Clan Donnachie
have arrived).*

ROSE

CREST BADGE : *A harp, azure.*
MOTTO : *Constant and true.*
GAELIC NAME : *Ròs, Ròis.*

THE CLAN ROSE were settled in the district of Nairn in the 12th century, and there is documentary evidence to prove that about 1219 Hugh Rose of Geddes was witness to the foundation charter of Beauly Priory. His son Hugh acquired the lands of Kilravock by marriage, and Kilravock remains with the family to the present day. In 1390 the family charters and other documents were destroyed by fire in the cathedral church of Beauly, where they had been placed for safety. In 1433 John Rose, 6th of Kilravock, received confirmation of his lands from James I. His son Hugh built the old tower of Kilravock in 1460. The barony of Kilravock was erected in 1474. Hugh, 10th of Kilravock, was taken prisoner at the Battle of Pinkie in 1547. He was sheriff of Ross, Constable of Inverness Castle, and sheriff-principal of Inverness. He died in 1597, aged 90 years.

The Roses of Kilravock were diplomatic in their relations with their neighbours and consequently lived peaceably compared with most other clans. They were loyal to the government during the Revolution and the Jacobite Risings of 1715 and 1745. Hugh, 15th of Kilravock, sheriff of Ross, voted against the Union of 1707, but was one of the commissioners to represent Scotland in the first British parliament.

Sir Hugh H. Rose, born in 1803, was in command of the Central Field Force during the Indian Mutiny, during which he fought sixteen successful actions, captured 150 pieces of artillery, took twenty forts, and captured Ratghur, Shanghur, Chundehree, Jhansi and Calpee. He was raised to the peerage as Baron Strathnairn in 1866, and was made Field Marshal in 1877. Kilravock Castle, built about 1460, is still inhabited by the chief of the clan.

ROSE

There is another tartan usually called the Green Rose.

ORIGIN OF NAME: *from the flower of this name.*
PLANT BADGE: *Wild rosemary.*

ROSS

CREST BADGE : *A dexter hand holding a garland of laurel, all proper.*

MOTTO : *Spem successus alit* (*Success nourishes hope*).

GAELIC NAME : *Ròs, Ròis.*

THE CLAN ROSS take their name from the province of Ross and are designated in Gaelic as Clann Andrias. Their traditional progenitor Fearchar Mac-an-t-sagairt (son of the priest), of Applecross, was a powerful supporter of Alexander II and, for his services, was created Earl of Ross about 1234. His grandson, William, led his clan at the Battle of Bannockburn, and Hugh, 5th Earl, was killed at the Battle of Halidon Hill in 1333. Hugh's successor, William, died without male issue and succession passed through the female line, a circumstance which later led to the struggle for the Earldom between the Lord of the Isles and the Regent Albany. In 1424 the Earldom reverted to the Crown but James I restored it to Margaret, mother of Alexander, 3rd Lord of the Isles, and it remained with the Lords of the Isles until the Lordship was forfeited in 1476 when the earldom became vested in the Crown.

On the death of William, Earl of Ross, the chiefship of the clan passed to his brother Hugh Ross of Rariches, who obtained a charter of the lands of Balnagowan in 1374, and for over three centuries the Rosses of Balnagowan remained the principal family of the clan. David Ross, the last of the direct line of Balnagowan, settled the estate on the Hon. Charles Ross, son of Lord Ross of Hawkhead, Renfrewshire. There was no connection between the two families. Balnagowan devolved upon George, 13th Lord Ross in 1745. On the death of William, 14th Lord Ross, unmarried, Balnagowan went to Sir James Lockhart, 2nd Bart. of Carstairs. Sir John, 5th Bart., assumed the name Ross, and on the sale of Carstairs in 1762 adopted the designation of Balnagowan. The chiefship is now vested in Ross of Pitcalnie, heir of the line of David, last of the old family of Balnagowan.

ROSS

There is also a hunting tartan.

ORIGIN OF NAME: *Place-name, Ross-shire.*
PLANT BADGE: *Juniper.*
PIPE MUSIC: *The Earl of Ross's March.*

SCOTT

CREST BADGE : *A stag trippant, proper, attired and unguled, or.*

MOTTO : *Amo (I love).*

GAELIC NAME : *Scot, Scotach.*

THE SCOTTS, one of the most powerful Border clans, take their name from a race who invaded Scotland at an early date and filtered into many other countries. Uchtredus filius Scoti witnessed charters between 1107 and 1128, and from him were descended the Scotts of Buccleuch and the Scotts of Balwearie.

The Buccleuchs exchanged Murdochston in Lanarkshire for Branxholm in Roxburghshire. Sir Walter, 13th Baron, was created Lord Scott of Buccleuch by James VI and his son was raised to the dignity of Earl of Buccleuch in 1619. On the failure of the male line the Countess of Buccleuch married the Duke of Monmouth, natural son of Charles II, who was created Duke of Buccleuch. His grandson became 2nd Duke, and the third Duke succeeded to the Dukedom of Queensberry.

Sir Michael Scott, knighted by Alexander II, obtained the lands of Balwearie by marriage with the heiress of Sir Richard Balwearie. Their son, Sir Michael, who died about 1300, was the famous wizard, actually one of the most learned men of his time. It is notable that of fourteen successive barons of Balwearie, thirteen of them were knighted. The Balwearie family are now represented by the Scotts of Ancrum.

Among the many prominent families of the clan are the Scots of Harden, of which family Sir Walter Scott, author of *Waverley*, was a scion. William Scott, who died in 1563, received the estate of Harden from his brother Walter Scott of Synton. Walter, 2nd of Harden, was the famous " Auld Wat of Harden," of whom many traditions still survive in the Border country, and he and his wife Mary Scott, " the Flower of Yarrow," are celebrated in Border song.

SCOTT

There is a hunting tartan and a black and white sett.

ORIGIN OF NAME: *National name.*
WAR CRY: *A Bellandean!*

SHAW
House of Tordarroch

CREST BADGE :. *A dexter arm, the hand holding a dagger in pale proper.*

MOTTO : *Fide et Fortitudine (By fidelity and fortitude).*

GAELIC NAME : *Mac Ghille-Sheathanaich.*

CLAN SHAW was one of the principal Clans of Clan Chattan. Shaw " Mor ", great-grandson of Angus, 6th Chief of Mackintosh and Eva of Clan Chattan was, by tradition, the leader of Clan Chattan at the battle on the North Inch, Perth, in 1396. Rothiemurchus was given to him as a reward but the lands were sold in the 16th century. His son, James, was killed at Harlaw in 1411 but his heir, Alasdair " Ciar " succeeded him.

Alasdair's brother, Adam (Ay), of Tordarroch was founder of Clan Ay. Tordarroch acted for Clan Shaw and at Inverness in 1543 and Termit in 1609 signed the Clan Chattan Bands. They supported Montrose and raised the Shaw contingent in the Jacobite rising of 1715.

Alasdair's second son, Alexander, was ancestor of Shaws of Dell; his third, James, of Shaws of Dalnavert; his fourth, Farquhar, was progenitor of Clan Farquharson and the fifth, Iver, ancestor of the Shaws of Harris and the Isles.

A new chief of Clan Shaw (21st) matriculated in 1970 after a vacancy of 400 years; Tordarroch in Strathnairn is still held.

SHEPHERD

THE SHEPHERD tartan is one of the most common, and perhaps one of the oldest in Scotland. It originated, most probably, from the use of the wool from white and from black or brown sheep. This did not require dyeing and consequently reduced the amount of work necessary to enable it to be woven into cloth.

This tartan is not illustrated, as the black and white check is familiar to all.

SHAW

ORIGIN OF NAME: *Gaelic seaghdha (pithy)*.
PLANT BADGE: *Red whortleberry*.

SINCLAIR

CREST BADGE : *A cock, proper armed and beaked or.*

MOTTO : *Commit thy work to God.*

GAELIC NAME : *Mac na Ceardadh.*

THE SINCLAIRS are of Norman origin, the first of the name being William de Sancto Claro, who received a grant of the barony of Roslin, Midlothian, in the 12th century. Sir Henry St. Clair of Roslin supported Robert the Bruce, and his son Sir William accompanied Sir James Douglas with the heart of Bruce, and died fighting the Moors in Spain.

Henry, son of Sir William Sinclair, obtained the Earldom of Orkney in 1379 through his father's marriage with Isabella, Countess of Orkney. William, 3rd Earl, founded Roslin Chapel in 1446, and received the Earldom of Caithness in 1455. In 1470 the Earldom of Orkney, which had previously been held from King Haco, was purchased from the Sinclairs by James III. The Earls of Caithness were engaged in a long succession of feuds with the Sutherlands, the Gunns, and other clans, and George, 6th Earl, being deeply in debt, granted a disposition of his title and estates to Sir John Campbell of Glenorchy. The Earl died without issue and Campbell took possession of the estates in 1676. His claim to the title was disputed by George Sinclair of Keiss. In a battle in 1680 the Sinclairs were defeated by the Campbells, but in 1681 George Sinclair's claim to the title was established. The Earldom thereafter passed through several families of Sinclairs.

The many prominent families of Sinclairs include the Sinclairs of Ulbster. Sir John of Ulbster (1754-1835) was one of the foremost agriculturists of his time, a voluminous writer of poetical works, and editor of the first Statistical Account of Scotland.

The Sinclairs of Argyllshire and the West of Scotland, known as " Clann na Cearda " or craftsmen, do not appear to be connected with the Sinclairs of the North.

270

SINCLAIR

There is also a hunting tartan.

ORIGIN OF NAME: *Place-name, French de Sancto Claro.*
PLANT BADGE: *Whin.*
PIPE MUSIC: *Spaidsearachd Mhic nan Cearda* (*The Sinclair's March*).

SKENE

CREST BADGE : *A dexter arm embowed, issuing from a cloud, hand holding a laurel wreath, all proper.*

MOTTO : *Virtutis regia merces (A palace the reward of bravery).*

GAELIC NAME : *MacSgian.*

THE traditional origin of the Clan Skene takes us back to the 11th century, when a younger son of Robertson of Struan saved the life of the king by killing a wolf with his sgian and was rewarded by the lands of Skene in Aberdeenshire.

John de Skene signed the Ragman Roll of 1296. His grandson, Robert, was a faithful follower of Robert the Bruce, from whom he received a charter erecting the lands of Skene into a barony. The chiefs were unfortunate in battle. In 1411 Adam de Skene was killed at Harlaw, Alexander fell at Flodden in 1513, and his grandson, Alexander, was killed at Pinkie in 1547. James Skene of Skene supported the Royalist cause during the reign of Charles I, and later served in the army of Gustavus Adolphus. In 1827 the family of Skene of Skene became extinct in the direct line, and the estates passed to James, 4th Earl of Fife, nephew of the last Skene of Skene.

Other prominent families of Skenes included those of Dyce, Halyards, Cariston, Curriehill and Rubislaw. Sir John Skene, a celebrated lawyer, was admitted a Lord of Session in 1594 and took the title Lord Curriehill. He was the author of several legal works, including *De Verborum Significatione*, and *Regiam Majestatem*, a collection of " The auld lawes and constitutions of Scotland." Lord Curriehill's son, Sir James Skene, was President of the Court of Session in 1626.

William Forbes Skene, the celebrated writer on Scoto-Celtic history, was born in 1809. He was the author of *The Highlanders of Scotland, Celtic Scotland,* and several other works. He was appointed Historiographer Royal for Scotland in 1881, and died in 1892.

SKENE

ORIGIN OF NAME: *Place-name, Aberdeenshire.*

THE
ROYAL TARTAN
('ROYAL STEWART')
STEWART

CREST BADGE : *A pelican argent winged or feeding its young proper.*

The crest shown here is that of the Earl of Galloway.

MOTTO : *Virescit vulnere virtus (Courage grows strong at a wound).*

GAELIC NAME : *Stillbhard.*

THE STEWARTS are descended from Walter, the son of an Anglo-Norman baron who came to Scotland in the 12th century, and who was appointed High Steward of the royal household by David I. Walter also received lands in Renfrew, Paisley, Pollock, Cathcart and elsewhere. The office of High Steward was made hereditary to the family by King Malcolm IV. James, 5th High Steward, bravely supported Sir William Wallace and Robert the Bruce in their struggle for Scottish independence. Walter, 6th High Steward, married Princess Marjory, daughter of Robert the Bruce, and from them are descended the Royal House of Stewart. The male line of the Royal Stewarts ended with the death in 1807 of Prince Henry, Cardinal Duke of York, brother of Prince Charles Edward.

Many noble families were descended from the Royal line, and Stewarts have held or hold the Dukedoms of Albany, Rothesay and Lennox, the Marquessate of Bute, and the Earldoms of Menteith, Angus, Atholl, Strathearn, Carrick, Buchan, and Galloway. Among other Stewart families were those of Bonkil, Blackhall and Greenock, Castlemilk, Balquhidder, Achnacone, Ardsheal, Ardvorlich, Dalguise, Fasnacloich, Grandtully and Invernahyle.

The Royal Stewart tartan was always regarded as the personal tartan of the Royal House of Scotland, and it is now considered to be the Royal tartan of H.M. The Queen.

ORIGIN OF NAME: *from the High Steward of Scotland.*
PLANT BADGE: *Oak, Thistle.*

STEWART, HUNTING

STEWART, DRESS

STEWART, OLD

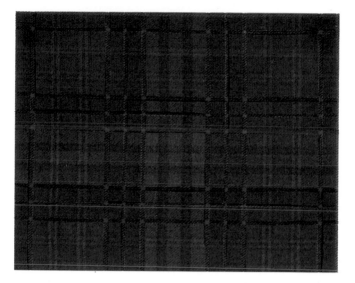

STEWART, PRINCE CHARLES EDWARD

STEWART OF APPIN

CREST BADGE: *A unicorn's head, crined and armed, or.*

MOTTO: *Quidder we'll zje* (*Whither will ye*).

GAELIC NAME: *Stiubhard.*

SIR JOHN STEWART OF BONKYL, son of Alexander, High Steward of Scotland, was the ancestor of this west Highland clan. One of his descendants obtained the Lordship of Lorn through marriage to the heiress of Lorn. Sir John Stewart of Lorn was murdered at Dunstaffnage Castle about 1463 and his son Dougal became 1st of Appin. Dougal unsuccessfully tried to recover the Lordship of Lorn and was supported by the MacLarens of Balquhidder. He strengthened his possession of Appin and for several centuries his followers were on terms of friendship with the MacLarens of Balquhidder. The first chief of Appin was killed when supporting the MacLarens. The clan fought at the Battle of Flodden (1513) and Pinkie (1547). At Pinkie the clan was led by Donald Stewart of Invernahyle, known as Donald nan Ord. They supported Montrose at the battle of Inverlochy and also fought at the battles of Auldearn and Kilsyth. The chief of Appin was outlawed and his lands forfeited, but they were returned to him at the Restoration. The clan joined Dundee's campaign in 1688 and supported the Jacobites in the Risings of 1715 and 1745. After the Battle of Culloden the banner of the Appin regiment was one of the few saved from destruction. In 1765 the estate was sold by the 9th chief who was succeeded in the chiefship by his cousin Duncan, 6th of Ardshiel, who became 10th of Appin, in 1769. In 1782 the 10th chief obtained the restoration of his confiscated paternal estate of Ardshiel. The ruined fortress of Castle Stalker, at the entrance to Loch Laich in Appin, once stronghold of the Stewarts of Lorn, passed into Campbell possession but was reacquired by a Stewart.

STEWART OF APPIN

PLANT BADGE: *Oak, Thistle.*
WAR CRY: *Creag ab Sgairbh (The cormorant's rock).*

SUTHERLAND

CREST BADGE : *A cat sejant erect guardant proper.*
MOTTO : *Sans peur (Without fear).*
GAELIC NAME : *Sutherlarach.*

THE territory lying to the south of Caithness was known to the Norsemen as Sudrland, in English Sutherland, and doubtless the inhabitants assumed their name from the district. The Earls of Sutherland, who were chiefs of the clan till 1514, are descended from Freskin, the progenitor of the Murrays.

The Earldom of Sutherland, claimed to be the oldest in Britain, is alleged to have been granted to William, Lord of Sutherland, about 1228. William was the great-grandson of Freskin, the ancestor of the Murrays of Atholl. William, 2nd Earl of Sutherland, fought for Bruce at Bannockburn, and his son Kenneth, 3rd Earl, was killed at the Battle of Halidon Hill in 1333. William, 4th Earl, married a daughter of Robert the Bruce. His successors had many feuds with neighbouring clans, particularly the Mackays. John, 9th Earl, died in 1514 without male issue, and the title passed to his sister, whose husband was Adam Gordon, of Aboyne.

The Gordon Earls of Sutherland encountered the same inter-clan enmities as their predecessors, and John, 11th Earl, and his Countess were poisoned by Isobel Sinclair at the instigation of the Earl of Caithness. William, 18th Earl, died in 1766, the last of the Gordon Earls of Sutherland. His daughter Elizabeth, Countess of Sutherland, married George Granville Leveson-Gower, afterwards Marquis of Stafford, who was created Duke of Sutherland in 1833.

Also an alternative pattern, similar to the Black Watch.

ORIGIN OF NAME: *Place-name, Scotland.*
PLANT BADGE: *Butcher's broom, Cotton sedge.*
WAR CRY: *Ceann na Drochaide Bige (The Head of the Little Bridge).*
PIPE MUSIC: *The Earl of Sutherland's March.*

URQUHART

CREST BADGE : *Issuing from a crest coronet, a female naked from waist up holding in her dexter hand a sword, and in the sinister a tree.*

MOTTO : *Mean, speak and do weil.*

GAELIC NAME : *Urchurdan.*

THE URQUHARTS derive their name from the district of Urquhart in the old sheriffdom of Cromarty, and although of minor importance are of ancient origin. The famous Sir Thomas Urquhart compiled his own genealogy and described himself as the 143rd in direct descent from Adam and Eve !

William Urquhart, Sheriff of Cromarty, at the beginning of the 14th century married a daughter of Hugh, Earl of Ross, and his son Adam added considerably to the family possessions. Sir Thomas Urquhart of Cromarty, who married Helen, daughter of Lord Abernethy, is alleged to have been the father of twenty-five sons, seven of whom were killed at the Battle of Pinkie in 1547. The eldest son, Alexander, received a charter in 1532 from James V granting him lands in Ross-shire and Inverness-shire. Alexander's son John, of Craigfintry and Culbo, was tutor to his grandnephew, Sir Thomas, and is the " Tutour of Cromartie " named in the *Roll of Landlords*, 1587. Sir Thomas Urquhart of Cromarty, the famous writer and cavalier of the 17th century, was notable chiefly for his translation of Rabelais, and for his epigrams. Col. James Urquhart, who died in 1741, was the last of the male line.

The chiefship passed to the Urquharts of Meldrum who are descended from John, the Tutor of Cromarty, who obtained the lands of Meldrum by his marriage with Elizabeth Seton. The chiefship became dormant in 1898.

URQUHART

There is an alternative pattern with a white overstripe.

ORIGIN OF NAME: *Place-name, Ross-shire.*
PLANT BADGE: *Wallflower.*

WALLACE

CREST BADGE: *A dexter arm in armour, embowed, in hand a sword, all proper.*

MOTTO: *Pro libertate* (*For liberty*).

GAELIC NAME: *Uallas.*

IN the old Latin documents the term Wallensis, or Walensis, was used to designate the Welsh, but in Scotland it was used more particularly to designate the Britons of Strathclyde who were of the same stock. From this word the name Wallace is derived.

Richard Wallace, in the 12th century, obtained extensive lands in Ayrshire, in the district now known as Riccarton. His son Henry Walays acquired lands in Renfrewshire and his descendant Sir Malcolm Wallace of Elderslie was the father of Scotland's greatest patriot, Sir William Wallace, who was his second son.

In his early years Wallace and his mother had to take refuge near Dunipace from the English, for the Wallaces refused to do homage to Edward I. While still very young, Wallace became the leader of a company of patriots, and his harassing tactics against the English earned for him the support of many nobles. His reprisal against the garrison at Lanark for the murder of his sweetheart, and the burning of " the barns of Ayr " in revenge for the murder of his uncle and other gentlemen who had been invited to a conference, gained him still more supporters. His military genius made him hated and feared by Edward I, and his only defeats were brought about by the jealousies and treachery of nobles forming his own armies. By treachery he was captured at Robroyston, near Glasgow, and delivered to Edward I by Sir John Mentieth. Wallace was brutally executed in London in 1305, but his example kindled a spirit of independence in Scotland that was never extinguished.

The Wallaces of Craigie, of Cessnock, of Kelly, and of Cairnhill were all descended from the original family of Riccarton in Ayrshire.

WALLACE

ORIGIN·OF NAME: *from Volcae, a tribe in North Gaul.*

JACOBITE *and* CALEDONIA

I T has frequently been claimed that Scots who do not bear a clan or sept surname may wear the tartan of their mother's clan or sept providing she possessed a clan surname. Although this practice is widespread it is incorrect. Clan membership rests upon name, and it follows that if no clan or sept surname is borne there can be no claim to the tartan of any clan. Those who bear surnames unconnected to a clan should, if they desire to follow the correct course, wear either a " District " tartan or the " Jacobite " or " Caledonia " tartans.

The Jacobite tartan was known as early as 1712 and is claimed to have been popular in 1707 when Lowlanders wore it as a protest against the Union of the Parliaments. It is a well-known fact that Edinburgh ladies took great pride in wearing tartan plaids at this time. This tartan was also worn by a participant in the Jacobite Rising of 1715, which fact may account for its name.

The Caledonia tartan was also popular in the 18th century and although its origin is doubtful, many claims have been made regarding its early use. One claim places it as contemporary with the Jacobite tartan and holds that it was also worn as a protest against the Union of the Parliaments. Another story is that it was worn by members of the Darien expedition and that the name indicates its connection with that ill-fated Scottish venture.

There are several variations of this tartan. The illustration in this volume is taken from a late 18th century pattern.

While these traditional tales do not, of themselves, prove that either the Jacobite or Caledonia tartans were in fact, used for the purposes claimed, they do support the contention that they were " general " tartans used by Scots who had no clan connections. Their preservation and use for many years has given them an antiquity of their own, and justifies their use by clanless Scots.

JACOBITE

CALEDONIA

REGIMENTAL TARTANS

Scottish Lowland regiments now wear what may be described as a semi-Highland uniform with tartan trews. Until 1881 there was little to distinguish those regiments from their counterparts in England, Ireland and Wales. When tartan trews were introduced the tartan was of the " Universal " or " Military " setting. All Lowland regiments now have their pipers. Highland regiments wear the kilt.

Details of the tartans now worn by Scottish Regiments of the Regular Army are as follows :

THE ROYAL SCOTS GREYS
" The Greys " have no regimental tartan.

SCOTS GUARDS
The pipers wear the Royal Stewart tartan. The offer, in 1881, of tartan trews for the regiment was declined.

ROYAL SCOTS
Trews of the Universal tartan were worn from 1882 to 1901 when the tartan was changed to Hunting Stewart. The pipers wear the Royal Stewart. The 7/9 (Territorial) Battalion wear kilts of the Hunting Stewart.

THE KING'S OWN SCOTTISH BORDERERS
From 1882 to 1898 trews of the Universal tartan were worn. The Leslie tartan was adopted by the Regiment in 1898 to commemorate its first commander. Since 1920 the pipers have worn the Royal Stewart tartan.

ROYAL SCOTS FUSILIERS
Trews of the Universal tartan were worn from 1882 until 1948 when the Hunting Erskine tartan was adopted in honour of the Regiment's founder, the Earl of Mar. In 1928 to commemorate the 250th anniversary the pipers were given the Erskine (red) tartan. *See* Royal Highland Fusiliers opposite.

THE CAMERONIANS
Trews of the Universal tartan were issued in 1882 but in 1892 the Douglas tartan was adopted for all ranks including the pipers and drummers. The Earl of Angus, who raised the Cameronians, was a Douglas.

THE BLACK WATCH
This regiment, the oldest of the Highland regiments, wears the Universal tartan. Sometimes called the Black Watch tartan, it is claimed to be a Campbell tartan and is worn as such (when woven in brighter colour shades), by the Duke of Argyll. The pipers wear the Royal Stewart tartan.

THE SEAFORTH HIGHLANDERS
This regiment wears the MacKenzie (Seaforth) tartan. The basis of the design is that of the Universal with the addition of white and red overstripes. This tartan is now accepted as Clan

MacKenzie tartan but it was first worn by the Regiment. See Queen's Own Highlanders below.

THE HIGHLAND LIGHT INFANTRY
This regiment became again in 1948 a kilted unit and wore the MacKenzie tartan with a seven-inch sett. See R.H.F. below.

THE GORDON HIGHLANDERS
The Universal tartan with a yellow overstripe as difference or distinguishing mark is worn by this regiment. This tartan is now called the Gordon.

THE QUEEN'S OWN CAMERON HIGHLANDERS
This regiment has the distinction of wearing a tartan completely unlike the Universal, now known as the Cameron of Erracht (q.v.). Since 1943 the pipers have worn the Royal Stewart tartan. See Queen's Own Highlanders below.

THE ARGYLL AND SUTHERLAND HIGHLANDERS
The Universal tartan is worn in lighter shades as the regimental tartan. It is sometimes worn as Clan Sutherland tartan.

THE ROYAL HIGHLAND FUSILIERS
Known as Princess Margaret's Own Glasgow and Ayrshire Regiment and formed on 20th January, 1959, by an amalgamation of the Royal Scots Fusiliers and the Highland Light Infantry. The regiment wear trews in the MacKenzie tartan (as the old H.L.I.) and the pipers wear Dress Erskine (as the old R.S.F.).

THE QUEEN'S OWN HIGHLANDERS (SEAFORTH AND CAMERONS)
Formed by the amalgamation of the Cameron and Seaforth Highlanders. All ranks will wear either the Seaforth kilt or Cameron tartan trews, as ordered. The pipe and military band will wear the Cameron kilt and Seaforth trews.

LESSER-KNOWN TARTANS
There are well over 600 named tartans but many of them are rarely found in manufacturers' lists or on sale by retailers. A few of the lesser-known patterns are as follows:

Aberdeen	Galawater	Nithsdale
Birrell	Galloway	Nova Scotia
Craig	Inverness	Paisley
Crief	Kidd	Strathspey
Dundee	Lochaber	Waggrall
Fort William	Musselburgh	Wellington

Confusion has been caused by some manufacturers and retailers calling tartans by names other than the name by which they should be known. Thus we find the Kennedy tartan sometimes called Cassells; the red Gordon the Abergeldie; the Ogilvie the Airlie, and so on. "The Merrilees" tartan is an example of how some have been named. In 1831 a Highland firm offered "Meg Merrilees" (the gypsy in Scott's *Guy Mannering*) tartan plaids for ladies' wear. A hundred years later the same tartan named Merrilees was on sale in Edinburgh.

Clan septs were of two classes: clansmen of the clan who were related by blood and formed separate branches and individuals and groups who sought and obtained the protection of the clan. This resulted in a clan having septs of different surnames, also persons with the same surname might be attached to different clans. Many septs now have tartans of their own, which are marked thus (*).

Even respected authorities differ on this complex question, therefore this list which has been carefully compiled cannot claim to be fully comprehensive or definitive.

Abbot, *Macnab*
Abbotson, *Macnab*
*Abercrombie, *Family*
Abernethy, *Leslie*
Adam, *Gordon*
Adamson, *MacIntosh*
Adie, *Gordon*
Airlie, *Ogilvie*
Alexander, *MacAlister,
MacDonald, MacDonell of
Glengarry*
Allan, *MacDonald of
Clanranald, MacFarlane*
Allanson, *MacDonald of
Clanranald, MacFarlane*
Allardice, *Graham*
*Allison, *Family*
Alpin, *MacAlpine*
Anderson, *Ross*
Andrew, *Ross*
*Angus, *MacInnes*
Arthur, *MacArthur*
Austin, *Keith*
Ayson, *MacIntosh*
*Baillie, *Family*
Bain, *Macbean, MacKay,
Macnab*
Bannatyne, *Campbell of Argyll,
Stewart*
Bannerman, *Forbes*
Bartholomew, *MacFarlane*
*Baxter, *Macmillan*
Bayne, *Macbean, MacKay,
Macnab*
Bean, *Macbean*
Beathy, *MacBeth*
Beaton, *MacDonald, MacLean,
MacLeod of Harris*
Bell, *Macmillan*

Begg, *MacDonald*
Berkeley, *Barclay*
Bethune, *MacDonald, MacLean,
MacLeod of Harris*
Beton, *MacDonald, MacLean,
MacLeod of Harris*
Binnie, *MacBean*
Black, *Lamont, MacGregor,
MacLean*
Bontein, Bontine, Bunten,
Graham
Bowie, *MacDonald*
Boyd, *Stewart*
Brewer, *Drummond, MacGregor*
Brieve, *Morrison*
Brown, *Lamont, Macmillan*
Buchan, *Cumin*
Burdon, *Lamont*
Burk, *MacDonald*
*Burnett, *Campbell*
*Burns, *Campbell of Argyll*
Caddell, *Campbell of Cawdor*
Caird, *MacGregor, Sinclair*
Calder, *Campbell of Cawdor*
Callum, *MacLeod of Raasay*
Campbell of Strachur,
MacArthur
Cariston, *Skene*
*Carmichael, *MacDougall,
Stewart*
*Carnegie, *Family*
Carson, *Macpherson*
Cattanach, *Macpherson*
Caw, *MacFarlane*
Chalmers, *Cameron*
Cheyne, *Sutherland*
*Christie, *Farquharson*
*Clark, Clerk, *Cameron,
MacIntosh, Macpherson*

NAME	CLAN
Clarkson, *Cameron, MacIntosh, Macpherson*	
Clyne, *Sinclair*	
*Cochrane, *Family*	
*Cockburn, *Family*	
Collier, *Robertson*	
Colman, *Buchanan*	
Colson, *MacDonald*	
Colyear, *Robertson*	
Combich, *Stewart*	
Combie, *MacIntosh*	
Comrie, *MacGregor*	
Comyn, *see* Cumming	
Conacher, *MacDougall*	
*Connall, Conne, *MacDonald*	
Conochie, *Campbell*	
Cook, *Stewart*	
Coulson, *MacDonald*	
Coutts, *Farquharson*	
Cowan, *Colquhoun, MacDougall*	
*Cranston, *Family*	
*Crauford, Crawford, *Lindsay*	
Crerar, *MacIntosh*	
Crombie, *MacDonald*	
Crookshanks, *Stewart*	
Cruickshanks, *Stewart*	
Currie, *MacDonald of Clanranald, Macpherson*	
Dallas, *MacIntosh*	
*Dalziel, *Family*	
Darroch, *MacDonald*	
Davie, *Davidson*	
Davis, *Davidson*	
Davison, *Davidson*	
Dawson, *Davidson*	
Denoon, *Campbell of Argyll*	
Deuchar, *Lindsay*	
Dewar, *Macnab, Menzies*	
Dingwall, *Munro, Ross*	
Dis, Dise, *Skene*	
Dochart, *MacGregor*	
Doig, *Drummond*	
Doles, *MacIntosh*	
Donachie, *Robertson*	
Donald, *MacDonald*	

NAME	CLAN
Donaldson, *MacDonald*	
Donleavy, *Buchanan*	
Dougall, *MacDougall*	
Dove, *Buchanan*	
Dow, *Buchanan, Davidson*	
Dowall, *MacDougall*	
Drysdale, *Douglas*	
Duff, *MacDuff*	
Duffie, Duffy, *Macfie*	
Dullach, *Stewart*	
*Dunbar, *Family*	
Duncanson, *Duncan*	
Dunnachie, *Robertson*	
*Dyce, *Skene*	
Edie, *Gordon*	
Elder, *MacIntosh*	
Esson, *MacIntosh*	
Ewan, Ewen, *MacEwen*	
Ewing, *MacEwen*	
Fair, *Ross*	
Farquhar, *Farquharson*	
Federith, *Sutherland*	
Fergus, *Ferguson*	
Ferries, *Ferguson*	
Ferson, *Macpherson*	
Fife, *Macduff*	
Findlay, Finlay, *Farquharson*	
Findlayson, *Farquharson*	
Findlater, *Ogilvie*	
Fleming, *Murray*	
Fordyce, *Forbes*	
*Forsyth, *Family*	
Foulis, *Munro*	
France, *Stewart*	
Fresell, Friseal, Frizell, *Fraser*	
Frew, *Fraser*	
Fullarton, *Stewart*	
Fyfe, *MacDuff*	
*Galbraith, *MacDonald, MacFarlane*	
Gallie, *Gunn*	
Garrow, *Stewart*	
Gaunson, *Gunn*	
Geddes, *Gordon*	
Georgeson, *Gunn*	

NAME	CLAN
Gibb, *Buchanan*	
Gibson, *Buchanan*	
Gilbert, *Buchanan*	
Gilbertson, *Buchanan*	
Gilbride, *MacDonald*	
Gilchrist, *MacLachlan, Ogilvie*	
Gilfillan, *Macnab*	
Gillanders, *Ross*	
Gillespie, *Macpherson*	
*Gillies, *Macpherson*	
Gilmore, *Morrison*	
Gilroy, *Grant, MacGillivray*	
*Gladstone, *Family*	
Glen, Glennie, *Mackintosh*	
Gorrie, *MacDonald*	
Gowrie, *MacDonald*	
Gray, *Stewart, Sutherland*	
Gregor, *MacGregor*	
Gregorson, *MacGregor*	
Gregory, *MacGregor*	
Greig, *MacGregor*	
Greusach, *Farquharson*	
Grier, *MacGregor*	
Grierson, *MacGregor*	
*Haig, *Family*	
Hallyard, *Skene*	
Hanna, Hannah, *Hannay*	
Hardie, Hardy, *Farquharson,*	
Mackintosh	
Harper, *Buchanan*	
Harperson, *Buchanan*	
Hawthorn, *MacDonald*	
Hendrie, Hendry, *Henderson,*	
MacNaughton	
Hewison, *MacDonald*	
*Home, *Family*	
Houston, *MacDonald*	
Howison, *MacDonald*	
Hughson, *MacDonald*	
*Hunter, *Family*	
Huntly, *Gordon*	
Hutcheson, *MacDonald*	
Hutchinson, *MacDonald*	
Inches, *Robertson*	
*Inglis, *Family*	

NAME	CLAN
Innie, *Innes*	
*Irvine, *Family*	
Jameson, *Gunn, Stuart of Bute*	
*Jardine, *Family*	
*Johnson, *Gunn, MacDonald*	
Kay, *Davidson*	
Kean, Keene, *Gunn,*	
MacDonald	
Kellie, Kelly, *MacDonald*	
Kendrick, *Henderson,*	
MacNaughton	
Kenneth, *MacKenzie*	
Kennethson, *MacKenzie*	
*Kilgour, *Family*	
Kilpatrick, *Colquhoun*	
King, *MacGregor*	
Kinnell, *MacDonald*	
*Kinnieson, *MacFarlane*	
Kirkpatrick, *Colquhoun*	
Lachlan, *MacLachlan*	
Lamb, *Lamont*	
Lambie, *Lamont*	
Lammie, *Lamont*	
Lammond, *Lamont*	
Lamondson, *Lamont*	
Landers, *Lamont*	
Lang, *MacDonald*	
*Lauder, *Family*	
Laurence, *MacLaren*	
Law, *MacLaren*	
Lawrie, *MacLaren*	
Lean, *MacLean*	
Leckie, Lecky, *MacGregor*	
Lees, *Macpherson*	
Lennie, Lenny, *Buchanan*	
Lennox, *MacFarlane, Stewart*	
Lewis, *MacLeod*	
Limont, *Lamont*	
Lobban, *Logan*	
Loudoun, *Campbell*	
Love, *MacKinnon*	
Low, *MacLaren*	
Lucas, *Lamont*	
*Lumsden, *Forbes*	
Lyall, *Sinclair*	

NAME	CLAN
Lyon, *Farquharson*	
MacAdam, *MacGregor*	
MacAdie, *Munro*	
MacAindra, *MacFarlane*	
MacAlaster, *MacAlister*	
Macalduie, *Lamont*	
MacAlester, *MacAlister*	
MacAllan, *MacDonald of Clanranald, MacFarlane*	
Macandeoir, *Buchanan, Macnab, Menzies*	
MacAndrew (*see* Anderson), *Mackintosh, Ross*	
MacAngus, *MacInnes*	
Macara, *MacGregor, Macrae*	
Macaree, *MacGregor*	
MacAskill, *MacLeod of Harris*	
MacAuslan, MacAusland, *Buchanan*	
MacAy, *Mackintosh*	
MacBain, *MacBean*	
MacBaxter, *Macmillan*	
*MacBeath, *MacBean, MacDonald, MacLean*	
MacBeolain, *MacKenzie*	
*MacBeth, *MacBean, MacDonald, MacLean*	
MacBrayne, *MacNaughton*	
MacBride, *MacDonald*	
MacBrieve, *Morrison*	
MacCaa, *MacFarlane*	
MacCaig, *Farquharson, MacLeod of Harris*	
MacCainsh, *MacInnes*	
MacCaishe, *MacDonald*	
MacCall, *MacColl*	
MacCalman, *Buchanan*	
MacCalmont, *Buchanan*	
MacCamie, *Stewart*	
MacCammon, MacCammond, *Buchanan*	
MacCansh, *MacInnes*	
MacCardney, *Farquharson, Mackintosh*	
MacCartair, *MacArthur*	

NAME	CLAN
MacCash, *MacDonald*	
MacCaskill, *MacLeod*	
MacCaul, *MacDonald*	
MacCause, *MacFarlane*	
MacCaw, *Stewart*	
MacCay, *MacKay*	
MacCeallaich, *MacDonald*	
MacChoiter, *MacGregor*	
MacChruiter, *Buchanan*	
MacClerich, MacChlery, *Cameron, Mackintosh, Macpherson*	
MacCloy, *Stuart of Bute*	
MacClure, *MacLeod*	
MacClymont, *Lamont*	
MacCodrum, *MacDonald*	
MacColman, *Buchanan*	
MacComas, *Gunn*	
MacCombe, *Mackintosh*	
MacCombich, *Stewart of Appin*	
MacCombie, *Mackintosh*	
MacConacher, *MacDougall*	
MacConachie, *MacGregor, Robertson*	
MacCondy, *MacFarlane*	
MacConnach, *MacKenzie*	
MacConnechy, *Campbell, Robertson*	
MacConnell, *MacDonald*	
MacConnichie, *Campbell, MacGregor, Robertson*	
MacCooish, *MacDonald*	
MacCook, *MacDonald*	
MacCorkill, MacCorkle, *Gunn*	
MacCorkindale, *MacLeod*	
MacCormack, *Buchanan, MacLaine of Lochbuie*	
MacCormick, *Buchanan, MacLaine of Lochbuie*	
MacCorquodale, *MacLeod*	
MacCorrie, MacCorry, *Macquarrie*	
MacCoull, *MacDougall*	
MacCowan, *Colquhoun, MacDougall*	

NAME	CLAN
MacCracken, *Maclean*	
MacCrae, MacCrea, *Macrae*	
MacCrain, *MacDonald*	
MacCraw, *Macrae*	
MacCreath, *Macrae*	
MacCrie, *MacKay*, *Macrae*	
MacCrimmon, *MacLeod of Harris*	
Maccrowther, *MacGregor*	
MacCuag, *MacDonald*	
MacCuaig, *Farquharson*, *MacLeod of Harris*	
MacCuish, *MacDonald*	
MacCulloch, *MacDonald*, *MacDougall*, *Munro*, *Ross*	
MacCunn, *MacQueen*	
MacCutchen, MacCutcheon, *MacDonald*	
Macdaid, *Davidson*	
MacDaniell, *MacDonald*	
MacDavid, *Davidson*	
MacDermid, *Campbell of Argyll*	
*MacDiarmid, *Campbell of Argyll*	
MacDonachie, *Robertson*	
Macdonleavy, *Buchanan*	
MacDowall, MacDowell, *MacDougall*	
Macdrain, *MacDonald*	
MacDuffie, *Macfie*	
MacEachan, *MacDonald of Clanranald*	
MacEachern, MacEacheran, *MacDonald*	
MacEaracher, *Farquharson*	
MacElfrish, *MacDonald*	
MacElheran, *MacDonald*	
MacErracher, *Farquharson*, *MacFarlane*	
*MacFadyen, *MacLaine of Lochbuie*	
McFall, *MacIntosh*	
MacFarquhar, *Farquharson*	
MacFater, *MacLaren*	
MacFeat, *MacLaren*	
MacFergus, *Ferguson*	
MacGaw, *MacFarlane*	
MacGeachie, *MacDonald of Clanranald*	
MacGeoch, *MacFarlane*	
Macghee, Macghie, *MacKay*	
MacGibbon, *Buchanan*, *Campbell of Argyll*, *Graham*	
MacGilbert, *Buchanan*	
MacGilchrist, *MacLachlan*, *Ogilvie*	
*MacGill, *Family*	
MacGilledow, *Lamont*	
MacGillegowie, *Lamont*	
MacGillivantic, *Macdonell of Keppoch*	
MacGillonie, *Cameron*	
MacGilp, *MacDonell of Keppoch*	
MacGilroy, *Grant*, *MacGillivray*	
MacGilvernock, *Graham*	
Macglashan, *MacIntosh*, *Stewart*	
Macglasrich, *MacIver*, *MacDonell of Keppoch*	
MacGorrie, MacGorry, *MacDonald*, *Macquarrie*	
MacGowan, see *Gow*	
MacGreusich, *Buchanan*, *MacFarlane*	
Macgrime, *Graham*	
MacGrory, *MacLaren*	
Macgrowther, *MacGregor*	
Macgruder, *MacGregor*	
Macgruer, *Fraser*	
Macgruther, *MacGregor*	
MacGuaran, *Macquarrie*	
MacGuffie, *Macfie*	
MacGugan, *MacDougall*, *MacNeill*	
MacGuire, *Macquarrie*	
Machaffie, *Macfie*	
*Machardie, Machardy, *Farquharson*, *MacIntosh*	

NAME	CLAN
MacHarold, *MacLeod of Harris*	
MacHay, *MacIntosh*	
MacHendrie, MacHendry,	
Henderson, MacNaughton	
MacHowell, *MacDougall*	
MacHugh, *MacDonald*	
MacHutchen, MacHutcheon,	
MacDonald	
*MacIan, *Gunn, MacDonald*	
Macildowie, *Cameron*	
Macilreach, *MacDonald*	
Macilrevie, *MacDonald*	
Macilriach, *MacDonald*	
Macilroy, *MacGillivray, Grant*	
Macilvain, *Macbean*	
Macilvora, *Maclaine of*	
Lochbuie	
Macilbraie, *MacGillivray*	
Macilvride, *MacDonald*	
Macilwham, *Lamont*	
Macilwraith, *MacDonald*	
Macimmey, *Fraser*	
Macinally, *Buchanan*	
Macindeor, *Buchanan, Macnab*	
Menzies	
Macindoe, *Buchanan*	
*Macinroy, *Robertson*	
Macinstalker, *MacFarlane*	
MacIsaac, *Campbell*	
MacDonald of Clanranald	
MacJames, *MacFarlane*	
MacKail, *Cameron*	
MacKames, *Gunn*	
MacKeachan, *MacDonald of*	
Clanranald	
MacKeamish, *Gunn*	
MacKean, *Gunn, MacDonald*	
Mackechnie, *MacDonald of*	
Clanranald	
Mackee, *MacKay*	
Mackeggie, *MacIntosh*	
MacKeith, *Keith, Macpherson*	
MacKellachie, *MacDonald*	
MacKellaig, *MacDonald*	
MacKellaigh, *MacDonald*	

NAME	CLAN
*MacKellar, *Campbell of*	
Argyll	
MacKelloch, *MacDonald*	
MacKemmie, *Fraser*	
MacKendrick, *see* Henderson	
MacKeochan, *MacDonald of*	
Clanranald	
MacKerchar, *Farquharson*	
MacKerlich, *MacKenzie*	
MacKerrachar, *Farquharson*	
MacKerras, *Ferguson*	
MacKersey, *Ferguson*	
MacKessock, *Campbell,*	
MacDonald of Clanranald	
MacKichan, *MacDonald of*	
Clanranald, MacDougall	
Mackie, *MacKay*	
MacKillican, *MacIntosh*	
MacKillip, *MacDonell of*	
Keppoch	
MacKim, *Fraser*	
MacKimmie, *Fraser*	
*Mackinlay, *Buchanan,*	
Farquharson, MacFarlane,	
Stewart	
MacKinnell, *MacDonald*	
Mackinney, *Mackinnon*	
Mackinning, *Mackinnon*	
MacKintosh, *see* Mackintosh	
Mackinven, *Mackinnon*	
MacKirdy, *Stewart*	
MacKissock, *Campbell,*	
MacDonald of Clanranald	
Macknight, *MacNaughton*	
Maclagan, *Robertson*	
MacLaghlan, *MacLachlan*	
MacLamond, *Lamont*	
MacLardie, MacLardy,	
MacDonald	
MacLarty, *MacDonald*	
MacLaverty, *MacDonald*	
*Maclay, Macleay, *Buchanan,*	
Stewart	
Macleish, *Macpherson*	
MacLeister, *Fletcher*	

NAME	CLAN
MacLellan, *MacDonald*	
MacLennan, see Logan	
MacLergain, *MacLean*	
Maclerie, *Cameron, Mackintosh,*	
Macpherson	
MacLewis, *MacLeod, Stewart,*	
*MacLintock, Family	
MacLise, *Macpherson*	
MacLiver, *MacGregor*	
MacLucas, *Lamont, MacDougall*	
MacLugash, *MacDougall*	
MacLulich, *MacDougall,*	
Munro, Ross	
Maclure, *MacLeod of Harris*	
MacLymont, *Lamont*	
MacMartin, *Cameron*	
MacMaster, *Buchanan,*	
MacInnes	
MacMath, *Matheson*	
MacMaurice, *Buchanan*	
MacMenzies, *Menzies*	
MacMichael, *Stewart*	
MacMinn, *Menzies*	
MacMordoch, *MacDonald,*	
Macpherson	
MacMorran, *Mackinnon*	
MacMunn, *Stewart*	
MacMurchie, MacMurchy,	
Buchanan, MacDonald,	
MacKenzie	
MacMurdo, *MacDonald,*	
Macpherson	
MacMurray, *Murray*	
MacMurrich, *MacDonald of*	
Clanranald, Macpherson	
MacMutrie, *Stuart of Bute*	
MacNair, MacNayer,	
MacFarlane, MacNaughton	
MacNee, *MacGregor*	
MacNeilage, *MacNeill*	
MacNeish, *MacGregor*	
MacNelly, *MacNeill*	
MacNeur, *MacFarlane*	
MacNider, *MacFarlane*	
MacNie, *MacGregor*	

NAME	CLAN
MacNish, *MacGregor*	
MacNiter, *MacFarlane*	
MacNiven, *Cumin, Mackintosh,*	
MacNaughton	
MacNuyer, *Buchanan*	
MacFarlane, MacNaughton	
MacOmie, *Mackintosh*	
MacOmish, *Gunn*	
MacOnie, *Cameron*	
Macoul, Macowl, *MacDougall*	
MacOurlic, *Kennedy*	
MacOwen, *Campbell*	
MacPatrick, *Lamont,*	
MacLaren	
MacPeter, *MacGregor*	
*MacPhail, *Cameron,*	
Mackintosh, MacKay	
MacPhater, *MacLaren*	
MacPhedran, *Campbell*	
Macaulay	
Macphee, Macphie, see	
Macfie	
MacPhilip, *MacDonell of*	
Keppoch	
MacPhun, *Campbell, Matheson*	
Macquey, *MacKay*	
Macquihirr, *Macquarrie*	
MacQuistan, *MacDonald*	
Macquoid, *MacKay*	
Macra, *Macrae*	
Macraild, *MacLeod of Harris*	
MacRaith, *MacDonald, Macrae*	
MacRankin, *MacLean*	
MacRath, *Macrae*	
MacRitchie, *Mackintosh*	
MacRob, MacRobb, *Gunn,*	
Innes, MacFarlane, Robertson	
MacRobbie, *Robertson*	
MacRobert, *Robertson*	
MacRobie, *Drummond,*	
Robertson	
MacRorie, MacRory,	
MacDonald	
MacRuer, *MacDonald*	

NAME	CLAN
MacRurie, MacRury, *MacDonald*	
MacShimmie, *Fraser*	
MacSimon, *Fraser*	
MacSorley, *Cameron, Lamont, MacDonald*	
MacSporran, *MacDonald*	
MacSuain, *Macqueen*	
MacSwan, *MacDonald, Macqueen*	
MacSween, *Macqueen*	
MacSymon, *Fraser*	
*MacTaggart, *Ross*	
MacTause, *Campbell of Argyll*	
*MacTavish, *Campbell of Argyll*	
MacTear, *Macintyre, Ross*	
*MacThomas, *Campbell of Argyll, Mackintosh*	
MacTier, MacTire, *Ross*	
MacUlric, *Kennedy*	
MacUre, *Campbell of Argyll, MacIver*	
Macvail, *Cameron, MacKay, Mackintosh, Macpherson*	
MacVanish, *MacKenzie*	
MacVarish, *MacDonald of Clanranald*	
MacVeagh, *MacDonald, MacLean*	
MacVean, *MacBean*	
MacVey, *MacDonald, MacLean*	
MacVicar, *Campbell, MacNaughton*	
MacVinish, *MacKenzie*	
MacVurie, *MacDonald of Clanranald*	
MacVurrich, *MacDonald of Clanranald, Macpherson*	
MacWalrick, *Kennedy*	
MacWalter, *MacFarlane*	
MacWattie, *Buchanan*	
MacWhannell, *MacDonald*	
MacWhirr, *Macquarrie*	
MacWhirter, *Buchanan*	
MacWilliam, *Gunn, MacFarlane*	

NAME	CLAN
Malcolmson, *MacCallum, MacLeod, Malcolm*	
Malloch, *MacGregor*	
Mann, *Gunn*	
Manson, *Gunn*	
Marr, *Gordon*	
Marshall, *Keith*	
Martin, *Cameron, MacDonald*	
Masterton, *Buchanan*	
Mathie, *Matheson*	
Maxwell, *Family*	
May, *MacDonald*	
Means, *Menzies*	
Meikleham, *Lamont*	
Mein, Meine, *Menzies*	
Melville (*see page* 254), *Family*	
Melvin, *MacBeth*	
Mengues, *Menzies*	
Mennie, *Menzies*	
Menteith, *Graham, Stewart*	
Meynars, *Menzies*	
Michie, *Forbes*	
*Middleton, *Innes*	
Miller, *MacFarlane*	
Milne-Gordon, *Innes, Ogilvie*	
Minn, *Menzies*	
Minnus, *Menzies*	
*Mitchell, *Innes*	
Moir, *Gordon*	
Monach, *MacFarlane*	
Monteith, *Graham, Stewart*	
Monzie, *Menzies*	
Moray, *Murray*	
More, *Leslie*	
Morgan, *MacKay*	
*Mowat, *Sutherland*	
*Muir, *Family*	
Munn, *Stewart*	
Murchie, *Buchanan, MacDonald, MacKenzie*	
Murchison, *Buchanan, MacDonald, MacKenzie*	
Murdoch, *MacDonald, Macpherson*	

NAME	CLAN
Murdoson, *MacDonald,* *Macpherson*	
Neil, Neill, *MacNeill*	
Neilson, *MacKay, MacNeill*	
Neish, *MacGregor*	
Nelson, *Gunn*	
Nicol, Nicoll, *MacNicol*	
Nicolson, *see* MacNicol	
*Nisbet, *Family*	
Nish, *MacGregor*	
Niven, *Cumin, MacIntosh,* *MacNaughton*	
Noble, *MacIntosh*	
Norman, *MacLeod of Harris*	
*Oliphant, *Sutherland*	
Parlane, *MacFarlane*	
Paterson, *MacLaren*	
Patrick, *Lamont*	
Paul, *Cameron, MacIntosh,* *MacKay*	
Peter, *MacGregor*	
Philipson, *MacDonell of* *Keppoch*	
Pitullich, *MacDonald*	
Polson, *MacKay*	
Purcell, *MacDonald*	
Rae, *Macrae*	
Raeburn, *Family*	
*Rankin, *MacLean*	
*Rattray, *Murray*	
Reid, *Murray*	
Reid, *Robertson*	
Reoch, *Farquharson,* *MacDonald*	
Revie, *MacDonald*	
Riach, *Farquharson, MacDonald*	
Risk, *Buchanan*	
Ritchie, *MacIntosh*	
Robb, *MacFarlane, Robertson*	
Robinson, *Gunn*	
Robson, *Gunn*	
*Rollo, *Family*	
Ronald, *MacDonell of Keppoch*	
Ronaldson, *MacDonell of* *Keppoch*	

NAME	CLAN
Rorison, *MacDonald*	
Roy, *Robertson*	
Ruskin, *Buchanan*	
*Russell, *Family*	
*Ruthven, *Family*	
Sanderson, *MacDonell of* *Glengarry*	
Sandison, *Gunn*	
Scobie, *Mackay*	
Scobie, *Mackay*	
*Seaton, *Family.*	
Shannon, *MacDonald*	
Sim, Sime, *Fraser*	
Simon, *Fraser*	
Simpson, *Fraser*	
Small, *Murray*	
Sorley, *Cameron, Lamont,* *MacDonald*	
Spalding, *Murray*	
Spence, *MacDuff*	
Spens, *MacDuff*	
Sporran, *MacDonald*	
Stalker, *MacFarlane*	
Stark, *Robertson*	
*Sturrock, *Family*	
Swan, *Macqueen*	
Swanson, *Gunn*	
Syme, *Fraser*	
Symon, *Fraser*	
Taggart, *Ross*	
Tarrill, *MacIntosh*	
Tawesson, *Campbell of Argyll*	
*Taylor, *Cameron*	
Thomas, *Campbell of Argyll*	
Thomason, *Campbell of Argyll,* *MacFarlane*	
Thompson, Thomson, *Campbell of Argyll*	
Tolmie, *MacLeod*	
Todd, *Gordon*	
Tosh, *MacIntosh*	
Toshach, *MacIntosh*	
Toward, Towart, *Lamont*	
Train, *MacDonald*	
Turner, *Lamont*	

NAME	CLAN
Tweedie, *Fraser*	
Tyre, *Macintyre*	
Ure, *Campbell of Argyll, MacIver*	
Vass, *Munro, Ross*	
Wallis, *Wallace*	
Walters, *Forbes*	
Wass, *Munro, Ross*	
Watson, *Buchanan*	
Watt, *Buchanan*	
Weaver, *MacFarlane*	
*Weir, *Buchanan, MacFarlane, MacNaughton*	
*Wemyss, *MacDuff*	
Whannell, *MacDonald*	
White, Whyte, *Lamont, MacGregor*	
Wilkinson, *MacDonald*	
Will, *Gunn*	
Williamson, *Gunn, Mackay*	
*Wilson, *Gunn*	
*Wotherspoon, *Family*	
Wright, *Macintyre*	
Wylie, *Gunn, MacFarlane*	
Yuill. Yuille, Yule, *Buchanan*	

PERSONAL NAMES IN ENGLISH AND GAELIC

Names of Men

Adam, *Adhamh*
Albert, *Albert*
Alexander, *Alasdair*
Allan, *Ailean*
Alpin, *Ailpein*
Andrew, *Aindrea*
Angus, *Aonghas*
Archibald, *Gilleasbuig*
Arthur, *Artair*
Aulay, *Amhladh*

Barry, *Barra*
Bartholomew, *Parlan*
Benjamin, *Beathan*
Bernard, *Bearnard*

Callum, *Calum*
Charles, *Teàrlach*
Christopher, *Gillecriosd*
Colin, *Cailean*
Coll, *Colla*
Conall, *Connull*

Daniel, *Daniel*
David, *Daibhidh*
Dermid, *Diarmad*
Donald, *Dòmhnull*
Dugald, *Dùghall*
Duncan, *Donnochadh*

Edward, *Eideard*
Evander, *Iamhair*, *Iomhar*
Ewen, *Eòbhann*, *Eoghan*

Farquhar, *Fearchar*
Fergus, *Fearghas*
Fingal, *Fionn*
Finlay, *Fionnla*, *Fionnlagh*
Francis, Frank, *Frang*

Gavin, *Gabhan*
Geoffrey, *Goieidh*
George, *Seòras*, *Deòrsa*
Gerald, *Gearald*
Gilbert, *Gilleabart*, *Gillebride*
Gilchrist, *Gillecriosd*
Gillies, *Gilliosa*
Godfrey, *Goraidh*, *Guaidhre*
Gordon, *Gòrdan*
Gregor, *Griogair*

Harold, *Harailt*
Hector, *Eachunn*
Henry, *Eanruig*
Hugh, *Aoidh*, *Uisdean*, *Huisdean*

James, *Seumas*
John, *Iain*, *Eoin*
Joseph, *Joseph*, *Seòsaidh*

Kenneth, *Coinneach*

Lachlan, *Lachunn*, *Lachlann*
Laurence, *Labhriunn*
Lewis, Louis, *Luthais*
Ludovic, *Maldònuich*
Luke, *Lùcais*

Magnus, *Manus*
Malcolm, *Calum*
Martin, *Màrtainn*
Matthew, *Mata*
Maurice, *Maolmuire*
Michael, *Micheil*
Murdoch, *Muireach*, *Murchadh*
Myles, *Maol-Moire*

Neil, *Niall*
Nicol, *Neacail*
Ninian, *Ringean*
Norman, *Tormoid, Tormod*

Oliver, *Olaghair*
Owen, *Aoghann*

Patrick, *Pàdruig, Pàruig*
Paul, *Pòl*
Peter, *Peadair*
Philip, *Philip*

Ranald, *Raonull*
Richard, *Ruiseart*

Robert, *Raibeart, Rob*
Roderick, *Ruairidh*
Ronald, *Raonull*
Rory, *Ruairidh*
Roy, *Ruadh*

Samuel, *Samuel, Somhairlè*
Simon, *Sim, Sime*
Somerled, *Somhairlè*
Stephen, *Steaphan*

Thomas, *Tòmas, Tàmhas*
Torquil, *Torcull, Torcall*

Walter, *Bhaltair*
William, *Uilleam*

Names of Women

Agnes, *Una*
Alice, *Ailis*
Amelia, *Aimili*
Angelica, *Aingealag*
Ann, *Anna*
Annabella, *Anabladh,*
    Barabal
Barbara, *Barbara*
Beatrice, *Beitiris*
Bessie (Elizabeth), *Ealasaid*
Betsy, Betty, *Beitidh*
Bethia, *Beathag*
Bridget, *Bride*

Catherine, *Catriona*
Cecilia, *Sileas*
Christina, *Cairistiona*
Clara, Clare, *Sorcha*
Diana, *Diana*
Dora, *Doireann*
Dorcas, *Deporodh*
Dorothy, *Diorbhàil,*
    Diorbhorgail

Effie (Euphemia), *Aoirig,*
    Eighrig

Eileen, *Eibhlin*
Elaenor, *Eilionoir*
Elizabeth, *Ealasaid*
Ellen, *Eilidh*
Emily, *Aimil*
Euphemia, *Aoirig, Eighrig*
Eve, *Eubh*
Flora, *Fionnaghal, Flòraidh*
Frances, *Frangag*

Grace, *Giorsal*
Grizel, *Giorsal*

Hannah, *Una*
Helen, *Eilidh*
Henrietta, Harriet, *Eiric*

Isabella, *Iseabal*

Jane, *Sine*
Janet, *Seònaid*
Jean, *Sine*
Jessie, *Sesi*
Johann, *Siubhan*
Judith, *Siubhan*
Julia, *Sileas*

Kate, *Ceit*

Lilias, *Lileas*
Lily, *Lili*
Louisa, *Liùsadh*
Lucy, *Liùsadh*

Mabel, *Moibeal*
Margaret, *Mairghread, Peigi*
Margery, *Marcail*
Marion, *Muireall*
Marjory, *Marsali*
Martha, *Moireach*
Mary, *Màiri, Moire, Muire*
Mildred, *Milread*
Molly, *Malai*

Muriel, *Muireall*

Nelly, *Neilli*

Rachel, *Raoghnailt, Raonaild*
Rosemary, *Rosmairi*

Sally, *Mòrag, Sàlaidh*
Sarah, *Mòr, Mòrag*
Sheila, *Silis, Sile*
Sophia, *Beathag*
Susan, *Siusaidh, Siùsan*
Sybil, *Sibeal*

Winifred, *Una*

55B.C. Julius Cæsar(102-44 B.C.)
landed in Britain.

80A.D. Julius Agricola invades
" Scotland."

84 Mons Graupius.

121 Hadrian's Wall.

139 Antonine's Wall. Also
known as Graham's
Dyke.

209 Campaign of Severus.

397 St. Ninian in Galloway.

501 Scots settle in Argyll.

563 St. Columba arrives at
the island of Iona.

575 Treaty of Drumceat.

597 Death of St. Columba.

606 Death of King Aidan of
Dalriada.

685 Battle of Nectansmere.

794 Beginning of Norse invasion of Scotland.

802 Danes plunder Iona.

843 Kenneth MacAlpin, king
of Picts and Scots.

942 Malcolm I crowned.

977 Battle of Luncarty.

1005 Malcolm II crowned.

1018 Battle of Carham.
Strathclyde annexed by
King of Scots.

1040 King Duncan murdered.
Macbeth crowned king.

1069 Marriage of Malcolm
Ceanmore and Mar-
garet.

1093 Deaths of Malcolm and
Margaret.

1098 Magnus Barefoot claims
Western Isles.

1107 Alexander I crowned.

1124 David I crowned king.

1130 Province of Moray forfeited to the Crown.

1138 Battle of the Standard.

1153 Malcolm IV crowned.
Rise of Somerled.

1160 Galloway subjected to
the Crown.

1164 Death of Somerled.

1174 Treaty of Falaise.

1179 Province of Ross sub-
dued by William the
Lion (1143-1214).

1180 Inverness received Charter from William the
Lion (1143-1214).

1214 Alexander II(1198-1249)
made king.

1222 Alexander II(1198-1249)
conquers Argyll.

1238 Glenmasan MS. written.

1249 Alexander II died at
Kerrera.
Alexander III crowned.

1263 Battle of Largs fought.

1266 Western Isles annexed
by the Crown.

1274 Robert the Bruce born.

1286 Death of Alexander III.

1290 Death of the Maid of
Norway.

1296 Invasion of Scotland by
Edward I of England.
Ragman's Roll issued.
Revolt of Wallace.
Franco-Scottish Alli-
ance signed.

1297 Battle of Stirling Bridge.

1298 Battle of Falkirk.

1305 Execution of Wallace.

1306 Red Comyn killed at
Dumfries by Bruce.
Coronation of Robert
the Bruce at Scone.

1308 Battle of the Pass of
Brander.

1314 Battle of Bannockburn.

1320 Letter to the Pope
asserting the Indepen-
dence of Scotland.

1326 First Scottish Parliament met.

1328 Treaty of Northampton.

1329 Death of Robert the
Bruce.
Accession of David II.

1332	Edward Balliol invades Scotland.
	Battle of Dupplin.
1333	Battle of Halidon Hill.
1346	Battle of Neville's Cross.
1371	Accession of Robert II, first of the Stewart Kings.
1388	Battle of Otterburn.
1396	Clan battle at Perth.
1406	James I (1394-1437) captured by English.
1411	Battle of Harlaw.
1412	Foundation of St. Andrew's University.
1424	James I allowed to return to Scotland.
1427	Parliament at Inverness when James I ordered the imprisonment of 50 Highland Chiefs.
1429	Battle of Drumnacoub.
1437	Assassination of James I at Perth.
1451	Foundation of Glasgow University.
1452	Earl of Douglas killed.
1455	Downfall of the Black Douglases.
1460–1530	William Dunbar, poet and priest.
1460	Death of James II.
1466	Battle of Blair-na-Park.
1468	Orkney and Shetland Islands acquired by Scotland from Norway.
1480	Battle of Bloody Bay, near Tobermory.
1488	Battle of Sauchieburn.
	Assassination of James III by rebels.
1493	End of the Lordship of the Isles.
	James IV visited Dunstaffnage and Mingarry Castles.
1495	James IV visited the Western Highlands.
	Foundation of King's College, Aberdeen.
1496	Education Act passed.

1498–99	James IV visits the Western Highlands.
1503	Insurrection of Donald Dubh.
1506–1582	George Buchanan, historian, humanist and reformer.
1507	Printing introduced to Scotland by Miller.
1512	Compilation of the Book of Lismore begun.
1513	Battle of Flodden.
	Death of James IV.
1529	John Armstrong and his followers hanged by order of James V.
1532-34	Expedition of James V to the Highlands.
1540	James V toured the Western Isles.
1542	Rout of Solway Moss.
	Death of James V.
	Birth of Mary, Queen of Scots, at Linlithgow.
1544	English Expedition to the Western Isles.
	Battle of Blar-na-leine.
1547	Battle of Pinkie.
1550	Death of Mackinnon, the last abbot of Iona.
1557	The First Covenant.
1561	Queen Mary returns to Scotland from France.
1562	Queen Mary visits Inverness.
1567	Knox's Liturgy translated into Gaelic by Bishop Carswell.
1568	Battle of Langside.
1569	Mary MacLeod (Mairi Nighean Alasdair Ruaids, 1569-1674) Gaelic poetess, born.
1570	The murder of Regent Moray by nobles.
1571	Regent Lennox slain.
1572	Death of John Knox.
	Death of Regent Mar.
1579	Bible printed in Scotland for first time.

1582	Foundation of Edinburgh University.
1587	Act for quieting the Clans of the Borders, Highlands, and Isles.
1588–89	Spanish Armada ship sunk at Tobermory.
1594	Battle of Glenlivet.
1597	Highlanders give assistance to Queen Elizabeth I of England.
1598	Highland Landowners ordered to prove their right to possess titles. Lewis granted to Lowland " Adventurers."
1600	Gowrie conspiracy.
1601	Lowland "Adventurers" in Lewis defeated.
1602	Battle of Glenfruin.
1603	Union of the Crowns.
1605	Renewed attempt to colonise Is. of Lewis by "Adventurers."
1607	MacKenzie of Kintail acquires Lewis.
1609	" Statutes of Iona."
1614	Islay granted to Campbell of Cawdor.
1625	Death of James VI.
1633	Charles I (1600-49) visits Scotland.
1638	The National Covenant.
1643	Solemn League and Covenant signed.
1644	Battle of Tippermuir.
1644–45	Campaign of Marquis of Montrose.
1645	Battle of Inverlochy. Montrose ravages Argyll. Battle of Philiphaugh : Montrose defeated. Battle of Auldearn.
1647	Garrison of Dunaverty massacred by General Leslie.
1649	Execution of Charles I. Charles II (1630-85) proclaimed king.
1650	Execution of Montrose. Battle of Dunbar. Battle of Invercarron.

1651	Battle of Inverkeithing. Battle of Worcester.
1653	Scotland taken under the Protectorate.
1660	Restoration of Charles II to the throne.
1661	Execution of the Marquis of Argyll.
1666	Pentland Rising occurred in the North.
1678	Invasion of the South-West of Scotland by the "Highland Host."
1679	Battle of Drumclog. Battle of Bothwell Bridge.
1685	Death of Charles II. Earl of Argyll's Invasion of Scotland. Execution of the Earl of Argyll at Edinburgh.
1689	James VII deposed. Battle of Killiecrankie. Battle of Dunkeld.
1692	Massacre of the MacIans by government troops at Glencoe.
1698	Darien Expedition.
1701	Alexander MacDonald (Alastair Macmhaighster Alastair, 1701-80) the Gaelic poet, born.
1702	Death of William II.
1707	Union of Parliaments.
1714	Death of Queen Anne. Rob MacKay (d. 1778) Gaelic poet, born.
1715	First Jacobite Rising. Battle of Sheriffmuir.
1716	Dugald Buchanan (1716-68) Gaelic poet, born.
1719	Jacobite Rising. Battle of Glenshiel.
1724	Duncan Ban Macintyre (1724-1812) born.
1725	General Wade appointed Commander-in-Chief in the Highlands of Scotland. Road construction begins in the Highlands.

1727	Death of George I.
1729	Independent Cos. begun.
1736	James Macpherson (Ossian) (1736-96) born at Ruthven.
1739	Black Watch raised.
1743	The potato introduced into the Highlands.
1745-46	Last Jacobite Rising.
1745	Prince Charles raises the Stewart Banner at Glenshiel. Battle of Prestonpans.
1746	Battle of Falkirk. Battle of Culloden. Highland dress proscribed by Parliament.
1759	Robert Burns (1759-96) born at Alloway.
1760	Death of George II.
1767	First New Testament in Gaelic printed.
1770	James Hogg, poet, born (1770-1835).
1771	Sir Walter Scott born in Edinburgh (1771-1832).
1775	Ewan MacLachlan, Gaelic poet, born. Penal Statutes against Clan Gregor repealed.
1777	Highland Light Infantry raised.
1778	Seaforth Highlanders raised
1779	John Galt, Scottish author, born (1779-1839).
1780	Thomas Chalmers, Scottish divine and humanist, born in Anstruther (Fife) (1780-1847).
1782	Act proscribing Highland dress repealed.
1783-1801	First Gaelic Bible published.
1788	Prince Charles Edward died (1720-88).
1793	Cameron Highlanders raised.
1794	Argyll and Sutherland Highlanders raised.

1794	Gordon Highlanders raised.
1802	Hugh Miller, geologist and author, born Cromarty (1802-56).
1804	Dr. John MacLachlan, of Rahoy (1804-1874), Gaelic poet, born.
1808	Evan MacColl (d. 1898), Gaelic poet, born. William Livingstone (1808-1870), Gaelic poet, born.
1813	David Livingstone born Blantyre (1813-1873).
1815	Battle of Waterloo.
1818	Dugald Macphail born.
1822	Visit of George IV to Scotland.
1824	George MacDonald born (1824-1905).
1834	Mrs. Mary Mackellar (1834-1890), Gaelic poetess, born.
1842	Queen Victoria's first visit to Scotland.
1843	Neil MacLeod, Gaelic poet, born.
1850	R. L. Stevenson born Edinburgh (1850-94).
1864	Neil Munro, author and poet, born (d. 1930).
1886	Crofters' Act passed.
1912	The Scottish Land Court entered on its duties.
1914-1918	The First World War.
1921	Scottish Railways absorbed into L.N.E.R. and L.M.S. lines.
1928	Grampian Hydro-Electric Power Scheme initiated.
1929	Union of Church of Scotland and United Free Church.
1934	Cunard White Star liner Queen Mary launched at Clydebank.

1938 Cunard White Star liner *Queen Elizabeth* launched at Clydebank.

1939-45 Second World War.

1947 Edinburgh Festival of Music and Drama, also Film Festival, inaugurated.

Marriage of Princess Elizabeth and Duke of Edinburgh in Westminster Abbey.

1948 King George VI confers dignity of " Royal" on Highland and Agricultural Society of Scotland.

1952 Death of George VI; Accession of Elizabeth.

1955 Crofters' Commission set up with headquarters in Inverness.

1959 Dounreay, world's largest atomic reactor, opened.

1963 Series of VHF sound and TV relay stations built in Highlands.

Highland Transport Board appointed to report on railway proposals.

1964 Forth Road Bridge completed.

Foundation of Strathclyde University.

1965 Highlands and Islands Development Board established to promote economic and social development of the crofting counties.

1972 North Sea Oil boom.

1973 U.K. joined the Common Market.

GLOSSARY OF SCOTTISH PLACE-NAMES, ETC.

including Gaelic and other elements

AIDS TO PRONUNCIATION

Initial Bh or Mh, equals *v*, but after a broad vowel
        equals *w*, as in English " now."
    ,,   C equals *k*.
    ,,   Fh is silent.
    ,,   Ph equals *f*.
    ,,   Sh or Th equals *h*.
    ,,   S after an t—is silent.
Final—aidh equals *y* as in *my*.
    ,, —idh equals *y* as in *duty*.
Th final or when flanked with vowels, is a strong
    breathing.
Ch in contact with *a*, *o* or *u*, is a strong guttural as in
    loch.
Ch in contact with *e* or *i*, is a guttural as in German
    ich.

The Article:—

A'	equals	*the* as	in	A' Chreag—*the rock*.
Am	,,	,,	,,	Am Boc—*the buck*.
An t-	,,	,,	,,	An t-Eilean Sgitheanach—*the isle of Skye*.
Na	,,	,,	,,	Na Bruthaichean—*the braes*.
a'	,,	*of the*	,,	Alt a' Choire Dhuibh—*burn of the black corrie*.
an t-	,,	,,	,,	Bàgh an t-Siosalaich—*Chisholm's bay*.
na	,,	,,	,,	Slochd na Beinne—*hollow of mountain*.
nan	,,	,,	,,	Meall nan Eun—*hill of the birds*.
nam	,,	,,	,,	Coire nam Bò—*corrie of the cows*.

Abbreviations:—G. for Gaelic, N. for Norse, Sc. for
Scots.

Aber, *confluence* as in Aberdeen, Abergeldie, and Abernethy, *confluences* of the Don, Geldie and Nethy.

Abhainn, Aibhne, and Amhuinn, Aimhne (avin), *river*.

Acair, Acairseid (akir), *anchor* and *anchorage*.

Achadh, Achaidh, *a field*.

Agh, Aighe, Aighean, *hind, heifer*.

Ail, Aileach, or Aillig, *a rock* or *stony place*.

Ailean, Ailein (alen), *green spot, enclosure, meadow*.

Airidh, Airidhe, or Airigh, Airighe (ary), *sheiling*.

Aisir, Aisre (ashir), *a pass*.

Ald, Alt, Ault, Auld, G. Allt, *a burn, stream*, as in Aldclune, G. Allt Chluain, *burn of the meadow*. Altnabrae, G. Allt nam Breac, *trout burn*. Aultbea, G. Allt Beithe, *birch burn*. Auldearn G. Allt Eireann.

Amat -Amaite, N. Á-mót, *river meet, confluence.*

Annaid, Annaite, and Annat, *a mother church.*

Aoineadh, Aoinidh (oonu), *steep brae with rocks, moraine.*

Aonach, Aonaich (oon-ach), *moor or market-place.*

Arbhar, Arbhair (arv'ur), *corn.*

Ard, Airde, *a height, promontory,* e.g., Ardlamont, *height of Lamont.* Ardmeanach, *mid-height.*

Aros, N. ár-ós, *river mouth.*

Àth, Atha, *a ford; a kiln.*

Auch, Ach, G. Achadh, *a field.* Achanalt, G. Achadh nan Allt, *field of the burns.* Auchnashellach, G. Achadh nan Seileach, *field of the willows.*

Avon, G. Abhainn, *q.v.*

Ay, *Island,* from N. ey.

Bà, bò, *cow.*

Bac, Bhaic, Bacaichean, *bank, peat bank.*

Bad, Bhaid, *a tuft, a clump of trees or shrubs,* also *a place.*

Bàgh, Bhàigh, *a bay.*

Baile, Bhaile (balu), *a town* or *hamlet, homestead.*

Bal and Ball as a prefix is from G. Baile, *q.v.,* e.g., Balnagown, G. Bail'a' Ghobhainn, *the Smith's town.*

Balgair, Bhalgair, *a fox, a dog.*

Balloch, G. Bealach (byal'uch), *a pass.*

Bàn, Bhàn, Bhàin, Bana, *fair, white.*

Ban-righ (baunri), *queen.*

Bar, *headland.*

Bàrd, Bhàird, (1) *a poet,* (2) *an enclosed meadow* (Scots word).

Barpa (Hebrides and Skye), *a rude, conical heap of stones, sepulchral,* Eng. *barrow.*

Bàta, Bhàta, Bàtaichean, *a boat, boats.*

Bàthaich, Bhàthaich (ba-hach), *byre, sanctuary* (in deer forests), *shelter.*

Beag, Bheag, Bhig, Bige, Beaga (beg), *little.*

Bealach, Bhealaich (byal'-uch), *a pass.*

Bealaidh, Bhealaidh, *broom.*

Bean, Mnà, Ban (ben), *wife, woman.*

Beàrn, *a gap.*

Beinn, Bheinn, or Beinne (ben), *mountain.*

Beith, Bheithe (be), *birch.*

Beithir, Bheithir, *e.g.,* Beinn a' Bheithir,(be-hir),*serpent,wild beast, monster, thunderbolt.*

Ben, G. Beinn, *mountain* (originally *horn, peak),* e.g. Ben Wyvis, G. Beinn Uais, *high mountain,* Ben Macdui, G. Beinn Mhic Duibhe, *Mc-Duff's mountain.*

Beul, Beòil, Bheòil (bial), *mouth.*

Biast, Béiste, *beast, monster.*

Bield, Sc. *shelter.*

Binnean, Binnein (binen), *small and peaked mountain,* e.g., Ban An (Trossachs), G. Am Beinnean, *the little pinnacle.*

Biolaire, Bhiolaire,*water-cresses.*

Biorach, Bioraiche (beerich), (1) adj. *sharp-pointed,* (2) noun *dog-fish.*

Blair, G. Blàr, *q.v., peatmoss.*

Blàr, Bhlàir, *cleared space, plain.*

Bó, Bà, *cow,* e.g., Bealach nam Bó, *Pass of the cattle.*

Bodach, Bhodaich, *old man; spectre.*

Bog, Bhuig, (1) adj. *soft;* (2) noun *a soft place.*

Bogha, Bhodha, or Bodha Bhodha (boa and voa), (N. Booi, *a breaker), sunken rock.*

Borg, N., *a fortress.*

Both, Bothan or Bothain, *a stone or turf house; bothy.*

Bradan, Bhradain, *salmon.*

Brae, Bread—G. Bràigh, *upper part.* Braemar, G. Braigh Mhàr, *height of Mar.* Breadalbane, G. Bràghad Albainn, *height of Alba (i.e.,* Scotland).

Bràigh, Bhraghad, *upper part.*

Breac, Bhreac, Bhric, Brice, Breaca(brec), (1) adj. *speckled,* (2) noun *trout.*

Breug, Breugach, or Bréige (breg), *false, applied to stone cairns erected on mountains as guides;* e.g., Buachaille Bréige, *false shepherd.*

Broc, Bhruic, *the badger.*

Brochan, Bhrochain, *literally gruel* or *porridge, but applied in place-names to anything broken up or comminuted, as:* Coire Bhrochain (Cairngorms), *the corrie of the broken stones.*

Bruach, Bhruaich, or Bruthach, Bhruthaich (broo-uch), *bank, brink, steep place, brae.*

Buachaille, Bhuachaille (boouchilu) *herdsman,* e.g., Buachaille Etive, *Watchman of Etive.*

Buidhe, Bhuidhe (buie and vuie), *yellow.* Buidheanaich, *yellow place.*

Bun (boon) *literally root, but in place-names generally applied to the mouth of a river or stream, as in* Bunaven (G. Bun na h-Aibhne), Bunawe, Bunchrew (Inverness), G. Bun chraobh, *bottom of the wood.*

Bùirich, Bhùirich, *roar, bellow,* e.g., Meall a' Bhùirich.

Cadha (caa), *steep place; a pass*

Cailleach, Caillich, *a nun; old woman; hag* (of bodach).

Caipleach, Caiplich, *place of horses.*

Cairn, G. Càrn, *heap of stones, rocky hill,* e.g., Cairntoul, G. Càrn an t-Sabhail, *hill of the barn.*

Cala or Caladh, *a harbour.*

Calltuinn (caultin), *hazel.*

Calman, Calmain, or Calaman, Calamain, or Columan, *a dove.*

Cam, Chaim, *crooked.*

Camas, Chamais, *a channel, a bay,* in inland places *a bend.*

Cambus, G. Camas, *q.v.,* e.g., Cambusmore, G. Camas Mór, *big bend.*

Canach, Chanaich, *cotton grass.*

Caochan, Chaochain, *a streamlet.*

Caol, Caolas, Chaolais, *narrow, strait, firth, kyle,* e.g., An Caol Arcach, *the Pentland Firth.*

Caora, Caorach (cooru), *sheep.*

Caorann, Chaorainn, *rowan tree* or *mountain ash.*

Capull, Chapuill, *horse* or *mare.*

Car, *bend,* e.g., Bealach Carach, *the winding pass.*

Càrn, Chùirn, or Chàrn (karn), *heap of stones, applied to round rocky hills.*

Càrr, or Càthair (kaar), *rough or broken mossy ground.*

Carse, Sc. *alluvial land beside a river.*

Cas, Caise, *steep.*

Cat, Chait, *a cat.*

Ceann, Chinn (kyann), *head, a headland.*

Ceapach, Cheapaich, *a tillage. plot.*

Cearc, Circe (kiarc), *a hen.* Cearc-fhraoich, *moor-hen, grouse.*

Cearcall, Chearcaill, *a circle, a hoop,* e.g., Coire Chearcaill.

Ceàrd, Ceardach, Cheàrdaich (kyard), *craftsman, smithy, forge.*

Ceò, Cheathaich, *mist,* e.g., Coire Cheathaich, *the misty corrie.*

Chullish, *strait.*

Cill, Cille, Ceall, *church, burying-place,* e.g., Cille Mhuire, *St. Mary's Church.*

Cìoch, Cìche (ciach), *a pap.* Beinn nan Cìochan, *hill of the paps* (old name for Lochnagar).

Clach, Cloiche, *stone,* e.g., Clach Dhìon, *shelter stone.*

Clachan, *place of stones, a stone house*, especially *a cell* or *church; hamlet.*

Cladach, Chladaich (kladuch), *shore, beach.*

Claidheamh,Chlaidhimh(clyiv), *sword.*

Claigionn (clycum), *skull head, rounded hillock.*

Clamhan, Clamhain (clavan), *kite, buzzard.*

Cleit, Chleit, N. *rocky eminence.*

Close, Sc. *passage leading to a " land."*

Cluain (cloo-ain), *a green plain, pasture.*

Clunie, Cluanie—G. Cluainigh, *meadow-place, e.g.,* Clunie in Badenoch.

Cnàimh, Cnàmha, *bones.*

Cnap, Chnaip (krap), *a hillock.*

Cneamh, Chneamh, or Creamh, Chreamha (crev), *wild garlic.*

Cnoc, Chnuic (krock), *a round hill.*

Coileach, Choilich (culuch), *a cock.*

Coill, Coille, *wood, forest.*

Còinneach, Chòinnich (co'ny-ach), *moss.* Chòinneachan, *place of moss.*

Coir', Coire, Choire, *a round hollow in mountain-side; cirque, a corrie.*

Con, Choin, *dog; see* Cù.

Craig, G. Creag, *q.v.,* Craig-house, *rock house.* Craigen-doran, G. Creag an Dóbhrain, *rock of the otter.*

Crannog, *lake-dwelling.*

Craobh, Craoibhe (croov), *tree.*

Crasg, Chraisg, Chroisg, *a crossing.*

Creachann, Creachainn, *the bare, wind-swept place about the top of a hill.*

Creag, Chreag, Creige, *a crag, rock* or *cliff.* Conchreag, *combination of rocks.*

Crìoch, Crìche (cree-uch), *boundary, e.g.,* Allt na Crìche, *burn of the boundary.*

Crò, Crotha, Croithean, *sheep cot, pen.*

Cròcach, Cròcaich, *branched, antlered.*

Crodh, Chruidh (kro), *cattle.*

Crom, Cruime, *crooked.*

Crosg, *see* Crasg.

Cruach, Chruach, Chruaich (cruach), *a heap, stack, bold hill.*

Cruachan (kruach'an), *a haunch,* Cruachan Beann, *haunch of peaks.*

Cù, Con, or Choin, *dog.*

Cuach, Chuaich, Cuaiche (coo-ach), *a cup-shaped hollow.*

Cùil (cool), *nook, recess.*

Cuilc, Cuilce (coolc), *a reed.*

Cuileann, Chuilinn, *holly.*

Cuith, Cuithe, *pit, wreath of snow, narrow glen.*

Cùl, Chùil, Cùile (cool), *back, hill-back, nook.*

Culloden, G. Cuil-lodair, *nook of the marsh.*

Cumhann, Cumhainn, Cuinge, *narrow; a strait.*

Dal, Dall—When used as a prefix it is from G. Dail; as an affix it is generally from N. Dair, *a dale, e.g.,* Dalna-spidal, G. Dail na Spideil, *field of the hostel.* Netherdale, N. Nedri-dalr, *lower dale.*

Damh, Daimh (dav), *ox, stag.*

Darach, Daraich, *oak.*

Dearcag, *a berry.*

Dearg, Dheirg (jarg), *red.*

Diebidale, N. *deep dale.*

Diollaid, Diollaide (jee-ulig), *saddle, e.g.,* Beinn na Diol-laide, *hill of the saddle.*

Doire, Dhoire, *grove, hollow.*

Doirlinn, Doirlinne, or Doir-ling, Doirlinge (dorlin), *isthmus, beach.*

Dour, *water.*

Drem, Drom, Drum—G. Druim, *q.v., e.g.,* Drumna-drochid, G. Druim na Dro-chaide, *ridge of the bridge.*

Drochaid, Drochaide, *bridge.*

Druim, Droma, *a ridge, the back.*

Drummond, G. Druiminn, old locative case of drum "*at ridge.*"

Dubh,Dhubh,Dhuibh,Duibhe, Dubha (doo), *black.*

Duine, Dhaoine, or Daoine (doonu), *a man, men.*

Dùn, Dùin, or Dhùin (doon), *fortress, castle, heap, mound.*

Dun, G. Dùn, *q.v., e.g.,* Dumbarton, G. Dùn Breatunn, *fortress of the Britons.*

Each, Eich (ech), *horse.*

Eadar, *between, appears in place-names as* Eadar Da Chaolas, *between two kyles.* Eadar Da Fhaoghail, *between two fords.* Eadar Da Ghobhal, *between two forks.*

Eaglais,Eaglaise(eglish),*church.*

Eala, Ealachan, *swan or swans.*

Earth-house, *Pict's house.* Weem, *a primitive drystone building constructed just under the surface of the ground.*

Eas, Easa, Easan (es), *waterfall; rough ravine* (Perthshire).

Easg (obs.), *a marsh.*

Eilean, Eilein, Eileanan (elan), *island or islands.*

Eilrig, *deer pass, place where deer were killed or captured.*

Ear (er), *East.*

Eccles, G. Eaglais, *a church, e.g.,* Ecclefechan, *Church of St. Fechan.*

Eun, Eòin (en), *bird or birds.*

Fad, Fhad, Fhada, Fada, *long.*

Fail, *cliff.*

Faire (feru), *watching.*

Fang, Faing, or Fhaing, *sheep-pen, fank.*

Faoghail, or Faodhail (faŏ-ul), *a ford in sea channel.*

Faoileag, Faoileige, *sea gull.*

Feadan, Fheadain, *narrow glen or hollow, streamlet.*

Fear, Fir, Fhir, *a man.*

Feàrn, Fhearna, *alder tree.*

Féith, Féithe (fæ), *bog, slowly moving stream* (lit. *vein*).

Fell, N. Fjall, *a rough hill;* appears as a termination Val, *e.g.,* Screval, *scree fell.*

Feu, *perpetual leasehold.*

Fiadh, Fhéidh, *deer.*

Fionn, Fyne (fyunn), *white.*

Firth, Frith, *arm of the sea, estuary.*

Fuar (foor), *cold, e.g.,* Fuar-ghlaic, *cold hollow.* Fuara-laich and Fuaralacha, *cold place.* Fuar-Mhonadh, *cold mountain.*

Fuaran, Fhuarain, *well, spring; a green spot.*

Gabhar, Gabhair, or Gaibhre, also Góbhar, Gobhair, or Goibhre (ga-ar), *goat.*

Gair, Gare, *short, from* G. gearr.

Gamhainn, Gaimhne, or Gamhna (gav'inn), *a stirk.*

Gàradh, Ghàraidh (garu), *wall* or *dyke,* also *a garden.*

Garbh, Gharbh, Ghairbh, Gairbhe, Garba (garv),*rough.*

Gart, *enclosure.*

Gèadh, Gheòidh, *a goose.*

Geal, Gheal, Ghil, Gile, Geala (gyal), *white.*

Geàrr, *short.* Geàrr, Geàrrsaich, *a hare.*

Gearraidh, *sheiling, outer pastures* (Lewis).

Geodha, Geo, Gio, N. Gjá, *a chasm, rift.*

Gill, N., *a ravine, e.g.,* Trailigil, Troll-ravine.

Gineamh, Gainimh, or Gaineamhach, Gaineamhaich, *sand.*

Giubhar, Giuthas, Ghiubhais and Ghiubhsachan (geoo-us), *fir, place of firs.*

Glac, Glaic, *a hollow.*

Glais, *a stream.*

Glas, Ghlas, Ghlais, Glaise, Glasa, *grey or green.*

Gleann, Ghlinne, *narrow valley, dale, glen.*

Glen, G. Gleann, *q.v.*

Gob, Ghuib, *point, beak.*

Gobha, Ghobhainn (go-u), *blacksmith.*

Gobhar, *see* Gabhar.

Gobhlach, Ghobhlaich (goll-ach), *forked.*

Goe, *creek.*

Gorm, Ghorm, Ghuirme, Guirme, *green* and *blue.*

Grian, Gréine, *the sun.*

Guala or Gualann, Ghualainn (goo-ulin), *shoulder of a hill.*

Haugh, Sc. *alluvial land by river.*

Holm, G. Tuilm, *an island in a river or near the shore, from* N. Holmr.

Hope, *small bay, inlet,* N. húp.

Howe, Sc. *hollow.*

Howff, *haunt, favourite tavern.*

Iar, *west.*

Imrich, Imriche (irmich), *removing, flitting.*

Inbhir, Inbhire (invir), *place of meeting of river, or where a river falls into the sea or lake, confluence,* cf. Aber, Amat.

Inch, G. Innis, *q.v.*

Inghean, Inghinn (inyin), *daughter, same as Nighean.*

Innis, Innse, (1) *island,* (2) *meadow by the side of a river haugh,* (3) *resting place for cattle, etc.*

Inver, G. Inbhir, *q.v., e.g.,* Inverness, Inverey, *confluence of the Ness and Ey.*

Iodhlann, Iodhlainn, or Iolainn, Iolainne (yoolun), *corn-yard, barn-yard.*

Iolair, Iolaire (yulir), *eagle.*

Iosal, Isle (ess-ul), *low.*

Ken, Kin—G. Ceann, *a head, promontory, e.g.,* Kingussie, G. Ceann a' Ghiuthsaich, *head of the fir wood.* Kintail, G. Ceann an t-sàile, *end of*

the salt water. Kendrum, *head ridge.*

Keppoch, G. Ceapach, *a tillage plot.*

Kil, *cell, church.*

Killie, *wood,* from G. Coille.

Knock, G. Cnoc (crock), *a round hill, hillock.*

Kyle, G. Caol and Caolas, *a strait.*

Lag, Luig, *a hollow.*

Lagan, Lagain, *a little hollow.*

Lagg, Laggan, G. Lag and Lagan, *q.v.*

Làir, Làire, *mare.*

Làirig, Làirige (larig), *a pass.*

Land, Sc. *building divided into tenements.*

Laogh, Laoigh, *calf, e.g.,* Beinn Laogh, *Calf mountain.*

Law, Sc. *conical hill.*

Leabaidh, Leapa, *a bed, a lair,* as in Leabaidh an Fhéidh, *the deer's lair.*

Leac, Lice, or Lic, *flat stones.* Leacach, *stony slope.*

Learg, Leirge, *a plain, hillside.*

Leathad, Leathaid, *a slope.*

Leathann, Leathainn, or Leathan, Leathain (le-hun), *broad.*

Leith (leh), *half,* as in Leith-allt, *half-burn, i.e., burn with one steep side.*

Leitir, Leitire, Leitreach (ley-tir), *slope, side of a hill.*

Leum, Leuma (lem), *a leap.*

Liath, Léith, or Léithe (lee-uh), *grey.* Liathanaich, *greyness.*

Linn, Linne, *a pool, e.g.,* Braclinn (Callander), Linn of Dee (Braemar).

Loch, Locha, Lochan, Lochain, *lake, lakelet.*

Logie, *see* Lag.

Loinn, Loinne, *an enclosure, land.*

Lòn, Lòin (in Galloway, Lane), *marsh, morass, meadow* (in Skye a *slow stream*).

Long, Luinge (loong), *a ship.*

Losg, Loisgte, *burnt ground.*

Losgann, Losgainn, *frog* (common in Lewis place-names).

Luachrach, Luachraich (loo-uch-ruch), *place of rushes.*

Lùb, Lùib (loob), *a bend.*

Machar, Machair (machir), *a plain,* e.g., A'Mhachar (Durness), Machrihanish (Kintyre).

Madadh, Mhadaidh (mad-u), *dog, wolf, fox.*

Magh, Mhaigh, Mhagha, *a plain, a field.*

Maigheach, Mhaighiche (my-uch), *a hare.*

Mains, Sc. *home farm attached to manor house.*

Màm, Mhàim, lit. *a swelling;* in place-names, *large, round, or gently rising hill.*

Manach, Mhanaich, *a monk.* A'Mhanachainn, *the monastery.* (G. for Beauly and Fearn in E. Ross).

Maol, Maoile (mul), *bare top.*

Meadhon, Mheadhoin (me-un), *middle.*

Meall, Mhill (miaw), lit. *a lump, applied to a round hill.*

Meanabh-Chrodh, Meanabh-chruidh, *small or young cattle,* properly Meanbh; hence Ben Venue, G. A'Bheinn Mheanbh.

Meann, Mhinn (mia-un), *a kid.*

Mèinn, Mèinne, *ore,* e.g., Allt na Mèinne, *ore-burn.*

Meur, Meòir (mer), *finger, branches,* applied to small streams.

Mìn, Mìne (meen), *smooth.*

Mnà (mra), *wife,* genitive singular of Bean, *q.v.*

Mòd, Mhòid, *generally applied to a small knoll where court of justice sat in ancient times.*

Mòd, *an assembly held annually in a different place with the object of promoting the Gaelic cult.*

Mòine, Mòinteach, or Monadh, *peat, mossy ground (outer pasture in Lewis).*

Mol, Mal (mal), *shingly beach.* M. Möl, *pebbles.*

Monadh (mon-u), *hill, mountain,* as in Monadh-Ruadh, *red mountains* (Badenoch).

Mòr, Mhòr, Mhòir, Moire, *large, great*

Muc, Muice, *pig.* A'Mhuclach, *the piggery.*

Muileann, Mhuilinn (mooylen), *a mill.*

Muir, Mhara, or Mara, *the sea.*

Mult, Mhuilt (moolt), *wether.*

Muran, Mhurain (mooran), *sea, bent.*

Na, nan, nam, *of the.*

Nathair, Nathrach, Nathraichean (na-hir), *serpent.*

Nead, Nid (ned), *a nest.*

Ness, nish, *nose, headland.*

Nighean, Nighinn (nee-un), *daughter, young woman.*

Ob, Oba, Oban, *a bay,* from N. Hóp, *a bay* whence Longhope (Orkney).

Ochter, *upper, high-flying.*

Odar, Odhair, Uidhre, Idhir, *dun-coloured.*

Oidhche (oech-a), *night,* e.g., Airidh na h-Aon Oidhche, *sheiling of the one night* (Lewis). Loch na h-Oidhche, *night loch, a loch that fishes best at night.*

Oitir, Oitire (oytir), *sandbank.*

Or, Oir, *gold.*

Ord, Uird, *round hill:* Ordan, *a little round hill.*

Os, Ois, or Osa, *river mouth or outlet:* in Lewis, *slowly-moving water.*

Pàirc, Pàirce (parc), *a park, a field.*

Pait, Paite, Paitean, *a hump, place, ford,* or *fords.*

Pend, Sc. *archway.*

Pet or Pit, *farm* or *piece of land*, sometimes *a hollow*, e.g., *Pit*maduthy, G. Pit 'ic Dhuibh, *Macduff's steading*. Pitlochry, G. Baile chloichridh, *stone steading*. Same as G. baile.

Pictish Tower, *a round tower of defence, dating from the early Iron Age and chiefly found in Shetland, Orkney, and North Scotland.*

Pict's House, *see* Earth-house.

Policies, *private grounds attached.*

Poll, Phuill, *a pool* or *pit.*

Port, Phuirt, *port, harbour, ferry.*

Phreas, Phris, *bush, shrub, copse.*

Quoich, *cup*, from G. cuach.

Raineach, Rainich (ren-uch), *fern.*

Ràmh, Ràimh (rav), *an oar.*

Rath (ra), *fort.*

Rathad, Rathaid (ra-ud), *road, a way.*

Reamhar, Reamhair, Reamhra (rav'ar), *thick, fat.*

Réidh, Réidhe (re), *smooth, level, plain.*

Rhinns (reen), *peninsula.*

Riabhach, Riabhaich (riuvuch), *brindled, greyish.*

Rìgh, Rìghe (ree), *king* (Banrigh, *queen*).

Roinn, Roinne, *point, promontory.*

Ròn, Ròin, *a seal.*

Roost, N. *tidal current.*

Ross, *peninsula.*

Rubha (roo-u), *a spit, a promontory.*

Ruigh, Ruighe, Ruidh, Ruidhe, *a run for cattle, a shieling, land sloping up to a hill.*

Sabhal, Sabhail (sav'ull), *barn.*

Sac, Saic, *horse load, sack.*

Sagart, Sagairt (sagart), *priest.*

Saidhe, Saigh, Saighe, *bitch.*

Sàil, Sàile (sal) (1) *heel*, (2) *salt water.*

Saobhaidh, Saobhaidhe, Saobhaidhean, *fox-den.*

Scuir, Sgurr, *scar, steep rock.*

Sealg, Seilge (shalg), *hunt, hunting.*

Seamrag, Seamraig (shemrag), *trefoil* or *shamrock.*

Sean, Seana (shen), *old.*

Seangan, Seangain (sheng-an), *an ant.*

Searrach, Searraich (sharuch), *foal, colt.*

Seilich, Seilach, *willow.*

Sgadan, Sgadain, *herring.*

Sgarbh, Sgairbh (scarv), *the cormorant*, from N. skarv.

Sgeir, Sgeire (sker), *a sea rock.*

Sgoilt, Sgoilte (scut), *split, e.g.,* Clach Sgoilte, *split stone.*

Sgor, Sgòrr, or Sgùrr, *rocky peak.*

Sheiling, *summer pasture*, or *hut occupied by herdsmen when cattle are driven to the hills for summer grazing.*

Sian, Sìne, *storm.*

Sidhean, Sidhein (shee-an), *a hillock, fairy knoll.*

Sionnach, Sionnaich (shoonuch), *fox.*

Sleac, Slic, *flat stones* (Badenoch), same as Leac.

Sleamhuinn, Sleamhna (slev'-inn), *slippery.*

Slochd, Sloc, or Sluichd, *deep, hollow.*

Sneachd, Sneachda (shnechc), *snow.*

Socach, Socaich, *snout, projecting place, mossy ground between forks of streams*, often Anglicised as Succoth.

Speireag, Speireig (sperag), *sparrow-hawk.*

Spréidh, Spréidhe (spray), *cattle.*

Srath, Sratha (stra), *a strath, valley.*

Sròn, Sròine, *a nose* or *point.*

Sruth, Srutha, Sruthan, Sruthain, *current, a stream* (let).

Stac, Staca, *steep conical hill.*

Stob, *a point*. Stob mór, *big point* (Cuillins).

Strath, G. Srath, *q.v.*

Strone G. Sròn, *a nose promontory*, *e.g.*, Strone (Firth of Clyde). Strontian, G. Sròn an t-Sidhein, *promontory of the knoll*.

Struan, G. Sruthan, *a stream*, *current*.

Stùc, *a peak*, *e.g.*, Stùc Garbh Mór, *the big rough peak*.

Suidhe (soo-yu), *sitting or resting place, level shelf in a hillside*, so also Spardan, *a roost*.

Tacksman, *tenant, lessee*.

Tairbeart, Tairbeirt, Tarbert, Tarbet (teruburt), *a narrow isthmus*, hence the Tarberts on the west of Scotland.

Tarsuinn (tar-sinn), *transverse, across*

Tempull, Teampuill, *a temple* or *church*.

Tigh, Tighe, Tay, Ty (ty), *a house*, *e.g.*, Tighnabruaich, G. Tigh na Bruaich, *house of the bank*. Tayloin, G. Tigh an Lòin, *house by the marsh*. Tyndrum, G. Tigh an Droma, *house of the ridge*.

Tipper, G. Tobair, *a well*.

Tir, Tyre, *land*.

Tòb, *a bay* (Lewis), same as Ob, *q.v.*

Tobar, Tobair, Tober, *a well*.

Tolbooth, *prison*.

Toll, Tuill, *hole*.

Tom Tuim, *a round hillock*, *e.g.*, Tomnahurich, G. Tom na h-Iubhraich, *hillock of the yew wood*.

Tòn, Tòin, *buttock, haunch*.

Torc, Tuirc, *a boar*.

Torf, Torra, *a heap, hill, castle*.

Tràigh, Tràighe, and Tràghad (tray), (*sand*), *beach*.

Tron, *public weighing machine*.

Tulach, Tulaich (tooluch), *a knoll, a hillock*.

Tunnag, Tunnaig (toonag), *a duck*.

Uachdar, Uachdair (uach-cur), *top, upper part*.

Uaine (ua-nui), *green*.

Uamh, Uamha, Uaigh, Uaighe (uav), *cave*.

Uchd, *breast, an ascent;* Uchdan, *a short steep bank*.

Uidh (ooy), *isthmus, land or water, slowly moving water*.

Uig, *a nook, hollow*, or *bay*.

Uisg, Uisge (ooshcu), *water*.

Ulaidh (ooly), *treasure*.

Ulbh, Ulbhaidh (oolu), N. Ulfr, *a wolf*.

Uruisg (oorushc), *human monster, goblin, brownie, e.g.*, Coire an Uruisg (Loch Katrine), *Corrie of the monster*.

Val, (1) N. Fjall, *a high hill*, (2) Hvall, *a knoll*.

Vat, N. Vatn, *water, e.g.*, Loch Langavat, *long water* (Lewis).

Vik, *creek*, from N. vikn.

Voe, *bay, inlet, fiord*.

Weem, *cave* or *earth-house, q.v.*

Wynd, *narrow street* or *passage*.

GLOSSARY OF HERALDIC TERMS

Affronté, *front to front; looking frontwise.*

Argent, *silver.*

Armed, *having claws or talons of a different tincture from adjoining parts; reproduced with teeth, etc.*

Attired, *furnished with horns.*

Azure, *blue.*

Beaked, *beak of fowl of different tincture from body.*

Cabossed, *borne full-faced (e.g. of head of stag, etc.) and cut off close behind the ears; trunked.*

Charge, *a bearing.*

Couped, *head or limb cut off clean.*

Crined, *having hair tinctured differently from body.*

Crosslet, *a small cross.*

Cubit (*arm*), *forearm.*

Demi-, *half-sized.*

Dexter, *the right hand (side).*

Displayed, *having wings expanded.*

Embattled, *having an edge shaped like a battlement.*

Embowed, *crooked like a bow.*

Ensigned, *marked with a crown, coronet or mitre.*

Erased, *head or limb cut off with jagged edge.*

Erect, *upright.*

Ermine, *white with black triangular spots.*

Expanded, *spread.*

Fess, *broad band drawn horizontally across shield.*

Fessways, -wise, *horizontally.*

Field, *surface of shield or one of its divisions.*

Fitched, -ly, *fixed; applied to cross the lower extremity of which is sharpened to a point.*

Frame saw, *thin saw stretched in a frame to give it rigidity.*

Fructed, *having fruit*

Gules, *red.*

Imperially crowned, *said of charge represented with imperial crown.*

Inflamed, *depicted as in flames.*

Inverted, *turned inwards or towards the middle of the field.*

Langued, *represented with tongue of specified tincture.*

Masoned, *marked with lines representing divisions between blocks of stone.*

Naiant, *swimming.*

Or, *gold.*

Orle, *narrow border within the shield but removed from its edge.*

Pale, *vertical stripe or band in middle of shield.*

Paleways, -wise, *vertically.*

Pheon, *broad barbed arrow.*

Pommel, *knob terminating hilt of sword or dagger.*

Proper, *represented in the natural colouring.*

Rampant, *said of beast standing upright on hind legs; rearing.*

Sable, *black.*

Salient, *leaping.*

Saltire, *a St. Andrew's Cross.*

Sejant, *in sitting posture.*

Sinister, *left hand (side).*

Statant, *standing in profile, with feet on ground.*

Surmounted, *having above or on top of.*

Tincture, *shade of colour.*

Trippant, *said of animals walking with one fore-paw raised.*

Tyne, *prong; branch.*

Unguled, *with hoof or claws of a different tincture from the body.*

Vert, *green.*

Vested, *clothed.*

SOURCES OF FURTHER INFORMATION

TARTAN COLLECTIONS

The Scottish Tartans Society, founded 1962, has, at Comrie, Perthshire, probably the most extensive collection of tartans of all periods in existence, supplemented by a valuable library of books on the subject, and comprehensive files of information not hitherto generally accessible. The Society has acquired several collections including the MacGregor Hastie and a large portion of that of J. Telfer Dunbar—the last includes the gift of over 2,000 late eighteenth and early nineteenth century MS letters of Messrs Wilson of Bannockburn—and it has received many smaller but valuable gifts. Research is constantly being carried on into this great mass of material by a small band of experts, and the results are gladly put at the disposal of any enquirer at a nominal fee. The Society is supported by Members' subscriptions and Enquiry Fees, assisted by grants made by regional and national Education Authorities towards approved purchases. An exhibition is open free to the public during the tourist season at Comrie, Perthshire, where visitors are welcome.

The undernoted list gives the names of some other collections.
THE COCKBURN COLLECTION
  In the Mitchell Library, North Street, Glasgow.
THE HIGHLAND SOCIETY OF LONDON COLLECTION
  In the possession of the Society.
WEST HIGHLAND MUSEUM COLLECTION
  (Including the late Alexander Carmichael's collection.)
  In the West Highland Museum, Fort William.
NATIONAL MUSEUM OF ANTIQUITIES COLLECTION
  In the possession of the National Museum of Antiquities, Queen Street, Edinburgh.
MESSRS. BOLINGBROKE & JONES COLLECTION
PROVOST MACBEAN'S COLLECTION
INVERNESS MUSEUM COLLECTION
  All three named above are in the Scottish Tartans Society Museum, Comrie, Perthshire.

BOOKS ON TARTANS

The undernoted list of books giving details and illustrations of tartans may be of interest to those wishing to make a detailed study of the subject. While some of these publications are now out of print copies can generally be obtained through public libraries.
THE SCOTTISH GAEL by James Logan. Published in 1831.
VESTIARIUM SCOTICUM by J. S. S. and C. E. Sobieski Stuart. Published in 1842.

THE AUTHENTICATED TARTANS OF THE CLANS AND FAMILIES OF SCOTLAND by W. & A. Smith. Published in 1850.

THE CLANS OF THE HIGHLANDS OF SCOTLAND by Thomas Smibert. Published in 1850.

THE BOOK OF THE CLUB OF TRUE HIGHLANDERS by C. N. McIntyre North. Published in 1881.

THE TARTANS OF THE CLANS OF SCOTLAND by James Grant. Published in 1886.

OLD AND RARE SCOTTISH TARTANS by D. W. Stewart. Published in 1893.

THE SETTS OF THE SCOTTISH TARTANS by D. C. Stewart. Published in 1950.

HISTORY OF HIGHLAND DRESS by J. Telfer Dunbar. Oliver & Boyd, 1961.

TARTANS by Christian Hesketh, 1961.

THE TARTANS OF SCOTTISH CLANS by J. D. Scarlett. Wm. Collins, 1975.

CLAN AND FAMILY HISTORIES

Readers wishing to study the history of Scottish Clans and Families in greater detail than can be given in these pages may find difficulty in obtaining title and publication details of books dealing with the Clan or Family they wish to study.

Scottish Family History by Margaret Stuart and James Balfour Paul, published in Edinburgh in 1930, is available in most Public Libraries and is an invaluable guide to works of reference on the genealogy and history of Scottish Families.

A union list of books on Scottish Family Histories held in upwards of 70 Scottish libraries has been published by the Scottish Central Library, Lawnmarket, Edinburgh 1. A copy may be consulted in most Scottish burgh and country libraries, and persons interested in acquiring a copy should approach the Scottish Central Library.

SURNAMES

The Surnames of Scotland; Their Origin, Meaning and History by George F. Black, published in New York in 1946, gives valuable information regarding the origin, meaning and changing spelling of Scottish surnames. It also records the earliest date when each surname was mentioned in written records. Most reference and public libraries possess copies of this book for consultation.

ANCESTRY

The Scots Ancestry Research Society, 20 York Place, Edinburgh EH1 3EP, gives valuable help and advice in genealogical problems. Those genuinely interested in tracing their ancestry should consult this organisation.

The following is a translation of the Gaelic Proclamation intimating the repeal in 1782 of the Act of Parliament passed in 1746 prohibiting the wearing of the Highland Dress.

LISTEN, MEN!

This is bringing before all the Sons of the Gael that the King and Parliament of Britain have for ever abolished the Act against the Highland Dress that came down to the Clans from the beginning of the world to the year 1746. This must bring great joy to every Highland heart. You are no longer bound down to the unmanly dress of the Lowlander. This is declaring to every man, young and old, Commons and Gentles, that they may after this put on and wear the Trews, the Little Kilt, the Doublet and Hose, along with the Tartan Kilt, without fear of the Law of the Land or the jealousy of enemies.

MACNICOL
MACKINNON
Isle of
Skye
MACLEOD OF HARRIS
MATHESON
CHISHOLM
L. Ness
MAC
MACGI
DAVI
COMY
Canna
MACDONALD
MACLEOD
OF HARRIS
MACLENNAN
MACRAE
GRANT
MACDONELL OF
GLENGARRY
FRASER
L. Lochy
MACPHER-
CUMMIN
Rum
Eigg
L. Morar
MACDONALD OF
CLANRANALD
MACDONNELL
OF KEPPOCH
MURR
Muck
MACDONALD
OF CLANRANALD
L. Shiel
CAMERON
MENZIES
Coll
MACDONALD
Fort
William
L. Rannoc
CAMPBELL
MACLEAN MACKINNON
MACGILLIVRAY MACLEAN
MACMASTER
HENDERSON
STEWART
LIVINGSTONE
CAMPBELL
L. Tay
FLETCHER
Tiree
MACQUARRIE
MACINNES
Mull
MACLEAN
MACGREGOR
M
Iona
MACDOUGALL MACINTYRE
Oban
MACNAB
MACALPINE
MAC-
NAUGHTON
MAC
DRU
MACLEAN
MACCALLUM
CAMPBELL
MACARTHUR
STEWA
GRAHAM
BUCHANAN
Colonsay
MACFIE
Jura
MACLEAN
MALCOLM
MAC-
COLL
MAC-
LACHLAN
COLQU-
HOUN
NAPIER
LIVI
Oronsay
MAC-
MILLAN
MACEWEN
L. Lomond
MACAULAY
LAMONT
Glasgo
Islay
MACDONALD
STEWART
ERSKINE
MONTGOMERY
CUNNINGHAM
WALLACE
Cly
Gigha
CAMPBELL
MACALISTER
MACDONALD
Bute
COOK
FULLARTON
HAMILTON
STEWART
MACNEILL
Kintyre
Arran
Ayr
KENNEDY
DO
North Channel
Firth of Clyde
NORTHERN
IRELAND
FERGUSO
Wigtown

SOUTH SCOTLAND

Scale: 1:2, 00,000

Miles

0   10   20   '30   40

Highland Line ———

IRISH SEA